# Leading the Pack

*Model Driven Leadership for the 21st Century*

by

**Rick (Eric) Johnson**

Bloomington, IN  Milton Keynes, UK

author**HOUSE**™

*AuthorHouse™*
*1663 Liberty Drive, Suite 200*
*Bloomington, IN 47403*
*www.authorhouse.com*
*Phone: 1-800-839-8640*

*AuthorHouse™ UK Ltd.*
*500 Avebury Boulevard*
*Central Milton Keynes, MK9 2BE*
*www.authorhouse.co.uk*
*Phone: 08001974150*

*First published by AuthorHouse 6/29/2006*

*ISBN: 1-4259-3923-6 (e)*
*ISBN: 1-4259-3922-8 (sc)*
*ISBN: 1-4259-3921-X (dj)*

*Library of Congress Control Number: 2006904639*

*Printed in the United States of America*
*Bloomington, Indiana*

*This book is printed on acid-free paper.*

# Acknowledgements

Summer Wolf photo credit: *U.S. Fish and Wildlife Service/photo by John and Karen Hollingsworth*

Cold Wolf photo credit: *U.S. Fish and Wildlife Service/photo by Tracy Brooks*

*NAW (National Association Wholesale Distributors) DREF (Distribution Research Education Foundation) Profiles in Wholesale Distribution Leadership*

*The Illustrations in Lone Wolf – Lead Wolf were created by James T. Harper*

e-mail <u>guyinzeback@yahoo.com</u>

Mike Marks, Indian River Consulting for resource utilization along with content contribution from Mike and Dr. Bobby Swaim

# Table of Contents

# Chapter I

## *Introduction*

Make no mistake---this book is about "Leadership." A sometimes-confusing subject at best". It is not about being a (Boisterous, Omnipotent, Self Indulging Sociopath) B.O.S.S. Academics can site numerous "Leadership Theories" that may or may not apply in real life. Hopefully, by the time you finish reading "Leading the Pack", you will have a better understanding of the complexity of leadership and be able to apply Street Smart Rational Leadership to different situations faced in the workplace. Knowing when to be a mentor, when to be a coach, when to be a confidant and when to make strong, decisive, autocratic decisions is key to becoming an effective leader.

Good managers get employees to respect them, effective leaders get employees to not only respect them but more importantly they get them to respect themselves.

"Effective leaders are driven by a model. A model is a tool used to predict future outcomes of current decisions. Effective leaders build their models on the sum of their experiences, knowledge and deeds as well as their mistakes." (Mike Marks,

IRCG) Several different models will be explored throughout the chapters in this book.

Effective leaders demonstrate a respect for employees. They believe their employees are their most precious asset and the employee's innovative use of planning and control systems demonstrates a unique ability to balance predictability with simplicity. A leader's model may range from the elegant to the powerful to the simple, but they all have several major factors in common. Effective leaders believe in their employees. They demonstrate that belief through respect and servant type leadership. They also have a keen sense of executive curiosity. Effective leaders believe in a culture that embraces empowerment challenging employees to be innovative and creative. An old school, autocratic, B.O.S.S. (Boisterous, Omnipotent, Self indulging Sociopath) mentality fails to recognize the value of employee involvement, employee commitment and employee empowerment. (See "Are You A B.O.S.S. Chapter III)

---

**Thought Provoker**

*"Employees will not have faith in their leader until their leader shows faith in the employees"*

*"Employees will not show respect for their leader until their 'leader ' shows respect for the employees"*

---

Organizations increasingly will be characterized by a large and incredibly complex set of independent relationships between highly diverse groups of people. To be successful, you must

determine how to get active involvement, innovation and creativity out of your employees. Success depends on more than just "best practice" success drivers with an autocratic B.O.S.S. mentality that dictates and demands compliance. Success demands a superior level of leadership—a level that requires deep commitment. This commitment will not flourish in workplace environments that are still dominated by the "slap and point" or the "carrot and stick" method of management often used in the past.

Our own expectations often shape our destiny and create the roadmap to what we become. This truth is at the core of learning how to be a winner instead of just being a survivor. Self-doubt appears most active in people with negative expectations. The culture and environment of the organization are going to have a major impact on self-expectations. This is a critical element that executives who are not successful fail to recognize. Organizational culture is extremely important to successful growth, and culture is defined by the style of leadership that exists within the organization. Yes, *leadership style does have an impact on the culture* and the environment that embodies the business.

Throughout the chapters in this book we will explore leadership in all phases of a company's life cycle including dealing with specific challenges under varying circumstances utilizing different leadership models. Creating change, managing during turbulent times, fostering growth after restructuring, creating competitive advantage, or dealing with changing market dynamics all depends on a balance of leadership styles. No one person can make a company successful. It takes a lot of people, but one person with a command of leadership can transfer enough influence, creating effective leadership within the management group, leadership that can guarantee success; The Lead Wolf Style of Leadership.

## What do Wolves and Leadership Have in Common?

So exactly what do wolves have to do with leadership? The wolf is a very social animal. They travel together, eat together, hunt together and play together. There are referred to as a pack. The pack is generally a larger family group. Wolves within the pack are related by blood line. Being accepted, respected and cared for by their siblings and parents is important to the wolf. ---- *Isn't being cared about, trusted and respected important to every employee of every successful organization in the country?*

Just as management hierarchies vary in size, wolf packs vary in size but average six to seven members. --- *Does that sound like an executive team? Each pack member plays a specific role with a very specific rank?* Some young wolfs go off on their own (Lone Wolves, entrepreneurs), in search of their status. Generally speaking, the older wolves in the pack tend to be the leaders and they command the respect of the pack. They make the decisions for the group. The pack protects itself and it protects one another.

The lead wolf plays the role just as it sounds. He leads the pack. In fact, they generally will travel in single file with the lead wolf blazing the trail and setting the pace. --- *Sounds like the role of the CEO doesn't it?* The lead wolf however, is not afraid to

share his role. He will at times step aside to allow another up and coming wolf to take the lead. Make no mistake; each wolf in the pack has specific responsibilities. Each know in their own right that even if they don't aspire to lead the pack, they must be prepared to step up to that responsibility if called upon. Does this have any relationship to bench strength and succession?

## Dominant Wolves

Dominant wolves in the pack that do aspire to be leaders establish them selves in various ways. They might be larger, stronger or simply have a more aggressive personality. Captive wolves have been studied for years indicating complex behavior with regard to governance within the pack. Their communication with one another is also more elaborated than most of the other animal species.

Wolves are very patient of themselves and of one another. They are very focused on their objective whatever it may be at the time. They respect each others role and depend that each wolf in the pack will live up to their individual responsibility. This in itself promotes group unity. Wolves are very careful that they do not enter into redundant duplicate efforts. Each wolf can be heard by the pack; a form of individual respect. -- - *Could we actually write a corporate mission statement from this paragraph?*

Wolves have a sense of urgency. They depend on one another. They are much focused hard workers when it comes to feeding themselves. They are one of the wild's most effective hunters and yet in spite of that they hunt to live. They do not live to

hunt. They live by an unwritten code that says the good of the pack comes first. --- *How often do we uncover unsuccessful companies that are unsuccessful because the CEO or ownership put personal needs ahead of business needs?*

Lastly, one of the most common characteristics of the most successful leaders in wholesale distribution today is the extreme sense of curiosity. Wolves share this incessant curiosity about the world around them. They investigate everything, taking nothing for granted. They seek out opportunity. They have established specific priorities. Isn't that what successful leaders in business do today starting with the development of a strategic plan?

I personally believe that wolves demonstrate a distinctive relationship to successful leadership in the world of business today. That is why I have chosen the Wolf as part of the CEO Strategist logo and brand identity.

## What About Visionary Leadership?

Yes, effective leaders do have a vision and they support the concept of long term strategic planning. I know that some of us consider long term planning as what we are going to do after lunch, but effective leaders look into the future with foresight and confidence in the team they have surrounded themselves with. Ask yourself these questions?

"Are you a B.O.S.S. or are you a Leader?"

"Do you have a Lead Wolf mentality?"

"Do you have an end game vision?"

And never forget, an effective leader is only as good as the team that he surrounds himself with. This book is about the leadership model that will be the most effective in the 21st century. The Lone Wolf autocratic style of the past just doesn't work today. Investing time in reading this book more than once and studying the chapters can provide tremendous value to you personally even if you currently believe and practice the Lead Wolf leadership mentality. These chapters will help you develop and refine your leadership skills under varying circumstances and scenarios. Mastering change, dealing with the death spiral, power and politics, transitional restructuring, strategic planning, corporate recreational mating, coaching and mentoring and creating a turn around plan are all discussed in "Leading the Pack". Case studies interspersed throughout validate the lessons learned.

# Chapter II

## *Changing Times*

Wholesale distributors range in size from very small "Mom and Pop" operations with revenue as low as $100,000 or less, to huge multi-million dollar distributors with locations all across North America. Wholesale distribution also has some mega-distributors with sales ranging from $1 billion to as much as $27 billion. The majority of wholesale distributors are family owned. Leadership in privately held family run businesses often face unique challenges.

Family owned organizations, both small and large, with succession issues, family preparation and second and third generation leadership issues have been subjected to the evolution of leadership. These organizations are often founded by an aggressive, highly talented entrepreneur. Many of the principles of leadership that helped build the success that the organization enjoyed in the past is not the type of leadership that will maintain that success through generations of ownership. Contrary to some "leadership authorities" beliefs, in my opinion, the Machiavelli theories on leadership just don't apply today.

Niccolo Machiavelli is considered by some a leadership guru. He lived during the renaissance period and is often quoted and written about today. Machiavelli believed that "Men are more ready for evil than good" and "A leader's goal is one of power and domination."

Times have changed, leadership has evolved. The days of the "Lone Wolf" leader at the top who dominates with power and intimidation are gone. Successful privately held organizations have gone through the leadership evolutionary process developing their own

unique leadership style based on a Lead Wolf model. They understand that today's leaders must create change in the organization to meet the needs of their customers, to meet the needs of their employees and to meet the needs of their vendor partners. It involves a particular life cycle change. This change varies according to the generation of leadership.

---

**Thought Provoker**

*More often than not, the "seat of the pants" leadership model of the founder based on intuitive judgment with highly autocratic methodologies won't work in today's business environment.*

---

Today's environment demands a stable administrative structure that requires a change in the nature of past leadership practices. Simply put, it's an evolution from a highly reactive, autocratic individualistic style to a more empowering people oriented proactive style. It's about going from a "Lone Wolf" leadership style to a "Lead Wolf" leadership style; a leadership style that demonstrates confidence in the employee's ability to make things happen; a style that empowers employees to get the job done.

Founders and even second and third generation successors may find it difficult to make the transition from the "Lone Wolf" to the "Lead Wolf" leadership style. Leaders that have not made this transition often put personal needs ahead of business needs and the organization is not managed in the best interest of its customers, its vendors, and its employees. Organizations that are still run by a "Lone Wolf" model have an owner at the helm that has a strong dominating personality that is likely to be a poor listener. This "Lone Wolf" syndrome is easy to recognize. The same problems seem to arise over and over. Market share deteriorates, cash flow problems exist, and even though there may be a vision, no plan exists to accomplish that vision. Anxiety may set in and the owner becomes defensive or even paranoid. Executive management may resort to blaming others for the lack of success or pending failure. Without outside intervention, executive coaching, a solid board of directors or an advisory group, the company may end up being sold or worse yet the company may go into a death spiral facing imminent failure. (See Chapter XI "The Death Spiral")

## The Lone Wolf Leader Still Exists

This doesn't mean that there aren't some "Lone Wolf" leaders that still exist today that are successful. Remember, they have a strong entrepreneurial spirit that makes them dynamic and decisive. They often have a clear vision and these traits can drive a company for some time. However, I submit to you that the "Lone Wolf" leaders that have not evolved cannot maximize the success of their organization. They will not leverage the competitive advantage that has become the life line of their survival. The strong traits that brought them success in the past can quickly become liabilities in today's environment. They don't believe in empowerment. They don't believe in long range planning. They are reluctant to develop structure, policy and procedure because it inhibits the ability to shoot from the hip and it slows them down. They mistakenly believe that shooting from the hip is part of their competitive advantage because it worked so well in the past. They can make reactive crisis-driven decisions with little or no help from their management team without recognizing that they must identify and correct the root cause. If they do have a board of directors, they are hand picked friends or family that basically does whatever they want. They fail to challenge management. The old school Lone Wolf autocratic model counts on only those that seem to be the most loyal and it motivates by fear and guilt. Sure, the Lone Wolf holds staff meetings but it's more of an exercise in power to report on crisis intervention or simply to chew people out. They have difficulty in letting go of the past.

## Today's Business Environment Created the Demand for Lead Wolf Executives

Successful growing organizations have gone through the experience of change and welcome this century's business environment. In fact, these organizations recognized the necessity to create change. That is what leadership is really about; the ability to create change. These successful organizations have developed their employees along the way. The Lead Wolf executives have earned the respect and trust of their employees by demonstrating respect and trust in the employees themselves.

## Lead Wolf Characteristics

The Lead Wolf employs a servant, situational leadership style that is based on an empowerment platform. They develop future leaders; make proactive decisions based on calculated risk. They employ root cause analysis even if they don't formally call it that. They employ best practices and make staffing decisions

based on responsibility, competency, training and capabilities. They develop a real board of directors that provide value to the organization, challenge the executive staff and hold them accountable. The Lead Wolf executives recognize and believe that leadership is an invitation to greatness that we extend to others. Successful leaders understand that they must give back what they have learned. They understand the concept of coaching and mentoring.

## Learning to Lead the Pack is a Growth and Development Process

Owner executives that have evolved to the Lead Wolf style of leadership have gone through an individual growth and learning process. They have accepted the fact that they may not have all the answers. More importantly, they recognize that they don't have to have all the answers. Many have found a mentor or an executive coach outside the organization. Changing a leadership style is not the easiest thing in the world to do. Coaching becomes a very useful resource. Seminars and other forms of training are just entertainment without on-going coaching. Factors relevant to Leading the Pack include:

- Enhancement of individual instinctive curiosity and a strengthening of the focus on being a customer driven organization. Service and quality become a way of life within the organization and it is used to support their competitive advantage.

- Taking their vision and redefining it as an end game which challenges their executive team to create a strategic plan to meet this end game. This plan incorporates growth and profitability as well as other specific goals and objectives.

- The recognition that employees are the most precious asset and backing up that recognition by the willingness to invest profits in the development of these employees.

- Empowerment that is accompanied by the resources necessary to succeed and accountability for results.

- Utilizing a board of directors as a resource while sharing management challenges seeking policy and guidance. Incorporating contingency planning and scenario planning as a regular exercise.

## The Lead Wolf Executive

Lead Wolf executives get results. They are high impact leaders. They are consistent, explicit and concise and they command a presence when they walk into a room. They have enough charisma to turn the dullest moment into a high-energy event. When they move on, others want to go with them. They have a following. Their openness and honesty create a legacy which people admire and look up to. They gain commitment and foster trust.

The Lead Wolf Executive figures out how to get more active involvement and creativity out of their employees. Questioning of the status quo and the generation of new ideas is a mandate of success; that success depends on a superior level of performance, a level that requires deep commitment.

Most of us are not born leaders. We are not adept at communication. However, a good percentage of us long to become leaders and make deep connections in our careers that lead to commitment, a commitment to success. For family owned organizations, leadership is passed on from generation to generation. To achieve objectives, each generation must understand the following basic principles of leadership.

- Honesty
- Integrity
- Respect
- Trustworthiness
- Sincere concern of others
- Willingness to take calculated risk

Once these principles are learned and practiced, leverage of these leadership skills to develop the management team is the next step. Lead Wolf family executives that have gone through the evolution of change understand this and they are clear as to what their responsibilities are.

The Lead Wolf executive understands the importance of making emotional connections with the management team that surrounds them. They must encourage these people to open up,

share dialog and reveal dreams. They must coach and mentor. Leveraging their leadership entails advancing their personal agenda by advancing the agenda of others. A good leader is not intimidated by the success of others. They encourage others to succeed and help them fulfill their wants and needs. Leveraging leadership helps determine the hidden factors in communication. Understanding inferences and assertions become a key component to understanding people. Lead Wolf executives have high questioning skills that allow them to drill down to real facts and issues. Leveraging their leadership allows successful leaders to establish emotional connections, which diminish fear and intimidation. This encourages enthusiasm and cooperation and that is what the Lead Wolf leadership model is all about.

---

**Thought Provoker**

**"The true test of a successful leader is that he leaves behind the conviction, the will and the understanding in others to carry on."**

---

To achieve our leadership objective of Leading the Pack, understanding the Three C's of Leadership is essential:

- Curiosity
- Creativity
- Commitment

**"Good judgment comes from experience, and experience comes from bad judgment. And life is a series—or a managerial life is a series of building your skills and your judgment on the back of the mistakes you've made." (Steve Kaufman, 2003 NAW Interview)**

## Curiosity

Every successful leader demonstrates a curiosity that would not be satisfied without personal examination of what exactly were the causes of failure to meet expectations. This was validated through NAW's (National Association of Wholesaler Distributors) research "Profiles in Wholesale Distribution Leadership. http://www.nawpubs.org/orderform.html . In this project, individual leadership models differed in their specific approaches. The common thread that linked every model together was their respect for the individual and the willingness and ability to listen with an understanding that embellished their own leadership contribution to the organization. The most obvious similarity between the seven exceptional leaders interviewed  was the fact that they were all curious, creative and committed.

Leadership is about curiosity, scenario planning, strategic planning and calculated risk taking. Effective leaders are excellent listeners that have tremendous questioning skills. The power of influence is often in the question and not in the answers. Effective leaders understand this concept.  A common trait found in every successful leader I have ever been associated with is unhesitant curiosity. Curiosity about their markets, their business, their industry, their employees and what it takes to grow, prosper and create competitive advantage. Much like the lead wolf, curiosity is a dominant success trait.

These leaders have accepted the fact that they may not have all the answers. More importantly, they recognize that they don't have to have all the answers. Changing a leadership style is not the easiest thing in the world to do. Development of

their leadership skills and their individual leadership model is a continuous process. This process includes:

- Enhancement of their instinctive curiosity and a strengthening of their focus on being a customer driven organization. Service and quality become a way of life within the organization and it is used to support their competitive advantage.

- Taking their vision and redefining it as an end game which challenges their executive team to create a strategic plan to meet this end game.

- The recognition that employees are the most precious asset and backing up that recognition by the willingness to invest profits in the development of these employees.

- Empowerment that is accompanied by the resources necessary to succeed and accountability for results.

- Utilizing a board of directors as a resource while sharing management challenges seeking policy and guidance, incorporating contingency planning and scenario planning as a regular exercise.

Wholesale distribution organizations increasingly are characterized by a large and incredibly complex set of independent relationships between highly diverse groups of people. To be successful, today's leader must determine how to get active involvement built on a model encompassing creativity, commitment and curiosity out of their employees.

## Creativity

Successful leaders take the time to listen, imagine and investigate numerous alternatives. With the involvement of people they forge creative solutions to difficult problems. They challenge their people to stretch, go beyond their previous boundaries and think outside the box. Successful leaders feed off their people and allow their people to feed off of them. They give credit where credit is due. They give recognition as a means of gaining respect. They believe individuals can make a difference. Through these methods they learn to create new insights and possibilities.

Successful leadership means creating a sense of urgency, getting mutual commitment to action. Action steps are always clearly defined and precise. Often, due to the personification of the leader's own personality and charisma, employees are eager to leap into action – without forethought. A successful leader recognizes this possibility and takes the necessary steps to avoid this pitfall by teaching precision in planning. They are clear and explicit. They communicate with encouraging clarity that commands ownership by everyone involved in the commitments made.

The successful leader is constantly building advantages into the organizations. The belief is that you don't always have to be better than your competition but you must be different. This concept demands creativity and innovations.

## Commitment

Commitment is a critical element to success whether the company is in a growth mode, a stabilizing mode or an acquisition mode or any other type of circumstance. Failure to demonstrate commitment by the leader can have negative consequences that inhibit success. Commitment is essential to developing trust. Trust is necessary to get people to reach down deep inside and give everything they have under the most difficult circumstances.

The reason people follow any leader, especially in the business world, is due to trust. The only way to develop trust is by demonstrating personal commitment to success. Talking to people with respect to gain their respect and demonstrating your personal work ethic is part of your commitment. Their respect is a key ingredient to developing trust. Trust is gained when people think the company cares about their welfare and recognizes the role they play in creating a profit.. People have to think that the company not only cares about their problems but that the leader and the company is committed toward making every effort to solve them.

Employees want to take pride in their leaders. They are eager to give their trust but demonstrating the kind of commitment as a leader that deserves that trust can not be over emphasized. Don't let the employees down. Commitment to the employees and the company is built around a true concern for the people within the organization. It is based on fairness and consistency.

The effectiveness of a true leader is not measured in terms of the leadership he or she exercises. It is measured in the leadership evoked. It is not measured in terms of power over subordinates but in terms of the power released in subordinates. Leadership is not measured in terms of goals and objectives but it is measured in terms of the accomplishment of others as a result of that leadership. Leadership is not measured in the decisions made, the costs cut, the plans made. It is measured in terms of the growth in confidence, sense of responsibility and acceptance of accountability of the employees that are a result of that leadership.

Leadership and commitment are intertwined. They go together. Leadership and commitment help create solidarity. Solidarity implies a unity within a group that enables it to manifest its strength and exert its influence as a group. Unity implies oneness, especially of what is varied or diverse in its direction or clarity. Unity describes the inner relationships of individual parts making up the whole. It is an achievement that demands the probability of action and leadership. That action, that leadership, if appropriate and precise, leads to trust. Demonstrate your commitment to the company, to your employees and to success in every possible way. Your employees need to know you are committed.

Once these principles are learned and practiced, leverage of these leadership skills to develop the management team is the next step.

*"Leadership is easy, just find a bunch of people going in the same direction and jump in front of them"*
*--------Willie Nelson*

Leaders must make emotional connections with the management team that surrounds them. They must encourage these people to open up, share dialog and reveal dreams. They must teach and mentor. It's not as easy as Willie Nelson would have you believe. A good leader is not intimidated by the success of others. They encourage others to succeed and help them fulfill their wants and needs. Leveraging leadership helps determine the hidden factors in communication. Understanding inferences and assertions become a key component to understanding people. Curious leaders have high questioning and prospering skills that allow them to drill down to real facts and issues.

Leveraging their leadership allows successful leaders to establish emotional connections, which diminish fear and intimidation. This encourages enthusiasm and cooperation.

> **Excellence in what you do, continuous improvement aren't words. They're a way of life. When you understand that they're a way of life, then the change that you have in the way you perform is beyond comprehension because you just wind up operating at a different level, and if you can find a way to capture that in the culture of your business, in the culture that you emanate to your people, then as this culture structure changes, you have an opportunity for a superior level of performance. Excellence, and that's what in the end it's all about. Excellence breeds a high level of profitability. Chuck Steiner (2003) his NAW interview,**

Success depends on more than just "best practice" success drivers. Success demands a superior level of leadership—a level that requires deep commitment. This commitment will not flourish in workplace environments that are still dominated by the "slap & point" or the "carrot and stick" method of management often used in the past.

# Chapter III

## *Are you a B.O.S.S.? (Boisterous, Omnipotent, Self-indulgent, Sociopath)*

Avoid the Lone Wolf B.O.S.S. syndrome with five leadership principles that translate academic leadership theory to real world, 21st century application. Become a Lead Wolf Executive.

There are many academic theories published on leadership. Some of these theories include:

- Participative Leadership
- Transformational Leadership
- Situational Leadership
- Fielders Contingency Model
- Path Goal Leadership
- Vroom-Jago Participation Model

### Participative Leadership

Patricia McLagan and Christo Nel state that, "leadership is about breaking new ground, going beyond the known and creating the future." They talk about new governance requiring

effective leadership to create a future. McLagan and Nel report that the shift to increased participation changes their view of effective leadership. They believe that leadership, as a concept, is unstable. They also believe that notions of formal leadership expected from leaders are confused with notions of the individual leadership expected from everyone in the institution.

## Transformational Leadership

Richard L. Daft raises the question, "What kind of people can lead an organization through major change?" Daft points out that transformational leadership is characterized by the ability to bring about change through innovation and creativity. This type of leader motivates people to not only follow their lead but to believe in the vision of corporate transformation, the need for revitalization, to sign on for the new vision and help institutionalize a new organizational process.

## Situational Leadership Theory (SLT)

SLT suggests that leaders adjust their styles depending on the maturity of their followers, indicated by their readiness to perform in a given situation. Readiness is based on both how able and willing people are to perform required tasks. The Heresy Blanchard theory developed a model that depicts the different leadership styles necessary, ranging from delegating (observe and monitor) to participating (encourage and problem-solve) to selling (explain and persuade) to telling (guide and direct).

## Fiedler's Contingency Model

The Fiedler leadership model is similar to SLT because it is based on a match between leadership style and situational demands. However, the similarity ends there as Fiedler's theory states that the amount of control a situation allows the leader is a critical issue in determining the correct style to use.

---

**Thought Provoker**

"Failure often results when leaders do not communicate clearly in language understood by their audience, and they are certain to fail if they ignore input from colleagues and direct reports."

**H.A. Wagner**
**CEO Air Products and Chemicals**

---

## Path Goal Leadership Theory (PGLT)

Robert House advances the PGLT that suggests an effective leader is one who clarifies paths though which followers can achieve both task-related and personal goals. Effective leaders help employees progress along these paths. House goes on to identify four leadership models in his theory. They include:

1. Directive Leadership: Clarity of expectations and clear directions
2. Supportive Leadership: Making work more pleasant
3. Achievement Oriented Leadership: Challenges goals, continuous improvement

4. Participative Leadership: Involving employees in decision making

## Vroom-Jago Leader-Participation Model

The Vroom-Jago Participation Model is designed to present a choice on the method used based on the nature of the issues at hand. Vroom-Jago developed three alternative decision methods:

1. Authority Decision: A decision made by leadership and communicated to the employees

2. Consultive Decision: A decision made by the leader after receiving information input and advice from employees

3. Group decision: A decision made with full employee participation

The key to this style of leadership is the ability to recognize which decision model fits each circumstance. Execution of each method becomes critical to avoid confusion.

## Let's Face Reality

Just the review of theories and models reminds us of the complexity of leadership. It also makes it clear that being in a position of power, does not, in itself, make one an effective leader. So what happens in the real world on a day-to-day basis with people in positions of power?

People who attain positions of power, whether it is C.E.O., Vice President of Sales, C.O.O., Sales Manager, Branch Manager or another position of authority, reach these positions for a variety of reasons. The reasons are not always a result of competency and hard work; these positions are not always earned. Alternative reasons for being promoted to positions of power include:

- Nepotism
- Politics
- Being in the right place at the right time
- Personal relationships
- Extraordinary suck-up behavior
- Being the tallest in the land of midgets
- Failure to recognize the onset of the "Peter's Principle" - Promoted beyond the individual's ability to handle the new responsibilities

Success is defined by the quality of leadership at all levels in the organization. Acting like a B.O.S.S. is not a demonstration of leadership.

If a company is to survive in this century, meeting all the challenges of today's environment, the Lead Wolf leadership model is essential. It is especially critical and quite clear that the company must have one leader at the top that will take the responsibility and accept being held accountable for the results. That doesn't mean the leader is a Lone Wolf. On the contrary, this requires a Lead Wolf mentality that includes the development of a team that embraces the concept of effective leadership throughout the organization at all levels. The issue, however, is in the term leadership. This leader must be a Lead Wolf executive, not a manager, not a CEO, not a president and not an owner. Oh, they can be called any of these things too, but first and foremost they must be a leader who has a vision and a passion to succeed; a Lead Wolf that builds a competent team and empowers them.

## Pride in Leadership

Employees want to take pride in their leaders. They are eager to give their trust, but demonstrating the kind of leadership character that deserves that trust cannot be over-emphasized. Don't let your employees down. Character is built around a true concern for the people within the organization. It is based on fairness and consistency. It is not based on the autocratic authority of the B.O.S.S. syndrome, a Lone Wolf authoritarian.

The effectiveness of a true leader, a Lead Wolf, is not measured in terms of the leadership he or she exercises. It is measured in the leadership evoked. It is not measured in terms of power over subordinates, but in terms of the power released in subordinates. Leadership is not measured in terms of goals and objectives, but it is measured in terms of the accomplishment of others as a result of that leadership. Leadership is not measured in the decisions made, the costs cut or the plans made. It is measured in terms of the growth in confidence, sense of responsibility and acceptance of accountability by the employees that are a result of that leadership. The final test of a true leader is that they leave behind in others the conviction, ability, eagerness and will to carry on.

## Five Principles of the Real World Lead Wolf Model

The following five principles can help translate academic theory into real world Lead Wolf application in order to guarantee avoidance of the Lone Wolf B.O.S.S. syndrome. These five principles can create a platform of transition from the Lone Wolf model to the Lead Wolf model of leadership.

## <u>#1. Communication</u>

Next to people, communication is the most critical element to success, whether the company is in a growth mode or facing challenges to maintain market share. Failure to communicate is like a virus that can lead to  total failure. Communication is essential to developing trust. Trust is necessary to get people to reach down deep inside and give everything they have under the most difficult circumstances. Trust will allow people to give their discretionary energy to meet objectives.

## Discretionary Energy

Effective communication helps release discretionary energy. What is discretionary energy? Discretionary energy is the energy an employee uses when going above and beyond the call of duty to complete a task or get the job done. Every employee has discretionary energy. The amount of energy released and employed at work depends on their attitude, how well they enjoy being at work, how they are treated, how they feel about the company and how well informed they are.

Discretionary energy can be the difference between doing what is expected and performing in an outstanding manner.

**Thought Provoker**

**You want every employee to release their discretionary energy at work to improve their individual performance and as a result improve company performance. The last thing you want is for an employee to do exactly what you tell them to do. Individual initiative is the fuel of competitive advantage. Competitive advantage creates profit.**

Therefore, telling a person what he is doing wrong is not specific enough.

Eliminating undesirable behavior without providing a new substitute pattern leaves the worker open to learn another undesirable set of responses and will encourage him to withhold his discretionary energy.

It is better to comment on improvement in performance than to comment on the employee's failure to meet goals.

## This can be accomplished by:

- Frequent feedback
- Reinforcing small approximations to the desired goal, gradually increasing the number of steps necessary to obtain the positive reinforcement
- Evaluating good performance and without too much time delay; employees deserve to know how they are doing no less than on a monthly basis

To see how this principle is applied to coaching, assume you were on a ride-a-long with a salesperson and you just concluded a sales call. You observed the salesperson neglected to ask for the order when making a closing statement. If in this critique you mention to the salesperson that he/she did not use the skill correctly you would, in fact, be punishing the salesperson.

A much better approach would be to use the concept of self-feedback. In other words, allow the salesperson to self-critique the use of his/her skills. In the above example, assume the salesperson used the supporting skill correctly. You would apply the positive reinforcement technique as previously discussed. Next, ask the salesperson to repeat his/her closing statement as best he/she can recall.

You might say, "Can you remember the closing statement you made? I wonder if you could repeat it."

Several things may happen here. First, the salesperson may repeat the statement and realize on his/her own he/she neglected to ask for the order – a self-realization. At this point ask him to ask for the order and positively reinforce his/her response. On the other hand, the salesperson may not realize he/she used the skill incorrectly, even after repeating it. In this case ask the salesperson what he/she thinks he/she could do to improve on the closing.

Confirm understanding and ask the salesperson to make another closing statement. Once again positively reinforce after correct skill usage. By utilizing this method you avoid falling in the trap of the "Psychological Sandwich." That is, after the salesperson received praise he/she is now waiting for the axe to fall, the praise becoming the antecedent to negative consequence.

---

**Thought Provoker**

**Doing annual performance reviews without regular performance feedback so the employee understands his strengths and what he needs to do to become more effective is just not acceptable if you are to become an effective leader.**

---

## Why Follow The Leader

The reason people follow any leader, especially in the business world, is due to trust. The only way to develop trust is through communication - talking to people with respect to gain their respect. Respect is a key ingredient in developing trust. Trust is gained when people think their employer cares about their

welfare and recognizes the role each plays in creating a profit. People have to think that the company not only cares about their problems, but that the company will make every effort to solve them.

## Leadership and Communication are intertwined

Together, they help create solidarity. Solidarity implies a unity within a group that enables it to manifest its strength and exert its influence. This is particularly true when a business is facing challenges from the competition, the external environment, changing market conditions, or economic pressures. Unity describes a oneness of diverse, individual parts making up the whole. It is an achievement that occurs only with appropriate and precise action and leadership.

*Communication is the first spark in leadership.* It will hold the company together. Nothing else is so crucial to survival and solidarity. It is especially important that the message is consistent throughout the management team. No single factor plays a more precious role in building and preserving trust amongst the employees than communication. It is a make or break issue. The Lead Wolf model makes communication a priority.

Miscommunication, rumors and garbled messages cause conflict and distrust. Don't settle for second-rate communication, it's too critical to success. Avoiding informing all employees, specifically on matters that affect their lives, is like playing with fire. This kind of action breeds resentment, distrust and paranoia.

---

**Thought Provoker**

*"Leadership without communication is like a gun without bullets. It looks impressive but it can't do anything!"*

---

## Why Do We Have Problems Communicating?

- We are always in a hurry.
- We do not listen well.
- We don't ask appropriate questions.
- We don't seek feedback or provide it.
- We use unclear words or symbols.
- We fail to anticipate.
- We think people can read our minds.
- We think people have the same perspective as us.

Difficulty in communications is enhanced when you are exceptionally busy or you face adversity of some nature. In normal times, communication is difficult in itself due to our individual psyche and motivations.

## Symbolic Interactionism ------ Herbert Blumer

In a two-way conversation between you and someone else, there are virtually six people involved.

1. **ME – AS I SEE ME**

2. **ME – AS YOU SEE ME**

3. **YOU – AS I SEE YOU**

**4. YOU – AS YOU SEE YOU**

**5. ME – AS I REALLY AM**

**6. YOU – AS YOU REALLY ARE**

Blumer's theory consists of three core principles: meaning, language and thought. These core principles lead to conclusions about the creation of a person's self and socialization into a larger community. Language gives individuals a means by which to negotiate meaning through symbols. Humans identify meaning in speech acts with others. Thought modifies each individual's interpretation of symbols. Thought is a mental conversation that requires different points of view. With these three elements the concept of the self can be framed. People use "the looking glass self": They take the role of the other, imagining how we look to another person. The self is a function of language, without talk there would be no self concept. People are part of a community where our generalized other is the sum total of responses and expectations that we pick up from the people around us. That is why a face to face conversation can involve virtually six different perceptions of who we each are.

## Communication tools are both verbal and non-verbal.

| VERBAL | NON-VERBAL |
|---|---|
| **Spoken word** | **Body language** |
| Languages | Eyes |
| Dialect | Gestures |
| Jargon | Facial expression |
| Volume, Tone and Inflection | Distance-gap |
| Written word | |

## The Basic Rules of Communication

Listening skills are especially important. Proof that you are listening is in your actions. Don't ask someone if they understand. Ask them what they are going to do. Listening should dominate your interaction with your employees. Distractions need to be removed. Trust must be developed. You must have a sincere desire to understand. You must be aware of individual needs. Be attentive and don't assume anything. Ask for explanations. Don't interrupt because you want to talk. Try to keep an open mind. Be compassionate and don't react too quickly. Avoid talking about yourself. Remember: You and the person you are communicating with are trying to create a shared meaning. Meanings are not in words, they are in people. Your goal is to ensure there is a shared definition, and hopefully, you will have a shared meaning.

## <u>What Not to Say During the Communication Process</u>

Communication is the primary tool in building relationship equity, trust and respect. Every time you have the opportunity to communicate, your first priority is to show concern for the other person's issues. The major objective in every exchange is to meet or exceed their expectations. Failure to meet employee expectations can lead to frustration, disappointment, confusion and even anger at times. When you are faced with a disappointed employee, your primary objective is to maintain relationship equity. Don't make the situation worse. Confrontational employees could make you forget everything you've learned about leadership and building relationship equity.

There are key words and phrases that you should avoid, such as:

- NO! – No is the strongest detriment to building relationship equity. That doesn't mean you never say no, but in a confrontational situation you should try to avoid this word. You can say no without saying no. If the employee says, "Can I leave early and enter those orders tomorrow?" Instead of NO, you can reply, "They need to be entered tonight so they can be picked tonight. Can you get someone to enter them for you?

- Can't – Never say you can't do something; instead explain what you can do and how that will benefit the situation. Can't is nothing more than a method to relieve guilt

- You must – Never tell the employee what he has to do. He doesn't have to do anything. You might simply need to explain their options.

- Policy – Avoid quoting policy. The employee isn't motivated by policy. Your goal is to get the employee to do his best and release his discretionary energy.

- It's not my decision. – It is your decision. No matter what the situation is, it is your decision to carry out policy and procedure. This includes requests and direction from top management and ownership. Their decisions become your decisions and you must support them as your own, even if you don't agree with them.

- Corporate is always _____. Never ever blame corporate for problems or situations. You are a manager. You are all on the same team.

## #2.  Commitment with Passion

Employee commitment will soar if the entire executive staff demonstrates a passion for success. Excitement breeds excitement. Success breeds success.  The more consuming the desire to succeed, the more leadership is demonstrated, and this draws support from the employees. The President, as the leader of the executive staff, sets the stage. Other managers throughout the organization must follow suit.  If the company fails to meet its objectives, chances are the leader did not set the proper environment for success. The leader's intensity, focus, drive and dedication, along with these same attributes from the executive staff, are the determinants of the level of commitment provided by the employees. Commitment won't survive if leadership doesn't exist. The leader must be proactive and publicly demonstrate leadership, confidence and commitment.

---

**Thought Provoker**

**"If you lead through fear and intimidation using the old 'Slap and Point' methodology, you will have little respect; but if you lead with confidence, integrity, commitment and respect, you will have little to fear and gain the respect necessary to accomplish your vision."**

---

This is what the evolution from being a Lone Wolf to becoming a Lead Wolf is really all about. This is what "Leading the Pack" is all about.

## #3. A Common Fallacy: Have All The Answers

A mistake many leaders make is the self-imposed responsibility to have all the answers. This is just not accurate. It is okay to admit to not having all the answers. Good leaders are willing to show their imperfections. Surround yourself with a solid executive team and you don't need all the answers. No one expects perfection, just leadership. Being a leader doesn't grant you supreme knowledge.

A cosmic truth states: give before you receive. Being the B.O.S.S. by mandating new rules, stipulations, threats and unreasonable demands does not promote unity or trust. It is destructive to the kind of attitude required to succeed. Employee consideration and input is absolutely essential to success. The company needs employee support, trust and respect. But, the company must give before they receive. The leader must know when to lead and when to listen before acting. It is often surprising how much employees can and will contribute if you give them the opportunity to do so. Allow your employees to grow and release their creativity. Leading the Pack doesn't mean you must have **all the answers**.

## #4. Employees: The Most Precious Asset

Developing a team is not that difficult if employee development is a priority.

Every employee wants to feel that they have a voice and can be heard. They want to know that management knows they exist and what their contributions are. They want the satisfaction of doing a good job. They want to prove their talent to achieve the desired results. If they are challenged, the majority will become self-motivated.

People enjoy other people. Most derive satisfaction from interaction with their peers. Recognition is icing on the cake. Employees find the social aspect of the workplace rewarding if the environment is positive and conducive to success. Make coming to work enjoyable for the employees. Create ways to challenge as well as entertain your employees. Provide the opportunity for social interaction. There are a number of ways to do this, from a once a week company sponsored lunch to monthly breakfast sessions with the president to talk about current issues and new events.

Recognition and praise raises self-esteem. Positive feedback and ample communication allow employees gratification and a newfound confidence in the organization. Employees need to feel some sense of power. Most employees derive satisfaction by having an influence over something or someone. A varying level of leadership is an inborn trait to a degree in every human being, some more than others. Allow the employees the opportunity to demonstrate leadership in some form or fashion. Create work teams, committees and projects that motivate by presenting the opportunity to make decisions and be a part of the overall process of meeting strategic objectives.

Organizations in the 21$^{st}$ century that dominate market share have characteristics that often create a large and incredibly complex set of independent relationships between highly diverse groups of people. They recognize the value of their employees. Organizations experiencing problems with staffing and retention may find it isn't due to bad hires or a low unemployment rate. In fact, such problems may be related to poor leadership insight by not recognizing employees as a core competency in the business strategy. Although employees may not fit the strictest definition of a core competency, it is a fact that employees are the ones responsible for creating many of the core competencies. It is an indisputable fact that failure to recognize the importance of employee contributions will ultimately lead to failure, regardless of your business strategy.

## #5. Empowerment

The Lead Wolf model allows the employees to take risks and demonstrate initiative. Empowerment is a trait used by most effective leaders. The rewards of empowering your employees are far greater than the risk. Give them some independence in choosing their work schedules or other factors that won't affect overall objectives. Empowering employees allows them to use their own initiative and creativity to accomplish things you never imagined they could.

Employees must take ownership in the success of the organization. This means they must become part of the strategy employed by the company. Acknowledge their presence and contributions, and praise them at every opportunity. But, be sincere. Jack Welch, former CEO of General Electric, had a favorite method of sending personal handwritten notes to employees who demonstrated some form of success. The employee issue cannot be emphasized enough.

Winning organizations continuously build leaders at every level in their organization. Leaders who actively attempt to mentor and build other leaders gain respect throughout the organization and transfer knowledge, ideas, values and attitude about success. Effective Leaders with the Lead Wolf mentality demonstrate the following attributes:

- A sense of urgency
- Project and articulate the vision
- Create stretch goals
- Develop trust and a spirit of teamwork
- Develop realistic expectations for success
- Promote an environment of success, trust and belief
- Honesty—to tell the truth—to do the right thing—no hidden agendas

- Integrity and respect—responsive—recognizing employee value—empowerment
- Passion - commitment
- Motivate and inspire

## Lead Wolf Executives Have an Edge

Effective leaders must have an edge. They must be courageous enough to take risk and have an unrelenting readiness to act. Popularity is not a requirement, but the ability to generate respect from the employees is, without a doubt, one of the most critical attributes. They must be relentless in their efforts, unconcerned about personal sacrifice of their time, and willing to go beyond normal expectations. Tough decisions are commonplace; uncharted territories will be the norm. Honesty and impeccable character are musts.

Leadership is key to harmonizing diverse group interest into a focus-specific mode that supports the mechanics of execution. Those mechanics must include empowerment. The focus is on the way managers orchestrate activities and events and engage others in tasks, empowering them so that the desired results are realized. Action is key and is implicitly equated to professional leadership. This skill is subjective and often artistic. It varies with every situation and every individual. Leadership skills can be enhanced and fine-tuned but a basic ingredient of humanistic understanding must exist to create a platform for leadership development.

---

**Thought Provoker**

**Effective leaders get results. They make things happen. They continually advance a clear agenda, get others to buy in and move the organization to accomplish specific objectives. They are explicit, consistent, concise and sincere. They generally have an abundance of charisma although some leaders gain success with a quieter influence.**

---

Leaders take charge and are not afraid of responsibility or risk. Most people want to follow them. A good leader develops openness, honesty, clarity of purpose and a sincere caring for the people they lead. They gain commitment and trust by demonstrating respect for the individual. They have a

keen sense of understanding. They believe in their task, they understand the objectives, they communicate clearly and they honestly project the understanding that they need the efforts of everyone to succeed.

Effective Leaders don't act like a B.O.S.S. (Boisterous, Omnipotent, Self Indulging Sociopath) It's not in their nature. Don't be a B.O.S.S. Be a leader. Copy the leadership thought provoker checklist (Exhibit I). Keep it handy for ready reference. It may prove helpful for your own personal leadership development in becoming or refining your Lead Wolf leadership skills.

## Exhibit I

"Leadership" Thought Provoker Checklist

1.  Making promises when you are not sure you can keep them can lead to a loss of respect.

Take making promises seriously. View a promise, as a commitment made with an understanding that circumstances might arise that would make it impossible to keep them. Make those circumstances very clear to the person at the time promises are made. Breaking a promise can lead to a loss of respect on the part of the employee. He may question your integrity. A leader must have an impeccable character to earn the confidence of his employees. Don't make promises you can't keep and in that rare circumstance that you do break a promise, face the employee eye to eye explaining in detail why you were not able to keep your promise. Be honest about it.

2.  Some employees whine, especially sales people. It's part of their DNA. That does not mean you should ignore complaints that you consider whining.

No employee thinks his complaint is insignificant even if you think it is whining. It is still a problem even if the complaint is taken lightly or ignored. In fact it may grow and fester. An effective leader will address the complaint and not be afraid to tell the employee it is whining or trivial by explaining why. Even though the employee may not hear the answer he is looking for, the leader will not lose respect due to inattention. Of course how he delivers the message is important and should be done without belittling the employee.

47

3. A leader must show consistency and fairness in his treatment of employees.

Do you vary your approach with employees, being lenient with some and strict with others? There is a fine line between treating all employees exactly the same and showing consistency in the treatment of employees. Employees are all individuals with different backgrounds, different values, different goals, different ideas and different motivational factors. The ability to recognize the differences in people and the ability to apply variable leadership methodologies is an important characteristic of effective leadership. That being said, it is extremely important that a leader does not show favoritism and give preferential treatment to employees. A lack of consistency in the leader's treatment of employees destroys teamwork and trust. Do not give special privileges unless a special situation warrants it, and everyone understands it.

4. Becoming buddies with your employees is not a good idea and Corporate Recreational Mating is an absolute taboo. That does not mean that you should be cold and aloof. Leadership is about relationships but you must not develop a personal relationship to the extent that it compromises your ability to take command and show control when necessary.

Aloofness can detract from effective leadership. You can be friendly without losing authority or compromising your position. A leader must demonstrate competence and vision and at the same time show a sincere interest in the well being of his employees. Anyone whose job is to influence people and

direct them in their work must maintain friendly contact with the group.

5. The ability to collaborate, share ideas and not be threatened by the transfer of intellectual capital is extremely important to promoting a team concept and an atmosphere that promotes confidence.

Sharing your thoughts, experiences, knowledge along with coaching and mentoring is showing confidence and self respect. This supports a culture of camaraderie. Share information whenever issues in your realm of responsibility affect operations in other manager's areas. Absolutely do not circumvent the authority of managers reporting to you and don't go around other managers.

6. Refusing an employees request without creating resentment is a tactful necessity of effective leadership.

The ability to say no without creating hostility is important. The key to accomplishing that objective is to recognize the request with sincerity and explain in detail why the request cannot be granted. Being sincere demonstrates concern and makes your personal regret believable.

---

**Thought Provoker**

**"The ideal leader is courageous, strong and persistent, wise – but what really separates him or her from the pack is passion and vision. It's not enough to be skilled administrator or a world-class manager. No, to be a true leader, we need the passion of our dreams – and a vision of how to make them real. Passion and vision are transforming forces that will fail unless we fuse them into one powerful source for change." (Jack Welch, the former CEO of General Electric)**

---

## "The Lead Wolf Leadership Creed"

- A leader doesn't follow others footprints—he is always first in line creating a new road map to follow

- A leader doesn't panic in a crisis-he becomes a pillar of strength for others

- A leader doesn't look for the light at the end of the tunnel—he carries the light

- A leader doesn't flaunt his title—he finds the time to be more than his title

- A leader doesn't get up early to make himself better—he gets up early to   help make others better

- A leader has a vision—he doesn't dream—he is the dream and he communicates his vision

- A leader isn't arrogant but he commands a presence-he is confident.

- The leader is not the one taking credit for success first-he's the first one to credit those who helped create success

- The leader may not be the most valuable player-he is the player most valued

- The leader does not like being called the reason for success-he realizes success depends on the people surrounding him --after all he is the leader

Eric (Rick) Johnson

---

**Thought Provoker**

"Leaders are humble individuals. They don't seek the spotlight. They respect the others on the team."

John Tyson
CEO Tyson Foods Inc.

---

# Chapter IV

# *Coaching and Mentoring*

A prerequisite for effective leadership is the ability to coach and mentor. There is a subtle difference between coaching and mentoring.

*__Coaching means__: Helping improve __performance__ by encouraging, motivating and directing others to achieve their goals.*

__Mentoring__ *__means__: Becoming a confidant – leading through the use of past examples and experience.*

Coaching is proven to work when the following factors are present. **First**, the employee is willing and wants to grow. **Second**, there is a gap between where they are now and where they want to be. These two basic factors are absolutely essential for the leader and the employee to solve problems, create a new life, turn a business around, double sales and profitability, and design and implement a plan of action.

Ultimately humans consistently do only that which they naturally and effortlessly love to do. Finding that passion again and determining what you really want for yourself and your business is your first task. Coaching will help distinguish between what the employee "should want" and "have to want" from what they truly want for themselves. Once you help them develop their vision, they are much more likely to naturally and consistently proceed in that direction.

Very few people ever learn the skills of how to think. In our schools, families, and social structures, we learn "how" and "what" to do and we learn "what" to think. Our world is full of individuals who have chosen dependent, me first, excuse-ridden attitudes. It has become a way of life. This type of attitude is a dead end for employees. It is unwanted, unproductive, and unprofitable. Possibility thinking through coaching opens the door to a whole new way of seeing and interacting within the environment of the business world we find ourselves in.

The old saying "No Pain, No Gain" is exactly the same as the scientific principle of cause and effect. The employees you select to coach and mentor will learn to produce more with less effort. They become more productive and more valuable to the organization. Coaching can

help employees eliminate roadblocks and help identify if not eliminate critical constraints that prevent success. Coaching helps employees intensify their focus and become more visionary and productive. Supportive and mutually beneficial relationships are what business and a friendly family culture are all about. Unfortunately, few people learn the communication, decision-making, and perception skills needed to nurture these incredible skills. It is amazing how simple they are to understand

and how difficult they are to implement. Coaching can increase the skill level in each of these areas.

## The Five Key Objectives of Coaching

1. Identify the obstacles to success and help the employee overcome them. Personal and professional success comes much more easily when you have a strong coach or mentor.

2. Better decisions are a result of the willingness to discuss ideas and concerns. Winners are always seeking feedback from others.

3. Expand the self imposed horizon and boundaries the employee has created for themselves.

4. Set individual goals and objectives.

5. Identify and work on individual weaknesses that can impede success.

## The Umbrella Principles

Think of coaching like an umbrella. There are several principles that fall under this umbrella that support the five key objectives of coaching, these include:

- Observing Behavior
- Effective Listening
- Providing Feedback
- Recognizing Performance
- Training

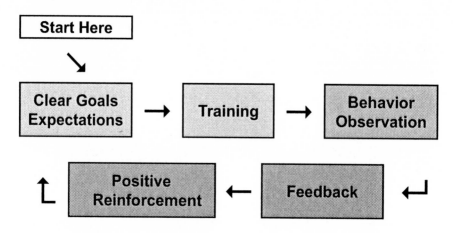

## Exhibit II

*Coaching is an ongoing process that should be done constantly. This process is demonstrated by the model in exhibit II.*

## The Five Steps in the Coaching Process

An effective coaching process requires that goals and expectations are clearly understood. It is essential that the employee being coached receive all the appropriate training based on his job responsibilities and future developmental needs. Behavior observation, communication and finally behavior modification are essential to success at coaching. This includes feedback and positive reinforcement.

**1. Set clear goals and expectations**. Setting goals and objectives is no easy task. They must be specific, measurable, attainable, relevant and tangible. (SMART) Goals and objectives are the very first step in effective coaching. The employee should participate in this process. After all, the goals should be specific to that individual and they must take ownership. As goals or expectations change, it is your job as coach to communicate these changes to your employees. The goal should be negotiated, not dictated.

---

**Thought Provoker**

**The best way to support behavior modification is to demonstrate the type of behavior expected through your own actions.**

**Lead by example!**

---

**2. Training**. To be an effective coach, you need to understand the employee's strengths and weaknesses. This includes a thorough understanding of their training needs and accomplishments. Do they have the necessary skills and knowledge to accomplish the goals and objectives that have been set? Making sure that the employee has the opportunity to get the required training to develop their skill set is a prerequisite to effective coaching. One of your basic challenging responsibilities as a coach is to identify the skills and knowledge the employee needs and then arrange for the appropriate training.

**3. Behavior Observation**. How does the employee react to a crisis? How do they handle themselves when they are placed in leadership situations? How do they react to peer pressure? As a coach observing the employee's behavior and noting specifics that need attention and discussion is a primary responsibility.

It is important that you collect and record both positive and negative performance along the way to add credibility to your feedback.

4. **Feedback.** Meeting with the employee regularly to discuss performance and other issues is absolutely critical to their development. The key is not in telling the employee what to do but it is helping the employee find the answers on their own. This can be done by asking very specific thought provoking questions. Make sure you give the employee kudos for all the positive behavior you have observed.

5. **Positive Reinforcement**. Believe it or not, employees want to be held accountable. If we re going to hold employees accountable, they have to know how they are performing. Specifically we should emphasize the positive aspects of their performance. Focusing on the good things an employee accomplishes will motivate them to continue to do good work, and in turn will ensure repeat performance.

## It's About Leadership

Make no mistake, coaching and mentoring is about leadership. It is difficult to be a coach or a mentor without leadership skills. Coaching and mentoring is all about the development of others. It requires effective development activities and projects related to current and future performance expectations. It requires the unique ability to recognize potential skill and ability in others that is worthy of development. A good coach or mentor possesses an innate ability to motivate and inspire others to achieve stretch goals. They have the ability, the knowledge and the sensitivity

to generate an adaptive style according to the individual and circumstances at hand earning respect and trust.

## Some of the key characteristics of coaches and mentors for the development of others include the following:

- The ability to help employees determine the skills and abilities necessary for growth
- Recognizes potential for leadership
- Creates appropriate development plans
- Skilled at constructive feedback
- Avoids the role of enabler and holds people accountable
- Rewards and recognizes success

## Delegation:

- Believes in the ability of employees and empowers them
- Provides opportunities for employees to develop
- Allows employees to take credit for success
- Provides guideline but does not get in their way

## Communication:

- Exceptional listening skills
- Maintains eye contact
- Takes notes
- Assures understanding by asking for clarifications
- Restates communication often to strengthen understanding of issue

- Uses servant style body language that is open and non threatening
- Speaks clearly and concisely
- Asks questions
- Maintains a positive attitude at all times

## Sensitivity:

- Demonstrates high self esteem and regard for others
- Encouraging attitude and concern for individual feelings
- Acknowledges accomplishments
- Always talks positive about others
- Aware of his own limitations
- Motivating influence

## Decision Making and Follow Through:

- Commits to a course of action
- Makes decisions openly
- Accepts responsibility
- Establishes priorities
- Sets completion dates with expected deliverables
- Anticipates needs and takes action
- Takes calculated risk but considers all aspects of the issue
- Develops alternative solutions
- Keeps appropriate people in the loop

## Preparation

Preparing for a formal coaching session is as critical as the actual coaching itself. Remember the old saying, "You will end up playing just like you practice." In spite of how well you know the employee and how confident you are in your coaching abilities; preparation and practice  determine how successful you will become. Coaching is not an easy task. People have different values, different principles and different life experiences. All these things combined and mixed with your company culture and work environment contribute to their response and performance on the job.

## Conducting Successful Coaching Session Suggestions

- Prepare by determining your key objectives.
- Put the employee at ease by being open and using positive body language.
- Define the reason for the discussion.
- Ask the employee how they feel about their progress.
- Express your concern about the area of performance you feel needs to be improved or discuss the area of performance that they excel in. Coaching is a

leadership skill. It applies to excellent performance, average performance and poor performance equally.

## If there is a performance problem:

- Describe the performance problem or the area that needs improvement and define the impact it has.

- Acknowledge and listen to the employee's feelings.

- Ask the employee's opinion for ways that can improve performance.

- Ask open-ended questions to engage the employee in helping come up with solutions to the problem.

- Give the employee ownership for solving problems and solutions.

- Obtain the employee's buy-in for the appropriate actions that need to take place.

- Schedule a follow-up meeting, with the objective being accountability on the employee's part to make changes and to provide feedback on improvement (within seven to ten days).

- Make a commitment to provide feedback on improvement (be sure to reward good performance in some way to reinforce the desired behavior).

Each of your employees has different personalities. Each employee is unique in his or her own way. This is why it is important to realize that you cannot coach every employee in the same way. You must get to know the people you are coaching and then determine the best coaching style to use.

Here are some guidelines to help you in determining the right coaching style for the individual and situation. Rate the skill and attitude level of the person you are coaching as high or low. Try to determine if they have released their discretionary energy in contributing to company success. Then select the appropriate coaching style based on the attitude—skill quadrant illustrated. This matrix can help you determine the style and level of coaching or mentoring that you may need to apply to different individuals.

## The Attitude/Skill Quadrant Matrix

| | Low Skill | High Skill |
|---|---|---|
| **Positive Attitude** | Coach and Mentor Train | Mentor Empower |
| **Negative Attitude** | Probation— Termination Manage | Coach- Manage Motivate |

# Use the coaching/mentoring attitude-skill quadrant matrix as follows:

## <u>Manage--(Low skill and Negative attitude)</u>

- Clarify expectations

- Establish expectations for future performance

- Provide training

- Comply with the review process providing feedback

- Probation

- Termination

Sometimes an effective leader needs to recognize when they have made a mistake. If the employee falls into this first quadrant, is not a new hire, has had all the training available to them, it is generally  expected that this employee may have to be thrown off the bus. Of course, as the leader you have to be able to look at yourself in the mirror and believe that you did everything possible to help this employee achieve success. If that is the case, you are doing the rest of the employees a disservice by keeping this employee. That is why probation and even termination exist within this quadrant.

## <u>Coach--(Low skill and Positive attitude)</u>

- Training

- Clarify expectations

- Seek employee input

- Learn from mistakes

Low skill with a positive attitude is one of the easier challenges in the coaching process. It is a lot easier to teach a skill than it is to change an attitude. You just can't teach attitude. In fact you cannot directly change attitude. You can only look for the possible causes and try to remove them. Employees that reside in this quadrant require additional training.

## **Coach-Mentor and Inspire (High skill and Poor attitude)**

- Identify the reason that the employee's attitude is poor: is it work related, supervision or personal issues affecting output?

- Look for reasons to compliment and praise

- Provide continuous feedback

- Track progress

- Try to remove any obstacles that may be contributing to the poor attitude

This is one of the more difficult challenges in the coaching mentoring process as it may require a combination of both coaching and mentoring dependent upon circumstances. It is absolutely critical that we determine the root cause for the poor attitude. This is where it can get difficult. Attitude can be affected by many different things including ones personal life and home environment. Tread softly here. Do not probe into the employee's life but be a good listener.

---

**Thought Provoker**

Leadership is an invitation to greatness that we extend to others. Successful leaders understand that they must give back what they have learned. They become mentors.

---

## Mentor--(High skill and positive attitude)

- Empower the employee
- Establish realistic objectives
- Challenge the employee to set stretch goals
- Don't micro-manage
- Stay out of his way
- Remove obstacles

This is the kind of employee we are all striving for. They are the future leaders of the organization. It is our responsibility as leaders to mentor these employees and help them develop their own greatness.

## Benefits of Coaching and Mentoring:

## 1.      Creates a platform for open communication

Communication skills are extremely important to the coaching and mentoring process. Listening is extremely important to understanding the individual employee needs regardless of the skill-attitude quadrant they find themselves in. Effective coaching and mentoring provides:

- An opportunity to communicate with each of your employees regarding their performance.

- Specific opportunity for you to provide both *constructive feedback* and *positive reinforcement.*

- Affords the employee an opportunity to express their concerns.

---

**Thought Provoker**

**Notice we use the term constructive feedback and not constructive criticism. There is no such thing as constructive criticism. Once an employee feels he is being criticized we have lost all chance of being constructive. Discussing weaknesses and poor performance is necessary but how we discuss that performance is a critical coaching skill.**

*"This is covered in more detail in chapter V."*

---

## 2. Helps determine strengths and weaknesses in a positive environment

- Gives you and your employees the opportunity to evaluate specific job related performance

- Addressing their strengths and weaknesses will help establish your expectations, so the employee will know what they are doing right and what they need to work on.

## 3. It is motivational

- Motivation and encouragement that creates enthusiasm and commitment.

- Clarification of goals that enable individuals to relate their personal goals to the organization's goals.

## Constructive Criticism
**There is no such thing as constructive criticism**

Feedback is *giving someone information on their behavior.* A person's behavior is either "on-target" or "off-target" from your expectations and standards.

## Feedback Guidelines

- Never interrogate, it just isn't necessary to ask a lot of questions during a feedback session.

- Trust is essential for candor and constructive feedback. If you haven't gained their trust you will not be effective.

- Maintain a conversational non-sales approach.

## There are two kinds of feedback:

1. Positive reinforcement
2. Constructive feedback given in a positive format

- **Positive reinforcement** is reinforcing or recognizing a desirable behavior by acknowledging the behavior. This is behavior that is expected from the employee. Positive reinforcement will stabilize performance activity and support continued behavior that meets expectations or exceeds it. This will increase the frequency of that behavior, as well as increase the employee's commitment and positive attitude.

---

**Thought Provoker**

**Positive reinforcement should always include:**

- **Specifics about the employee's performance.**
- **Timely feedback as close to the behavior as possible.**
- **Clear recognition of the employee on a personal basis.**

---

- <u>**Constructive feedback**</u> is information communicated from the manager of the employee regarding a behavior or task that does not meet performance standards and needs improvement. How this is communicated is critical. It is not constructive criticism. Criticizing an employee serves no purpose. Look for the good first and then explain the better performance desired.

It is human nature for employees to seek validation and approval. Believe it or not, employees want to be held accountable. Employees want to know how they are doing. When you know how and when to give positive reinforcement and are comfortable doing it, you are well on your way to helping your people to achieve to their fullest potential.

Feedback is *giving someone information on their behavior.* A person's behavior is either "on-target" or "off-target" from your expectations and standards.

## Why is it important to provide your employees with feedback on their job performance?

Employees have a right to know how there performance is regarded by their supervisor. If they are performing well, acknowledging that is positive reinforcement for continued high performance. If they are not doing well, they need help in addressing those areas that need improvement. Now we are referring to a behavior that is "off target" from your expectations and standards. *Constructive feedback*, on the other hand, is more difficult to provide because many times it is met with resistance. If given properly, constructive feedback will eliminate the undesirable behavior and change it to a more desirable behavior. It's all in the delivery. ***It is not Constructive Criticism.***

---

**Thought Provoker**

Constructive feedback must start with positive recognition of on-target performance that is related. Criticism is not acceptable. Discuss the situation and how changes in the approach or action may provide different results.

- Be specific.
- Don't get emotional.
- You are not a judge and jury—you are a coach.
- Don't exaggerate.
- Speak from your heart.

---

## Putting the Pieces Together

| Situational Behavior | ▶ | Reinforcement Planning and Discussion | ▶ | Agreed Upon Action Plans | ▶ | Results |

Feedback Modifications ↵

## Exhibit III

## Performance Adaptive Feedback Model

When providing feedback to an employee it is imperative that you discuss the **situation**, their **behavior**, and the **impact** the behavior is having in a broad sense.

**1. Determine the Cause**: Ask probing questions to determine why the employee acts in a specific manner

**2. Address the Problem**: Open honest discussion that solves problems and develops improvement action planning

**3. Agree on Next Steps**: Both the supervisor and the employee should agree on the action plan for improvement. Schedule the next follow-up meeting.

---

**Thought Provoker**

**Following up is critical. You must hold the employee accountable for the agreed solution, and you must monitor progress.**

---

## The Mentoring Process

## Mentoring

*Becoming a confidant—leading through the use of past examples and experience. Mentoring is providing guidance, support and training to expedite the development of someone that has the potential to become an effective leader. Mentoring helps define ones purpose, values, skills and unique talents.*

Classroom training is not the only answer to improving our effectiveness as leaders. In fact, it may have the smallest impact on our progress. Actual experiences and learning from those experiences is a key part of the learning process. Mentoring is essential to this experienced based learning. Good judgment is based on experience and experience is based on bad judgment. (Steve Kaufman) The key is learning from our bad judgment. This is a much more effective process if there

is a mentor involved that can help you through the experience based learning process.

There aren't many successful people in life that haven't had the help of someone along the way; that help may have appeared in the form of a role model, the support of a particular group, a personal friend and confidant or a  hands on mentor. Finding that resource, the right person, is often very challenging. We may end up connecting with a mentor purely by accident, through circumstance or we may actually seek out someone to mentor us.  Mentoring involves commitment and a long-term relationship that an experienced leader makes to support the professional development of a protégé. It can be a formal or an informal process. Since this process is so valuable, many companies are looking for ways to create formal mentoring programs. It is really all about leadership development.

Mentoring can take the form of challenging assignments that create unique opportunities to gain experience in specific leadership areas. Another tool that is becoming more popular in the formal mentoring programs is the 360-feedback review. This is a performance evaluation of the mentored individual by his peers, his manager and his subordinates. This however, should not be an isolated feedback process. Improvement planning and evaluation validation must be a part of this process. The mentor and the individual's supervisor, if they are different individuals, must actively support this process. Incomplete information and lack of follow-up and support can destroy the benefits of this process. Timing is also very critical to this process and it should always carry a positive reinforcement message to the person being mentored.

## Leaders Must Be Mentors

1.  Write down the name of your mentor, someone who taught you something about leadership (personal or professional):

_____

_____

2.  What leadership principles did you learn from this person?

_____

_____

_____

_____

3.  What have you intentionally done or intend to do to mentor others in their bid to become leaders?

_____

_____

_____

_____

## Balance

Balance is important in life. The mentor must keep in mind that people cannot "Live to Work" they must "Work to Live." This is about keeping family life and personal values in perspective. A healthy lifestyle is important to success. This in itself will not only help minimize stress

but will allow the employee to deal with stress as it occurs. We live with stress every day. The deadlines, the crisis after crisis and facing unexpected problems and events create stress in our lives. Stress does serve a purpose. It helps us become more effective. It provides the "Thrill of Victory" when we succeed at something. But uncontrolled stress and too much stress can be damaging not only to our business success but also to our health in general. We often run our bodies at maximum speed constantly and expect success. Stress kills. If you are constantly running at full speed, you may not even recognize tell tale signs that lead to failure. It is a primary responsibility of the mentor to not allow this type of stress level to occur. Uncontrolled stress produces many warning signs including:

1. Impatience
2. A deep sense of being tired
3. Abusive and dogmatic behavior
4. Irrational expectations
5. Difficulty in concentrating

6. Depression

7. Pessimism

8. Withdrawal from the limelight

9. Feeling tired and worn out

When you reach the twilight of your life you want to be able to say:

*"I not only stopped to smell the roses, I tore off the petals and threw them into the wind!"*

## Why become a Mentor or seek out a Mentor?

Mentoring is a form of learning that goes back to ancient times when an experienced and successful teacher would take on a specific pupil to teach him everything he knew to duplicate his success. Remember the movie "The Karate Kid"? This methodology was the most effective form of creating succession. It was the original form of succession planning. By mentoring, the experienced teacher could shortcut mistakes, wrong turns and other costly set backs that others make without the privilege of having a mentor? Mentoring is an honorable, old way of learning that had been forgotten but is now being rediscovered as an extremely valuable leadership development tool.

Some people say success has a lot to do with luck. The harder you work the luckier you get. Mentoring can help find the virtues, the attitude and the values necessary for success. Virtues and values are very definable. They can be defined as:

- Integrity
- Honesty
- Respect
- Compassion
- Character

However attitude is a state of mind. Something that changes based on circumstance and the environment. Attitude is extremely important when mentoring or being mentored. Success is very dependent on an attitude that embraces the following:

- Impatience
- Abstract unconventional thinking
- Insightfulness
- Happiness
- Calculated risk taking
- Hunger for achievement
- Decisiveness
- Self awareness

**Impatience** in the world of success can be a virtue. Don't be so patient and tolerant about everything that you lose your passion. Life is too short to drink cheap wine. Don't allow others to dictate your schedule or control your life. It's your life and life is short. Success comes to those who proactively go out and make things happen. They don't sit around waiting for something to happen.

**Abstract Unconventional Thinking** creates vision. Be a little crazy. Go against conventional wisdom when you feel it in your gut. Remember, many geniuses were once considered crazy. Don't always go along with the majority. Challenge the status quo.

**Insightfulness** means demonstrating passion for your ideas. Excitement breeds excitement. Success breeds success. Believe in yourself. Believe in your ideas and don't be afraid to express that confidence but express it without demonstrating cockiness or arrogance.

**Happiness** is absolutely an essential ingredient to becoming successful. You must have fun and be happy doing the work you do. If you do not enjoy what you are doing, you will not do it well. Money is not, I repeat, money is not the barometer of success. It's just a way of keeping score. Unless you are happy with your work, your life and you have created a balance, money doesn't mean anything. Learn how to laugh. Laugh at the challenges life often puts in front of you.

**Calculated risk taking** means avoiding the fear that doesn't allow you to stretch, to reach for something extra, to take a chance on something. Calculated risk is thought out. It is not whimsical or foolish. The odds are in your favor. The greatest risk in life is not taking any risk. Mediocrity must not become a standard in your life. Success takes guts. That means you have fortitude and a lot of character. Tell yourself, when the day comes that you retire, you will not look back on your life with regrets.

**Hunger for achievement** means you will not give up. You have drive. You want to succeed so badly that you think about it all the time. Being hungry means you are focused on what it is going to take for you to succeed. You have a passion, a desire and a willingness to learn.

**Decisiveness** is the ability to make a decision and stick to it. Execution and implementation are two important keys to success. If you have a mentor, utilize the knowledge you are gaining from the relationship. Be original in utilizing the experience and knowledge you are gaining.

**Self-awareness** is the ability to understand you. Know your strengths but more importantly know your weaknesses. Capitalize on your strengths and work on your weaknesses. Don't ignore them. But be happy with who you are. You wouldn't have or be a mentor if you didn't have the potential to help create success.

## Finding a Mentor

Most often you will find the mentor you are looking for at your place of employment. Picking the right person to mentor you is important. First of all, they must have gained the respect of others in your organization. They must be recognized as a leader in the organization and demonstrate the Lead Wolf model of leadership that excites people making them want to follow their lead. Accept no substitute, no stand in. However, most importantly, the candidate you select must be willing and able to take on the responsibility of mentoring you. This is not something either of you should take likely. A mentor is not just

someone you can go to for advice. A real mentor is interested in you, your life, your progress and your success. They take a proactive role in your development and your leadership effectiveness. Don't accept substitutes. Study ahead and read everything that is available that your mentor has produced prior to working with you. Make your time and your mentor's time as productive as possible. Create an action plan with your mentor that defines the activities in great detail. Details that you need to complete to create the success that you and your mentor have defined. Specific goals and objectives with a definitive timeline are key components to the mentoring process. You may recall having a mentor in your past, even in your childhood. In the following "Personal" story several mentors played a dominant role in shaping my life. "Thank God!"

## <u>The TOLEDO STORY—Who Invented the Moon Walk?</u>

*If they couldn't sell a newspaper, they'd shine shoes. If that didn't work, they'd dance to music on the jukebox hoping the drunks and semi-drunks on skid row would throw nickels and dimes at them. In fact, it wasn't Michael Jackson who invented the moonwalk; it was Louie Jones who first did it in a little bar called the Erie Café in Toledo, Ohio.*

> *A number of years ago a 10-year-old boy roamed the streets of Toledo, Ohio. He grew up on those streets learning life's lessons. Like many of us, he came from a broken home. His daddy left him and his four brothers and one sister when he was five. His Dad died when he was nine. He was the youngest, the baby of the family.*

*You can imagine that times were tough; feeding six hungry kids wasn't easy, especially without a father figure. In fact, he was on welfare during his entire adolescent period until he joined the military at age 17.*

*At the age of 10 he sold newspapers in downtown Toledo. He crafted his abilities, his drive, on those streets. He didn't have a plan, he didn't have anyone to show him the way. He only had himself and he had his best friend, an African American kid named Louie Jones. They didn't have a normal paper route like most kids, delivering to the same house every day in nice, quiet neighborhoods. This young boy and his friend, Louis, did what was known as blue jacking and their territory happened to be skid row. They carried a canvas sack filled with the Toledo Blade. The bag weighed almost as much as they did.*

*They went bar to bar. "Paper mister, shine. Paper mister, shine?" "Here's a quarter kid. Get the Hell outta here."*

*This kid was developing scar tissue. At the age of five he lived in an abandoned house trailer with no heat or running water and an outhouse. Their was big hole cut in the ceiling with a 55 gallon drum under it so they could build a fire to keep warm and the smoke would go out of the hole. At eight years old he lived in a condemned house that was actually located right on the city dump. That house had rats bigger than cats running around at night with their beady eyes shining in the dark. He used to shoot marbles at them with his sling shot. It was a game.*

*The young man didn't realize how bad he had it back then even though at times he would crouch down and hide behind trash cans and cars as he walked home from school until the rest of the kids were gone so they didn't see him go into that condemned house on the city dump. In fact, although he was embarrassed about where he lived he actually was more upset about his big ears. To him they felt like he had two kites tied to his head. He could feel them move when the wind was strong. Grade school kids can be cruel and they teased him all the time. They were relentless. Many times he would come home crying. But he couldn't tell his mother about it. He couldn't tell her why he was crying. Because-- **SHE HAD BIG EARS TOO**. She thought it was because they had nothing and lived in such a state.*

*Before his 11th birthday, His oldest two brothers had left home and joined the military and the third went to live with an aunt.*

*At the time the young man didn't realize what life should be like. He just didn't know. He was relatively happy, upbeat. They say ignorance is bliss, well; this young man's ignorance was only of his surroundings. He was quite an entrepreneur and became more successful on the streets as he grew. People create their own success, but it's a whole lot easier if you have a direction and a mentor. His mother referred to him as Dr. Jekyll and Mr. Hyde. He graduated high school in the upper ten percent of his class even though he was suspended three times during his senior year. He started his first business at the age of 15 selling used car parts. He would take orders by day and fill them by night.*

*"You need hubcaps for a '57 Chevy, not a problem; a carburetor for a '55 Ford, you'll have it in two days."*

*Then a life changing event occurred, he graduated from high school and, at the age of 17, he had no clue what to do with his life. But he did know what he didn't know. He knew that if he continued on the path he was on he would end up in deep trouble, maybe even prison. He knew he needed something to change the direction he was headed in. Something to change the path he was on. He needed a plan, a roadmap. He wasn't proud of his past, but it was his survival.*

*It has been said that high impact leaders don't go down existing paths, they create new ones for others to follow. This kid hadn't become a leader yet, he needed a path to follow, a road map to follow. He needed guidance and discipline.*

*The United States Military provided that guidance and discipline. After graduating from high school at 17, he entered the military where he was trained in Jungle Survival; not a whole lot of difference in the techniques he learned in street survival. Not a whole lot different then the techniques you must learn to be successful in wholesale distribution.*

*Those four years were filled with defining moments in his life. Although he didn't recognize it at the time, several mentors had influenced his development. He had no idea what to do when his four year in the military were up. The separation counselor told him his job experience in the military meant that he qualified to be a forest ranger or a Hunting & Fishing guide in civilian life.*

*That just wouldn't work. He didn't like to camp and he didn't hunt. One thing he did learn from the military though, if you are going to succeed, you've got to prepare and you've got to have a plan. His very first mentor in adult life, Tech Sergeant Stamp told him once — "if your gonna get ahead boy—you've got to be hungry. You've got to want it more than anything you've ever wanted. You've got to be hungry. You've got to be huuuuuungry!" He drilled it into him.*

*-He was hungry. He answered an advertisement for a job as an inside salesman for a steel distributor.*

*He walked in:*

*"Mr. Marshall, I'm here to apply for that job you advertised for an inside salesman."*

*------ "Do you have any experience son?"*

*"No sir Mr. Marshall—but I'm smart and I learn fast."*

*----- "Do you have a college education son?"*

*"No sir."*

*"I'm sorry but, we're looking for someone with experience. Or Someone with a college education."*

*He went back home—he told his wife the story and she said; "You aren't giving up are you? Remember what SSgt Stamp told you. He told you you've got to be **huuuuuungry.**"*

*So he went back the next day.*

*"Mr. Marshall. I'm here to apply for that job as inside salesman."*

*"Weren't you here yesterday son?"*

*"Yes sir".*

*"Didn't I tell you we were looking for experience or a college education?"*

*"Yes sir."*

"Then get on out of here."

*"But, Mr. Marshall —I thought about it and I do have experience."*

- *"I have life experience."*
- *"I spent four years in the military. I think that's better than any college education you can get."*
- *"I learned respect."*
- *"I learned discipline."*
- *"I learned tenacity. "*
- *"I learned to never give up".*
- *"I learned to demonstrate confidence in my fellow man and to show him he could always count on me regardless of the severity of the situation."*
- *"I learned how to smooze the generals and discipline the privates".*

- *"I know what it takes to survive in the jungle ---I know what it takes to survive on the streets."*

*"Mr. Marshall, I guarantee you it wont take me long to learn how to not only survive but to excel in sales. If you don't hire me Mr. Marshall it will be the biggest mistake you can make and you probably won't get another chance because there's somebody out there that knows they can use the skill sets that I bring to the table."*

### He was HUNNNNNGRY.

*Mr. Marshall looked at the lad in amazement and finally he said; "Can you start Monday young man?" He was hungry.*

*He learned quickly and became very successful, being a little dysfunctional helps in this business. At 32 years old he started his own steel processing and distribution business. He grew it to $25 million in sales in nine years and then he sold it.*

*He didn't get his Bachelor's degree until he was 42 years old and his MBA at the age of 50 and his PhD at 58, but as I write this book today, I am absolutely certain that I wouldn't be writing it if someone hadn't provided coaching, mentoring and the guidance for the journey I was to undertake in my life.*

*That journey continued after leaving the military and it did seem like a jungle out there in civilian life. And the roadmap the military had provided was now gone. The principles, the character, the discipline and the integrity remained but I no longer had the structured guidance or the mentor influence on my life. It was tough and as I look back I can recall many*

*names and many faces that helped me avoid the landmines. They helped me learn from my mistakes. As I began my civilian career, new mentors began to emerge.*

## Mentors

Mentors-----we learn a tremendous amount from them. They helped me become successful enough, confident enough to start my own distribution business.

That confidence comes from within---ultimately it depends on you—But having someone to coach or mentor you sure makes things a lot easier.

**_Some executives actually hire professional business coaches. The right coach can become an excellent mentor. But coaching alone will provide an edge to maximizing success. Any mentoring relationship just adds to the success formula._**

Consider the following questions to understand how you can make the most of your opportunity to be coached or mentored.

## BUSINESS

- Is your family and career out of balance (working too much)?
- Do you need to get your creative juices flowing again?
- Do you need to become more organized?
- Do you want to increase productivity?

- Do you need help strategizing/problem solving?

- Do you need to set clear goals and get more focused?

- Identify the specific challenges you face in your job.

- Are you confused about wanting to change what you do?

- Do you want to become more successful in life?

## PERSONAL

- Are you facing relationship/family challenges?

- Do you have a hard time coping with stress?

- Do you have a hard time getting things done (follow through)?

- Do you feel stuck and confused?

- Has something recently altered your lifestyle?

- Are you in the midst of a life/career transition?

- Do you need to release the past?

## GOALS

- Have you discovered what you really want in life?

- Do you need to build a strong personal foundation?

- Have you discovered and expressed your unique talents?

- Do you need to create more focus and results?

- Do you need to enhance your communication skills?

## In addition to finding a mentor, you may need to become a mentor for others...

## Are You Ready to Become A Mentor?

**Circle the number that you believe describes your leadership ability.**

| Category | Description | Never 1 | 2 | Sometimes 3 | 4 | Always 5 |
|---|---|---|---|---|---|---|
| 1. Setting an example | When you coach/mentor you also listen well. You can identify things you learn during this process | | | | | |

| | | | | | | |
|---|---|---|---|---|---|---|
| 2. Clarity | You can clearly articulate your point of view and use relevant examples. This includes discussions on ideas, values, communication, respect and the sense of urgency required in becoming a leader | | | | | |
| 3. Commitment - a non-threatened view | You personally believe a commitment to develop your subordinates is good for you, the company and the individual | | | | | |
| 4. Scope | When mentoring others you focus on the total leadership equation – both hard, analytical issues and intangible issues such as how to create a sense of urgency | | | | | |

Scoring sixteen or higher means you may be a candidate to become a mentor. This is only a guide however, being a mentor requires that you have all the characteristics of effective leadership described throughout this book.

## Exercise I
## Coaching and Mentoring a Sales Representative

### Situational Guidelines

Objective:     To accomplish a specific call objective and also improve the competitive positioning of the distributor field sales representative. Your call must be planned in advance, paying particular attention to:

- Primary calling objective

- Secondary calling objective (if the first one doesn't work)

- Roles to play by rep and manager

- Code word or sign to signal "be quiet"

- You need to balance the discussion between all three parties. If the buyer only talks to you, ask the rep directly for more information about the buyer's questions (gives the rep a chance to talk).

- It is important for the buyer to believe that the sales representative has considerable power and influence within the organization. Do not make any customer commitments without checking with the rep first.

- Make reference where possible to achievements of the sales rep. They can't blow their own horn, but you can do it for them.

- The rep should position your visit to the account in advance as a visit from a "brilliant, successful and important industry expert."

- If a "good guy, bad guy" approach seems to be appropriate, the sales rep is ALWAYS the good guy. By setting this up and letting the rep "win," a customer will often be impressed with the clout of the sales rep.

- Managers should always pick up any social expenses, meals, bar tabs, etc. never the sales representative.

- If a supplier is involved, preplanning is absolutely necessary to ensure that everyone is working toward the same objectives.

- When the call is complete, always discuss the results. Ask the sales representative what he thinks. What went right? What went wrong? What could have been done better? Do not criticize. Let the rep find the answers through effective questioning.

## Exercise II
## Coaching and Mentoring a Sales Representative

### Situational Guidelines
### Territory Reviews and Territory Planning

Objective: To determine priorities for future time allocation, improve effectiveness of activities and ensure that necessary resources are available for critical tasks.

Establishing your intent is critical and must include:

- Your desire to increase their commissions
- Your desire to achieve business objectives
- Your desire to help them be "risk prone"
- Your desire to remove obstacles

The more time spent ensuring sales representative understanding of business objectives, the less time spent in disagreements on time allocation. Review forms should require the sales rep to write in actual results on your business objectives so they understand their own performance.

Working through customer development difficulties and obstacles is best done in a group setting for team building and synergy (off site?). The sales rep is good at describing new opportunities. You need to be good at finding the opportunities that are dying. Taking time away from dying opportunities is the only way to resource new opportunities.

Action plans should include:

- Which accounts will get less sales time
- Which accounts will get more sales time
- Call objectives on major opportunities
- Alert program for internal peers (credit, inside sales, product, warehouse)
- Objectives for next month's supplier work
- Targeted buddy calls
- Tier Level Selling (TLS) Penetration Strategy

It is important to present a balanced view of performance so be sure to fully discuss what is going right. Be sure to use the review to find out from the sales rep how you are doing as the manager. Is there anything that you could do more of, better or different to help improve their performance?

---

**Thought Provoker**

"No one will follow you if you do not listen to their concerns. Of all the skills I think people fall short on, it is the skill of listening. No one will follow you if they feel they are insignificant. Therefore, it is important to make sure that everyone you are privileged to lead understands their role. People should also be held accountable. This will engender respect as well."

**Errol B. Davis Jr.**
**CEO Alliant Energy**

---

# Chapter V

## *Employee Performance*

First of all, if all you ever do is an annual performance review for your employees, they are worthless. Put every last one of them in a big pile and burn them. The scenario of annual performance reviews often goes like this; "I have nine reviews I have to get done by the end of the month. As a result, I feel more pressure about completing the review than I feel an obligation to the employees to let them know how they are really doing. How I can help them."

Additionally, since you only do one review a year, chances are you are only going to base your judgment about the employee's performance on the last two months or so. If the employee happened to have done something wrong during that two month period, they get a poor review. Conversely, if they did everything right in those two months, they get a good review. A good review even if they performed very poorly early in the year. Is that really justice?

Some critics promote the theory that reviews are worthless and should be abolished altogether. However, that really isn't an option. Performance reviews are and have been a corner stone for managing performance. It is about accountability. In reality, performance reviews don't hold people accountable, managers do. Employees must understand what the employers expectations are of them. This can not be accomplished in a once a year meeting.

The purpose of a performance review is not to build a case for termination. Nor is its purpose to write a hallmark moment about how wonderful the employee is. The purpose of a performance review is to let the employee know where they stand. How they are doing. To determine what the company can do to help them become the best at what they do. To recognize their contributions and also to help them recognize their weaknesses and where they may need additional training and development. You cannot accomplish those objectives if you are pressured to complete multiple reviews under pressure. You can not accomplish those objectives if you only think about the last several months of the employee's performance.

As managers, as leaders, we owe it to our employees to help them develop their talents. It's good for them, it's good for us and it is good for the company. We need to make an individual commitment to every one of our direct reports that we will spend a minimum of thirty minutes per month discussing their performance. What they are doing well and what they need to work on. A simple four by six card noting our discussion thrown into their file provides tremendous insight when it comes time to do their annual review. You now have twelve individual documented discussions to refer to when completing their review. It also will show their progress. How they follow direction? What kind of support, training, mentoring or coaching that has taken place over the course of a year?

Reviews will never be 100% accurate and 100% honest. It's a good idea if reviews are reviewed especially if they only occur annually. Another concept for making reviews more accurate is the utilization of 360 degree reviews. This includes having employees reviewed by their supervisor., their peers and subordinates if applicable. Keeping reviews as objective as possible with definitive key performance measurements also reduces the human factor. Yes, performance reviews will probably never go away. We must not lose sight of the fact that the more critical aspect of leadership, coaching and mentoring is the actual setting and understanding of expectations.

## Why are performance reviews important?

As mentioned in an earlier chapter. Employees want to be held accountable. Employees want to know how they are doing. Employees can not strive for excellence if they do not know where they stand. Performance reviews can guide an employee's progress. They can identify the employee's career path and they can identify area's of performance that need improvement and create a plan with input from the employee to correct the problems. In order for employees to improve and maintain their job performance and skills, it is **necessary to periodically** review their performance and **provide** appropriate **feedback**.

The starting point of any coaching process is setting goals and expectations and then observing *behavior* and *providing*

*specific performance feedback.* That is what a performance review is all about. When you are reviewing performance, there is a process that you should follow. It is illustrated in Exhibit IV the performance review cycle.

## Exhibit IV

## The Performance Review Cycle

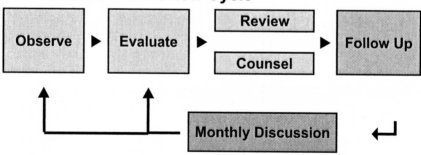

### *Observe*

When reviewing performance it is necessary to observe your employee's behaviors throughout the year. A monthly coaching discussion will keep the employee informed and will allow you to make an objective assessment of the employees performance and progress.

## Here are a few tips to observing performance:

Performance observance can happen in numerous different ways depending upon the employees job function. Outside sales is easy. A Ride Along by the Sales Manager creates a great opportunity to observe performance. Other observation techniques include:

- In Basket e-mail training (The employee is asked to handle every e-mail you receive in a day and make a decision as to what action should be taken)
- Reviewing specific metric Key Performance Indicators (KPI's)
- Working side by side with the employee by assigning a special project

---

**Thought Provoker**

- **Observe Behavior at every opportunity.**
- **Document the behavior and have monthly coaching sessions.**

---

## Evaluate--------Tips on Performance Reviews

- Be fair and objective by assessing job performance against pre-determined job-related performance standards.
- Involve the employee in the development of the action plan.

- Include specific and measurable goals with action plans on how to reach them. Set time frames to review accomplished goals, identify possible obstacles and identify ways to overcome them.

- Encourage feedback from your employee.

- Review a summary of your feedback by beginning with the employee's strengths and then tactfully move into the weaknesses.

- End the review by summarizing the action plan for improvements, so your employee clearly understands what's expected of him or her. End on a positive note and set a date for the next review.

The outcome of this review should come as **no surprise** to the employee, if you are **continually reviewing, evaluating, and providing feedback.**

## Conducting the Review

Create a self review. Have your employee rate them self by filling out a Performance Evaluation prior to their review. Tell them to provide specific examples to back up their ratings. Review their evaluation before you meet. This will provide for a more interactive meeting. Always focus on a positive before you discuss a negative. Keep the review as objective as possible utilizing facts and data. Follow your company review form precisely. It is organized in the fashion it is in for a reason. Do not speculate; make assumptions or offer opinions as to cause. Do ask a lot of questions. Focus on the differences between the self review and your review of the employee. Create a continuous follow up schedule.

**Checklist for Conducting Performance Appraisals**

**Objective:** To maintain or improve good performance in employees by providing specific performance feedback.

Assumptions of employees are about getting "in trouble" so there is a tendency to be defensive and avoid issues.

Physical surroundings can offset nervousness of both parties.

When evaluating performance, four areas must be considered:

1. Actual performance (numbers, results, etc.)
2. Conditions of performance (market change)
3. Your managerial support provided
4. Attitudes, values and feelings demonstrated

As a manager, you have prepared for the discussion with written notes (i.e. critical events file) and have spent 20 quiet minutes before the meeting on your objective.

You should have a handwritten objective about employee beliefs and conclusions at the end of the meeting. The most critical part of the appraisal process is establishing your managerial intent:

- The objective stated above
- Your desire to be helpful
- Your responsibility for problems

The key success criterion is that both parties feel better. Feedback on performance areas of concern is constructive only when:

- It is future focused?
- You don't ask "Why?"
- You itemize merits as well as concerns.
- You provide alternatives.
- You apologize for delayed feedback.

The action plan developed must have dates and expected results which include:

- What the employee is going to do?
- What you are going to do to help?
- What training will be provided?

An annual appraisal should only be done if you have discussed monthly employee performance with the employee.

## Behavior Modification and Leadership

## General

The objective of coaching and mentoring is to make the individual an effective leader rather than just a better employee. The method utilized to accomplish this objective and make you a better coach/mentor is to familiarize you with both the concept and the practical application of behavior modification theory.

## Definitions

Behavior Modification involves the application of knowledge from various disciplines and theories for the purpose of changing behaviors. Behavior is what a person does. It must also meet the following criteria:

- It must be observable
- It must be measurable
- It must be describable

The basic assumption is that most behaviors are learned (rather than being innate) and that these learned behaviors could, therefore, be increased or decreased utilizing certain learning theory principles.

## There are two types of behaviors. These are:

1. **On task behavior** – what we want our people to do, or desirable behavior.

2. **Off task behavior** – what we don't want our people to do, what we want to get rid of, or undesirable behavior.

## On Task Behavior Examples: "Common Sense"

1. Coming to work on time
2. Dressing "appropriately"
3. Saying "Thank you"
4. Performing daily job functions
5. Completing an expense account

6. Making a phone call

7. Going on a service call

8. Writing a report

9. Paying someone a compliment

10. Finishing any unit of work

11. Keeping work area neat

12. Completing a billing

13. Using safe equipment

14. Following a (new) procedure

## Off Task Behaviors Examples

1. Coming to work late

2. Dressing "inappropriately" (sloppy or sexy)

3. Excessive talking with co-workers

4. Speaking without looking at customer

5. Having accidents

6. Missing work deadlines

7. Ignoring people

8. Speaking "too loudly" or "too softly"

9. Leaving work incomplete

10. Making repetitive mistakes

11. Interrupting another person

12. Walking out of meetings

13. Looking out the window not paying attention

## Concepts and Behaviors

Before proceeding it is necessary to make a clear distinction between the terms "Concepts" and "Behaviors"

---

**Thought Provoker**

**You will recall a behavior is what a person does and must be observable, measurable and describable. These last two criteria help to distinguish a behavior from a concept. You can coach behavior but you can't coach concepts.**

---

It is important to make this distinction because to be an effective mentor/coach you must deal with behaviors rather than concepts.

As an example, to say, *"The sales representative works hard,"* is a concept. On the other hand, to say, *"The sales representative makes 12 calls a day,"* is a behavior. It is measurable and definable. Concepts can therefore be thought of as summary statements of behaviors.

**Exercise IV** Indicate whether the sentences below describe concepts or behaviors:

1. He is discourteous._____

2. He interrupts people when they are talking._____

3. He says hello to everyone he meets._____

4. He wastes time._____

5. He takes half hour coffee breaks._____

6. He uses everyone's name when he speaks to people.___

_____

## Concepts and Behaviors

<u>**Concepts**</u>

1. Hardworking
2. Cooperative
3. Unmotivated
4. Creative
5. Touchy
6. Careless
7. Nervous

<u>**Behaviors**</u>

1. Makes typing errors
2. Follows other's suggestions
3. Looks away when spoken to
4. Rolls up shirt sleeves
5. Rests hand on other employees
6. Makes jokes
7. Has spots on clothes

## Behavior Modification

There are three elements to consider when analyzing a situation to determine what is happening. These are:

**A**ntecedents -Things that come before behavior

**B**ehavior – What a person does

Consequences – The immediate or long-term consequence to the employee as a result of their behavior, i.e. reward punishment, etc. These consequences may be positive, negative or neutral.

An example of the above ABC's might be:

- Giving a new employee instructions on how to do a task (Antecedent)
- The employee completes the task (Behavior)
- The supervisor compliments the employee for completing the task (Positive Consequence)

---

**Thought Provoker**

**The principle of behavior modification is that behavior followed by a positive consequence is more apt to be repeated in the future. A positive reinforcement is a reward. It is something satisfying or enjoyable to the individual, i.e. money, praise, time off, vacations.**

---

If you, as the coach/mentor, compliment an employee for using a skill correctly, you are positively reinforcing their behavior and it is more likely he will continue to use the skill correctly in the future. In other words, you are rewarding on-task or desired behavior. The same principle holds true for off task or undesirable behavior. As an example, if in our case the employee used a skill incorrectly but you are unaware of what the correct skill use should be, then praising the salesperson for incorrect skill use would increase the likelihood that he would continue to use the skill incorrectly in the future. Therefore, it

is necessary for you to understand correct skill use before you can be an effective coach.

## Positive Reinforcement Application

After an employee's behavior is observed, they are then critiqued in terms of correct or incorrect skill use (desired or undesired behaviors).

Those skills, which the employee used correctly, should be positively reinforced.

As an example, you might say to the person, "During the sales call, the customer brought up a need which you first agreed with then introduced an appropriate value proposition of our product which could satisfy that need. That was an excellent supporting statement. In other words, you are positively reinforcing a desired behavior vs. dealing with concepts and generalities like, "you did a good job during the call." The first approach will make you a more successful coach and increase the likelihood that the employee will continue to use the skills correctly. When you first begin the coaching process do not say anything about incorrect skill use if you observe the employee utilizing some skills poorly.

## <u>Frequency</u>

Some additional principles of positive reinforcement should also be considered here. First, the shorter delay between behavior and reinforcement, the more effective the reinforcement will be (i.e. praise given immediately after a job is completed will be more effective than praise given on the annual employee appraisal form.) Also, the greater the magnitude of the reinforcement, the more probable the behavior will reoccur. Finally, the higher the frequency of the reinforcement, the more probable the behavior will reoccur. When a task is first being learned, it is best to reinforce frequently (100% fixed interval or ratio, if possible) whereas once a behavior has been learned, an intermittent schedule (i.e. less than 100%) is preferable.

## Available Options

An individual can become satiated with any one reinforcement; therefore, it is important to vary reinforcements and to control the frequency and magnitude by which a given reinforcement is obtained. The following list is provided to give you some ideas of other kinds of positive reinforcement.

### *Reinforcements __not__ involving monetary expenditures*

1. Verbal praise from the supervisor, higher company official and/or co-workers

2. Praise in front of co-workers

3. Letters of commendation or recognition (put copy in employee's work file)

4. Opportunity to choose own working hours

5. Opportunity to choose day(s) off wanted

6. Reserved parking space

7. Opportunity to train others

8. Nice office

9. Ability to select personal office furnishings

10. Opportunity to sit in an participate in higher level meetings

11. Opportunity to wear a variety of clothes to work

12. Being a member of the strategic planning team

13. Opportunity to express opinions and ideas

14. Opportunity to choose work partner

15. Rotating job duties

16. Job promotion (not involving pay increase)

17. Special assignments showing trust and confidence

## Reinforcements Involving Company Time

1. Time off to attend conferences

2. Time off during working day to conduct personal business

3. Long breaks

4. Longer lunch or dinner time

5. Bench marking other companies

## Monetary Incentives

1. Promotion with corresponding salary increase

2. Paid holidays

3. More vacation time with pay

4. Profit sharing

5. Opportunity to buy company stock

6. Bonus

7. Company car or gas for personal car

8. Pay for sick days not taken

9. Pay for overtime accumulated

10. Tickets to sporting events, theater, and art shows, etc.

11. Regularly given awards for good job performance

12. Group medical/dental insurance plans

13. Company retirement plan

14. Awards/money for suggestions that save the company money.

15. Tuition reimbursement

16. Chances in a raffle or lottery on the basis of job performance

17. Furnishings for office (e.g. plants, pictures, books, telephone)

18. Gift certificates to large department store

19. Dinner for family at nice restaurant

*There are hundreds of ways to reward employees. The decision to use a fixed schedule of reinforcement (where the reinforcement is given consistently at a certain point), or a variable schedule of reinforcement (where the presentation point of the reinforcement varies) and whether this schedule should be based on time (i.e. an interval schedule) or on the number of responses necessary to obtain the reinforcement (i.e. a ratio schedule) must be carefully analyzed.*

**Thought Provoker**

**When conditions permit, variable schedules of reinforcement should be used because the behavior being reinforced tends to maintain it longer.**

*Praise on the job , in most cases, should be given on a variable ratio or variable schedule of reinforcement.*

## Modifying Undesirable Behavior

### The Catch 'em Game

So far, you have learned that positive consequences cause behavior to be repeated and that there are two forms of behaviors, on-task and off-task.

The "Catch 'em Game" refers to the management practice of catching people in off-task behaviors and punishing them. This is the out-dated "slap and point" style of leadership that just doesn't work in the twenty first century. It clearly violates the principles of the Lead Wolf model. We need to employ the servant—situational Lead Wolf style of leadership that gives the employee the benefit of the doubt.

In order to motivate the employee we should reverse this process and "catch" people doing well. *In other words, avoid the tendency to punish off-task behavior and instead reward on-task behavior.*

# Punishment

Behavior followed by a negative consequence (i.e. a negative reinforce) is less likely to be repeated in the future. A negative reinforcement is a punishment, something one would like to avoid or get rid of (i.e. pain, criticism, ridicule).

Although punishment (presenting a negative reinforcement) can lead to a decrease in undesirable behavior, there are certain side effects that can occur and detract from the overall effectiveness of using punishment:

- The behavior may only be temporarily suppressed
- The punished behavior will tend to reoccur when the punisher is absent
- The individual punished will tend to avoid the punisher
- The punished individual may become "anxious" and strike out at someone else in his environment
- The individual will only do what is absolutely mandatory to avoid punishment and you will not get him to use his discretionary energy in a positive way

# Chapter VI

## *Diagnostics*

One of the many responsibilities of a Lead Wolf Executive is to be a problem solver. But, before you can solve problems, you must first accurately diagnose them. It's often easy to recognize that a problem exists, but it's much more difficult to put your finger on its exact cause.

As Lead Wolf Executives, we utilize tools that help monitor performance. The most basic of these tools is the profit and loss statement. It tells us how much gross profit we are making, what our expenses are and what our net profit is. We can use this tool to calculate various financial analyses, from quick ratios to Gross Margin Return on Inventory (GMROI). Other tools include the industry PAR report, or something similar which compares our company performance to other companies in our industry. Using this tool, we can set benchmarks for our company and compare ourselves to the highest performers. These tools, in addition to many other key performance indicators are all available. We just need to use them. Yet, we still have a difficult time pinpointing problems and performance

issues that may hinder our success. Why is problem definition and resolution so frustrating?

## The Answer is Simple

The answer is weak diagnostics! If you have made it to the executive management level of your company, you have obviously demonstrated success. So, it is generally not incompetence that clouds the issues. Instead, it's usually that we get so caught up in the day to day activity of running our business, so caught up in the emotional investment in our employees, so caught up in our vision for growth or defending our competitive position, and so caught up in our self-proclaimed answers to the perceived constraints that we can't see the *"forest through the trees."*

Lead Wolf executives deal with the urgency of running the business on a day-to-day basis. The very practices and characteristics that help accomplish this feat may hinder your ability to see the whole picture with a fresh, open mind. Therefore, this diminishes your diagnostic skills.

An assessment by an outside pair of eyes with in-depth industry experience can provide tremendous return by helping identify the most serious challenges you face. It's all about knowing what your true critical constraints are and then focusing your efforts to solve

these real problems. This is not a sign of weak leadership. In fact it is a sign of an effective leader demonstrating a leadership not so restricted by ego that the value in an assessment process is recognized.

## Examples of issues that are easy to misdiagnose include the following:

- You may believe you have a sales compensation problem. In fact, the real problem may be due to management, a training issue, or recruitment and retention.

- You may believe stagnant growth is due to either diminished support on the part of your vendors, poor sales management, a lack of enthusiasm, or even poor marketing. However, in reality, it may simply be a lack of accountability.

- You may believe you have an organizational development problem, when in fact it should be labeled as a *"family in the business"* problem.

- You may believe your problems are a result of dual distribution, when in fact they may solely rest on your lack of competitive advantage.

## Let's Talk Assessment

It's almost like going to the doctor for an annual physical. Generally a patient is showing symptoms but may not see the entire problem or understand its cause. A doctor provides a diagnosis for his patient; likewise, a trained, objective business expert does the same for a client. An assessment from an

outsider's perspective allows for total objectivity. Using a proven industry expert is also critical. The result is an often surprising clarity to a company's issues and problem causes. A CEO from a building products distributor said, *"It's like taking a punch in the gut, but it will open your eyes to reality."* It's important that the expert assessment is performed by someone who is honest, but not necessarily nice. This means they won't sugar coat the issues.

| Step 1: Get the best people |
|:---:|

↓

| Step 2: Give them clear objectives |
|:---:|

↓

| Step 3: Stay out of their way |
|:---:|

*"Management Theory 101"*

| **Exhibit V** |
|:---:|

A confidentiality agreement is necessary at the onset since the first step is to provide a care package to the assessor that contains items such as financials, strategic plans, sales demographics, compensation plans, and any other data specific to the perceived issues that have been identified or suspect. This allows for homework, research and analysis prior to the actual assessment visit.

After the package review and an on-site visit, an Assessment Review Report with realistic details on your operations and issues should be provided.

## Assessment Examples

Let's look at excerpts from some real assessments that have been disguised to protect confidentiality. These have been re-worked to represent one fictitious company when in fact;

they are a combination of several different assessments from various companies.

## Dolby's Distribution Enterprises: A Consultant's Report

*Organization:* The current organizational structure is not consistent with the planned growth that ownership anticipates. It is somewhat of a flat-line structure, which tends to encourage a Lone Wolf style of micro-management. This structure will not support the strategic initiative of expansion and growth. A strategic plan emphasizing accelerated growth calls for a solid management team that empowers their employees and encourages them to use their own initiatives. However, the employees have not taken ownership of the strategic initiatives.

*Leadership:* Employee confidence in company leadership, and perhaps the company itself, has faltered. It is imperative to regain the confidence of your employees, rejuvenate their initiative, and empower each and every one of them to contribute to Dolby's success. The entire executive staff must commit to the business with a passion. People must set high personal and departmental objectives and achieve them. Communication of the new direction, the new vision and the new mission is essential. This communication must be continuously repeated. Share information,

*show appreciation, celebrate your success and most importantly, listen to your employees and allow your staff to demonstrate leadership.*

*Contingency Planning: In reviewing your business plan and the annual budget, it became apparent that it lacked a "what if" analysis. Additionally, the plan is not complete and has not been formalized. Although the concept of the plan addresses the basic issues of cost containment, creating a break-even at current revenue levels, it neglects to address the possibility of failure to meet budget expectations. A contingency plan must be developed addressing tactical maneuvers that result in black line budgets with stagnant growth and black line budgets with a 5-10% revenue decline. This pessimistic plan should be far-reaching and include reductions in executive staffing and branch consolidations. In fact, review of the decision not to close the Alaska branch may be prudent in the plan. Core competencies should be matched to customer expectations with the minimum amount of overhead required to maintain a lower revenue stream.*

*Strategic Planning: Dolby Distribution does not currently have a workable strategic plan. This means a defined "end game" vision that is translated all the way down into detailed departmental business plans. As a smaller company, Dolby has been able to overcome the lack of a documented strategy by virtue of its strength at the top, the founder. However, to achieve further growth, and perhaps even survival at the current size, Dolby must perfect strategic planning and execution as core competencies.*

*The strategic plan development should also address some of the "poor communication" issues that were reported on the survey and in our management interviews. Although it is common to hear general complaints about insufficient communication in most companies, we believe that Dolby suffers from a lack of clearly defined roles and job duties that manifests itself as "bad communication." This is typical in a Lone Wolf leadership culture,*

***Succession Planning:*** *There is currently no succession plan for the President, or other senior executive managers at Dolby. This is potentially the most urgent deficiency in the organization. The Board is arguably failing in its fiduciary responsibility by not having a clear plan for dealing with the unexpected loss of a senior executive or the "Founders" retirement.*

*The lack of an explicit succession plan for the President causes enormous uncertainty and anxiety amongst the executive staff. It also opens the door to rumor, speculation and the potential for dashed expectations.*

*It is apparent that there is no one within Dolby Distribution who currently has the experience, the education and the knowledge to replace the president. "Currently" is defined as the next 24 months. There may be personnel within Dolby that have potential if an accelerated, top quality executive internship is administered. We also believe that, in the interest of its shareholders and employees, Dolby must look for the most qualified successor. This may involve an extensive outside search. The President's successor must be a change agent capable of introducing the Lead Wolf leadership style to the entire management team. An empowerment culture is a must.*

*Systems: The company uses a system that is three generations behind the technology curve. The largest issue is that there is no one within the organization that has any real knowledge of what IT resources actually exist or how to use the toolset. The organization is limited by what other people tell them. This is potentially a very dangerous situation.*

*Example Summary: It is obvious that the Dolby's direction is solely determined by Lone Wolf "reactionary" responses to circumstances and trends. The issues addressed in this assessment are critical to the future success of Dolby Distribution. The quantity and the magnitude of the issues discussed suggest that the critical mass of the company alone has been a sustenance to profitability in spite of the Lone Wolf leadership style and the problems and challenges faced by the company, even though the level of profitability has been unsatisfactory. Time may be running out. Doing nothing is not an option. Dolby Distribution must get up to speed and grow market share. They must avoid the downside risk associated with these problems that could leave them at a serious competitive disadvantage. Ultimately, that disadvantage could send Dolby into a "death spiral," forcing the unplanned sale of the company or crisis restructuring under a panic response management mode.*

## Typical Executive Reactions to an Assessment

Sometimes reality can be tough. It may mean firing your brother or laying off a number of family members. It may mean replacing your Vice President of Sales. It may mean accepting the fact that you haven't put business needs ahead of personal needs in the past. It could even be as extreme as finding out you are the problem and you have to hire someone else

to run your business for you. You may even question your own competence.

Of course, it's easy to site the *extreme* examples. More often than not, once the assessment is complete, the Lead Wolf executive clearly understands the issues, agrees with them and embraces them eagerly. They are excited about solving the problems now that they have a clear picture of the direction they must take. It's now time to really get their money's worth and start formulating specific action steps. It may feel like a burden has been lifted from your shoulders – a burden of doubt, uncertainty and frustration. The picture becomes much more clear since there is no baggage attached to an experienced consultant, the outside pair of eyes..

## Other quotes from former clients include:

"Not surprisingly, they really nailed the issues we knew we had to deal with and several more that escaped our radar screen," Jim P., CFO of a $350 million distributor.

"I should have done this years ago – maybe I could have circumvented some of these issues," John H., VP/Sales of a $64 million distributor.

## Lessons Learned

What are the take-aways from the assessment process? Based on past experiences from assessments across many industries throughout distribution, you can expect to learn the following:

- A realization that cherished beliefs are not always true

- An understanding that change is a function of future state minus current state, as well as plan clarity and resistance  Formula for change: C *f* [(F-N) * P] > R *(Dr. Robert Swaim)*

- A gap existing between "world view" and "world reality" will be defined

- Organization structure is a function of work

- People truly are your most precious asset

- Success must have a platform created from the bottom up, not the top down

- The old Lone Wolf autocratic style of leadership just doesn't work in today's environment

Going through an assessment is not an easy task. It's not for the faint of heart or someone that lacks self-confidence and self-esteem. More often than not, you will face the reality that your assumptions and conclusions were inaccurate. It then becomes a comparison between a realistic view defined by an outside, experienced source versus your own perceptions that may be too close to the source to properly diagnose. Once that gap is defined, creating action plans and solutions becomes far less difficult. You become sure of the direction to take. You know the right problems to solve and have proper data on how best to solve them.

Now that we have discussed how a consultant (using an outside pair of eyes) can be very beneficial in the assessment process, let me add a few words of caution.

## Consultants Can Be Scary — Utilize the Discovery Analysis to Ease Your Fear of Using a Consultant

Consultants can provide real value on many occasions but they can also be your worst nightmare. Some clichés include:

*"A consultant will ask you for the time and then steal your watch."*

*"Two things you don't want to watch ----- Sausage being made and a group of consultants trying to solve a problem."*

### Worst Nightmare

**The Hanging-on Strategy** - Consultants can become your worst nightmare in many ways. Some consultants have perfected hanging-on and use it as a proactive growth strategy. When a project starts nearing its end, new problems seem to mysteriously get identified. It may start as a training issue; the training issue grows into a management issue, a technology issue, a channel issue. Each issue can turn into another consultant project or an extension of the original project. Before you know it your costs for the consultant's advice and assistance becomes a major factor on the expense side of your profit and loss statement.

**Unclear expectations** - Some consultants are so skilled at presentations and proposal writing that deliverables become very intangible and they are not measurable. If they are not measurable, accountability goes out the window. This alone can turn your consulting experience into a nightmare. The scope of the project may have a continuous creep that costs you more and more money. Deliverables should be clearly defined and documented. However, even if you have done your homework and feel you have clear expectations things can go wrong.

**Employee involvement** - Your risk of failure is exponentially higher if you have not involved your key employees in the decision making process of hiring a consultant. It is essential that you have employee buy in when you decide you need a consultant.

**Accountability** - Consultants like to say they can lead a horse to water but they can't make them drink. In other words, consultants can't execute the plan for the company. As a result, it is very difficult to hold consultants accountable for the results. Often times the consultants make a fantastic presentation and sell their firm based on expertise they don't really possess. They are skilled at quick research and can be convincing in demonstrating their breadth of knowledge about your business based on this quick research. On many occasions the impressive partners of the firm may seal the deal and then send in a bunch of MBA kids to do the work. It's a fantastic learning process for the MBA's that you end up paying for.

**Who is in control** - Hiring the wrong consultant can be dangerous, it can cost you sales, profits and even employees if you are not careful. Don't turn your business over to a consultant. Don't make the mistake of thinking they know your business better than you. There isn't any consultant out there that knows your business better than you and your employees know your business. If you do hire a consultant stay involved and manage the process.

**A variety of flavors** - Consultants come in a variety of flavors. They consist of former sales people, former vice presidents, MBA graduates, former CEO's, former accountants, and **even former waiters**. There are many professional career based consultants that have developed  impeccable reputations. There are also a lot of consultants that are consultants because they are between jobs or retired and bored. Most consultants can be very convincing of their expertise and many can back it up with performance. But, there are those that sound impressive simply because they are exceptional speakers and presenters. Some quote problems similar to what you may be experiencing from work with prior clients. That in itself does not guarantee that they can help solve your problems. Some can, some can't. Some may do an excellent job for you but some may not.

**Walk the Walk** -The problem with some consultants is the fact that they haven't really walked the walk. They haven't

walked in your shoes. Most have some business experience but many have never owned their own business. Many lack the entrepreneurial experience of starting a business from scratch and growing a substantial revenue stream. Many lack the experience of running a family owned business, meeting payroll or managing cash flow. Some are well educated, some are not.

## The Value of an Experienced Consultant

The right consultant can provide tremendous value to your firm. Just having an unbiased, outside pair of eyes look at your firm can reveal things that you as president and your executive staff can't see. This is not uncommon because you're caught up in the day to day operation of your business. Additionally, a consultant does not have the emotional, compassionate attachment to people and processes that you and your management team have developed. As a result, the consultant can help you identify and resolve issues that have gone unnoticed or ignored.

Consultants provide value, not because they can do things you don't know how to do, but they often provide value because you and your team may not have the bandwidth to devote the time necessary to address many issues your company may face. This is especially true if those issues involve market or channel research. Research projects and technology projects are often the types of engagements that fall into this category. Training and employee development support are two other area's where consultants provide exceptional value. The consulting industry is a huge and growing industry that is fast approaching the $100 Billion Dollar mark. A market of this size attracts many

players. There are many professional, competent and trust worthy consultants out there but there are also some that may not be able to live up to your expectations. Sales and Marketing Management Magazine Surveys have indicated that over 75% of business executives responded that consultants are necessary for business success. These same survey results concluded that over 50% of the firms utilizing consultants were dissatisfied or only somewhat satisfied. Companies with less than $10 million in revenue reported a much higher confidence level in consultants than companies with over $10 million in revenue.

## So What Do You Do if You Think You Need a Consultant?

Start by utilizing the creativity and initiative of your own staff to identify the extent of your internal issues. The perfect vehicle to do this is called a "Discovery Analysis." The discovery analysis utilizes a questionnaire that stimulates a thought-provoking process designed to identify issues and challenges that impact company profitability. The following **sales discovery analysis** is an example of this process. It will identify issues and challenges within the sales functions of the company. A sales specific discovery analysis means that you must involve key sales personnel in the process. The independent answers to the questions posed should direct you to very focus-specific areas within your organization that need attention. The Owner/ President, Vice President of Sales, Sales Managers and both inside and outside sales representatives should complete this discovery analysis.

A discovery team meeting should be held to review the results of this process. Each team member should prepare an independent Strengths, Weaknesses, Opportunities, and Threats (S.W.O.T.) analysis based on their responses after completing this questionnaire. Only the three most critical areas in each category should be recorded:

*Strengths:* The three biggest strengths the company has that create competitive advantage.

*Weaknesses:* The three most critical weaknesses that must be addressed to maintain or create new competitive advantages or at a minimum put you on a level playing field with the competition.

*Opportunities:* The three biggest opportunities for your company to create competitive advantage, improve market share, increase revenues or create cost reduction through process improvement.

*Threats:* The three biggest threats created by either the internal or external environment. This may include government regulations, internal politics, competition activity or other external influences.

All responses should be collated from each group. Common areas of concern should be highlighted. A minimum of a one-day retreat attended by all management and key personnel is encouraged to ensure that proper attention and discussion is given to every area of concern that is identified through this

discovery analysis. The following ten questions are examples of the seventy-five questions on the ***sales discovery analysis questionnaire***. A discovery analysis can also be used for human resource issues, planning issues, operations and profit and margin management. (See appendix II for additional discovery analysis examples.)

## Sample Sales Questions:

1. Do you record and monitor customer complaints?

2. Do you maintain a customer complaint database to track patterns and identify recurring problems?

3. Do you use this information to improve performance and increase customer satisfaction?

4. Do you solicit customer feedback?

5. Do you provide customers with a single point of contact?

6. Do you track customer satisfaction with internal operating statistic fill rates?

7. Can you identify waste in operating costs, such as the high cost of errors?

8. Do you receive phone system statistics to analyze calling behavior?

9. How do you measure customer satisfaction? Do you have a formal system, such as a report card?

10. Does your sales force involve suppliers in the selling process?

You may find that  using this process identifies the issues clearly enough to address them without the help of a consultant or you may just need to hire a **"Team Coach"** to help you and your team find solutions and act on them.  At the very least you will have identified the problems clearly enough to set specific deliverables, deliverables that are measurable, for discussion with potential consultants. If you decide to go forward, seeking the assistance of a consultant, interview several. Check references and *ask for a reference from the consultant from a client where the project failed to meet expectations.* Don't accept the answer that none of their projects ever failed. Every consultant has had projects that did not meet expectations. Find out why from their clients. Armed with your information from the discovery analysis process,  you are now in a better position to define the results expected from the consultants. Ask for a proposal that has clearly defined deliverables. Don't be afraid to put a portion of their fee at risk based on results. Make sure that you and the consultants agree on a specific timeline (Important --- Ask for a fixed price proposal).

There are some highly qualified, highly effective consultants specializing in wholesale distribution. The more you are able to define your expectations, the better your chances of being pleased with the results.  Do your homework.  (See Appendix II for additional Discovery Analysis questionnaires.)

**Thought Provoker**

"You'll never succeed alone. You must surround yourself with a diverse group of motivated, talented, energetic people. You must send a clear vision; ensure everyone understands that vision and what their role is in helping achieve that vision. Then you've got to stay on top of their progress, keep them focused on that vision and the actions must be undertaken to achieve it. Then praise, coach and work with them every step of the way. That's the nature of leadership, and it requires the ability to assess people and to motivate them to action."

**Charles Morgan, Chairman**
**Acxiom Corporation**

# Chapter VII

## *Lead Wolf Planning*

### Scenario Planning

Lead Wolf executives are visionaries. They believe in preparation and being ready for almost any circumstance both internal and external. They understand that changing market dynamics can turn competitive advantage into a disadvantage. One of several tools many Lead Wolf executives use in preparation for both internal and external change is called scenario planning.

There are a number of approaches to scenario planning, and they differ greatly based on the people doing the planning and the type of industry for which the planning is done. Some of the best examples come from Citibank and Royal Dutch Shell and although the basics of each are the same, the actual scenarios will be very different. For example, Shell would be concerned with the Middle East cutting off oil supplies to one political entity or another while Citibank might be more concerned with Japan, China or the European economy going into a recession.

The most important thing to remember is to challenge your assumptions and create a new and hopefully more realistic view of the future from which to begin the strategic planning process. In many companies, the entire concept of "strategic planning" has been changed to "scenario planning." If you can successfully test and restructure the assumptions of the decision makers, you have a much better chance of generating creative scenarios and, therefore, strong and aggressive strategic plans. The idea is not to "get it right" but to expand the thought process.

Scenario planning IS NOT the logical projection of historical data so you can say, "In the next five years growth will average 3.5% a year, blah, blah, blah" - and from there write a strategic plan.

Scenario planning IS a creative method of examining possible futures and building the one that is desired while taking into account what COULD happen and how it would affect the plan. A major advantage of using scenarios to set up strategic planning is to gain ideas and insights that would be missed by using the traditional projection process. It is also a method of forcing the planning team to look at more than the "desired" outcome and, therefore, be prepared for or even aggressively plan for, events out of the ordinary.

What do we need to do to keep ourselves from being on the outside looking in? How is e-commerce and e-business going to impact our relationships with our customers, and what can we do to position ourselves for whatever we need to accomplish in that eventuality?

If you could predict the future you would be telling fortunes instead of working in the distribution industry.

## A Management Tool

So what is this thing called Scenario Planning all about? Scenario planning is just a tool. Like any other management tool it is only valuable if you understand it and put it to use. Scenario planning has progressed to the point of becoming a popular management tool to support and even replace, in some cases, the strategic planning process. It is a useful, practical and uncomplicated way to think about the future. Scenario planning allows you to look at an array of alternative plausible futures (although it is recommended that these alternatives should be limited to six maximum).

The purpose of scenario planning is not to imminently decide which scenario is correct. Look at each plausible future scenario and examine how prepared your company is for the potential change and consequences. Ideally you should try to establish markers or milestones that may occur in each scenario that would alert you to which scenario is actually unfolding. By knowing in advance due to these pre-determined benchmarks, you put yourself ahead of your competition in not only reacting

to the events but actually having an outline of a plan in place to take advantage of the situation.

To be successful at scenario planning, you and your scenario planning team must be able to suspend your disbeliefs in all possible futures.

Remember, the cosmic truth of scenario planning rests on the belief that the future cannot be predicted absolutely. Therefore, who is to say what is and isn't really possible? To help in the suspension of your disbelief, consider the following:

"Silicon intelligence is going to evolve to the point where it will get hard to tell computers from human beings." (Gorden E. Moore, Intel Corp.)

"Silicon will even give birth to new kinds of life. The advantage of this new silicon life is immortality and unimaginable brainpower. Inspired scientists will forge composite human-silicon life forms with a common conscious that transcends all living beings." (Robert E. Newham, Scientist, Penn State University)

"Super brainy machines could make the science fiction nightmare come true.

The human brain has only a short time left as the smartest thing on earth. The speed and complexity of computers will continue to double every 18 months through 2012. The density of computer circuits will have jumped 1,000 fold and the raw processing power of a human brain will fit into a shoebox. "(Kevin Warwick, Cybernetics Research)

Now that we've stated our case in Cyber Power terms, perhaps any disbelief about potential evolutionary change can be put to rest and we can look at the process of Scenario Planning.

## Determine Your Objectives

Look at specific objectives based on your own end game five years into the future. Ask yourself questions related to your specific objectives: should I diversify and take on additional products outside the traditional line? Should I merge with XYZ? Don't worry too much about the types of questions that come to mind. Exploring all these questions may lead you to discovering the right ones that fit your specific objectives.

Remember, looking into the future can lead to lots of uncertainty as you try to determine the impact of roll ups, big box competition and factory direct channel confusion, for example. However, in spite of the uncertainty, it is no longer acceptable to just try to run your business the way you have in the past. Evolution in the distribution industry brought on by the new century is forcing us to set a course in advance, to steer through the cloudy issues on the horizon and put a stake in the ground by investigating different scenarios. You cannot afford to wait for certainty to appear. By then it may be too late. Consequently, scenario planning can help us make decisions in the midst of uncertainty. That makes it a valuable tool.

## Identify External Factors

Factors such as market size, market trends, industry trends, consumer spending, new construction, home sales, remodeling,

government regulations, undiscovered market niches and even the level of consumer debt should be considered in the process. Given the impossibility of knowing precisely how the future will evolve means that you must adopt a strategy that is flexible enough to work well over several different scenarios.

## Identify the Driving Forces

Forces within your organization and within the industry are critical to your scenario planning. Ask yourself which of these forces are the most critical to your future objectives. Some may affect the scenarios equally. Some may lead you to altering options within the scenario. The purpose of identifying these forces

is not to pinpoint future events but to highlight forces that may push your company or the industry in different directions.

## Ready, Set, Go

So, we've taxed our brains and determined our "end game" for our strategic planning session. It's now time to get a team together to take a shot at this thing called Scenario Planning. How do we start?

Establish an initial planning team. This will likely include all those involved in the strategic planning process, key decision makers and stakeholders.

Pick a comfortable, hospitable location to conduct a one or two day retreat.

Include an individual from outside the industry, perhaps a board member.

Establish the rules:

- Respect
- No idea is crazy or bad
- All alternatives are documented
- Outside the box thinking is encouraged
- Look at the past and the present as a platform for building future scenarios
- Do preliminary scenario planning in small breakout sessions
- Discuss breakout session scenarios in the large group and play out the conversations
- Build on the concepts

In a fluid and changing environment, scenarios prepare us for shocks and surprises. We have to develop a very flexible idea of strategy. It is no longer the fixed five year plan, but a vision of the road ahead that is capable of being modified at every twist and turn of events, yet still allows progress toward our objectives.

In our fluid environment, there are many possible futures depending on the industry you are in. It is somewhat like the weather. It may be fine; it may rain; what if it snows? Strategy

must now embrace the "what if" questions that go outside the reach of our habitual mindset. This requires us to think about multiple futures. Each "what if" question requires a different story about the future. This becomes a scenario. Each story will be equally plausible if we can entertain its assumptions. Scenarios are distinctly structured views of the future that are self-consistent and plausible. We must document two to six of the scenarios your team has come up with. A bullet point list of potential action items should accompany each scenario. These documented scenarios with the list of action items become the basis for a contingency action plan that helps us prepare for the dynamics that may shape the future of the distribution industry.

## The Benefits of Scenario Planning

There are several important benefits from taking the scenario planning approach:

**First**, it helps us to avoid the trap of rigid strategy, which carries us too far down a given road that inhibits change.

**Second,** it helps us get out of reactive decision-making in which the environment has the upper hand over our mission. The daily grind can all too easily take our eyes off the future and confine us to a vicious cycle.

**Third,** strategic thinking with scenarios is a good way to enhance the capability to become a learning organization, especially if the scenario work is shared widely.

**Fourth**, it is a powerful way of developing deeper alignment (not necessarily consensus) in management teams, even those that have worked together over long periods of times.

Although it is important not to view scenarios as any kind of forecasting of the future, organizations that practice it do get better at spotting the driving forces that can change the industry, putting them a few steps ahead of those who don't see it coming. This is especially true of discontinuities. In many situations, the gaining of even a few months of extra lead-time to meet eventualities represents serious competitive advantage.

Finally, it offers a significant contribution to transforming an organization into an alert, objective, focused distributor. Scenario planning is based on the assumption that the end game vision and the strategic plan are flexible. Consequently, a robust flexible strategy that would perform well over different scenarios is essential. This is why it is important to identify specific action items for each scenario. These bullet pointed action items become the challenging factors to test the flexibility of the strategic plan.

## Tips For Scenario Team Leaders

Scenario planning is similar to brainstorming - in fact, brainstorming can be very effectively used PRIOR to scenario planning to come up with scenario topics or to kick off the process. The concepts of brainstorming such as no boundaries and no "pooh poohing!" should apply. Nothing should stop the flow and the creativity.

## A. Avoid Plots Which Follow the "Most Likely" Progression

The idea behind scenario planning is to get beyond the standard forecasting done for typical strategic planning sessions. Therefore, it is imperative that participants "think outside the box." Wild scenarios can always be reined in after the original ideas are extracted from them, but mundane scenarios will always be mundane, and will not contribute to growth. Thinking outside the box in the simplest terms means that we should not start with today and work forward for our scenario. We need to look to the future and write the scenario as if we are already there.

---

**Thought Provoker**

**Remember: "In order to Think Outside the Box ... You must know what's going on Inside the Box"**

**Rick Johnson**

---

## B. Don't Allow "Probabilities" to be Assigned to Scenarios

As soon as participants see probabilities assigned to their scenarios they will begin to think inside the box again. They will try to "win" by getting the highest score, which undoubtedly will be for the scenario closest to the "normal" progression. Defeat this by valuing all scenarios equally by not assigning values at all.

## C. Be Creative with Scenario Names to Stimulate Imagination

This entire concept is oriented to "outside the box" thinking. Therefore, every effort must be made to stimulate original and creative thought, both in the scenario creation process as well as the strategic planning process that follows it. Use of dramatic and creative names for scenarios will reinforce the creative thought process and add to the excitement.

## D. Demand Ownership of the Scenarios

Managers at every level MUST accept ownership of the scenario process and the scenarios that are generated by it. The final direction taken by the company may be far from the plots in the scenarios, but the final result will be crafted from the imagination and the findings in the scenarios.

## E. Be Creative in Communicating Scenarios

The scenarios created are the basis for the planning process. If they are dull and communicated poorly, the enthusiasm with which they were created will be lost in the strategic planning process. Relate the strategies in a creative fashion - as a TV news broadcast, a skit, or some other creative outlet.

Scenario planning can be fun. Scenario planning encourages creativity and it will challenge managers to get beyond old paradigms. Use it as a platform to begin your strategic planning process. You may find it much easier to determine your "end game" once you've completed a day of scenario planning. Try it, you might like it. Besides, you have everything to gain and nothing to lose.

## The Strategic Planning Process

The old school Lone Wolf leader generally had some type of plan. Unfortunately, their plan usually only existed in their head. It was seldom documented into a formal strategy. In their mind, this may have represented flexibility, considering "shooting from the hip" a competitive advantage. In some cases they may have been right. However, in today's environment leadership has to be more focused. Competition is greater and competition is smarter. Customers demand more and the business environment today is dynamic and constantly changing.

Strategic planning is a key process that adjusts an organization's direction in response to a changing environment. It supports the fundamental decisions and actions that shape and guide an organization. A sound strategic plan can help define and focus a distributor's efforts to move the company in the right direction, using the best methods.

Discipline is a prerequisite since it requires laser-like persistence to bring about a productive strategic planning initiative. The process raises a sequence of questions that helps planners examine current reality, test assumptions, gather and incorporate

information about the present, and perform a trend analysis to assess the future.

In simplest terms, a strategic plan is a set of decisions about what to do, why to do it, when to act, and how to proceed. However, the process that creates a detailed plan is a time and resource consuming endeavor that involves many people throughout the organization.

## Managing Change and Uncertainty

Before a company begins the process it needs to secure a commitment on the part of executives and owners, resolve any serious issues, and embrace a willingness to commit the necessary resources. In addition, it needs to assume an attitude of flexibility - a willingness to think outside the box and examine new approaches. Finally, as previously mentioned, the staff needs to acquire a basic understanding of scenario planning procedures.

The key resources a company must commit to the project include staff and executive management time, and finances for market research and consultants.

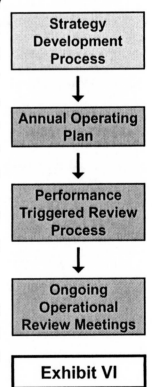

## Look At the End Game

The project's scope will depend entirely on each distributor's unique needs so it's important to begin by taking a look at the end game. That means determining what the company should look like in five to seven years. Start by asking the following questions:

- What markets will the company serve?
- What products will it distribute?
- Who are its primary competitors?
- What are its strengths?
- What are the competitors' strengths?
- How has the marketing strategy changed?
- What are the firm's core competencies?
- What is the size of the revenue stream?
- How is the revenue stream segmented?

Assessing the end game also includes a "what if" analysis - What if the firm loses its major product line? What if the three biggest competitors become part of a consolidator roll up? What if the distributor should decide to dramatically change its product or service offering? Finally, don't neglect to consider the impact of e-business. If your strategic planning is preceded by scenario planning, these questions may have already been answered.

Once this initial phase has been completed, the end game vision is presented to the strategy team. This team has the responsibility and an obligation to challenge, adjust and make recommendations on the end game to ensure ownership by all. It can become a negotiation process between the management team and ownership. The end game then becomes the

basis for building the strategic plan. The strategic document addresses tactical issues such as sales strategies, performance accountability, compensation, and details the firm's tactical action planning process.

The executive strategy team then presents the strategic document to the owners or board for approval. Once approved, the strategic document becomes the basis for launching the tactical planning process.

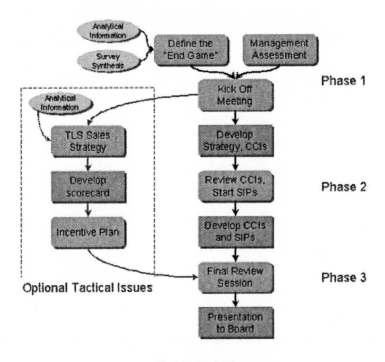

**Exhibit VII**

## Mapping the Strategy Development Process - (see diagram)

A strategy development process map will include the following components:

- CCIs = *Critical core initiatives* define how the end game vision will be achieved. What are the key strategic action items that are essential to meeting specific end game objectives?

- SIPs = *Strategic implementation plans* are definitive drill-down actions items that are necessary to support the accomplishment of the critical core initiatives. They define what is to be done, how it is to be done, when, and who is responsible.

## TLS – Tier Level Selling

*Tier Level Selling* is a specific sales penetration strategy that provides focus, process, and discipline for targeting accounts with high growth potential, including prospects. TLS is identified in the flow chart Exhibit VII to acknowledge the necessity to create specific growth oriented activities.

## The Strategy Development Process

During the first phase of the planning process the executive strategy team may want to conduct a web-based survey focusing on all aspects of the organization. The survey generates valuable, precise feedback from the employees which is synthesized, analyzed, and discussed at a strategy team meeting.

At the outset of the kickoff meeting, a brief 60-minute presentation should be conducted by the facilitator to train participants on the strategic planning process to establish goals and procedures. Meeting participants will brainstorm, engage in additional scenario planning, and distill the end game vision into a well thought out core strategy statement with specific objectives. This core statement now supports and defines the top level of the strategy development pyramid. All subsequent activities will create a foundation supporting the end game.

The time devoted to the planning process may vary from a two-day retreat to an extended period of time.

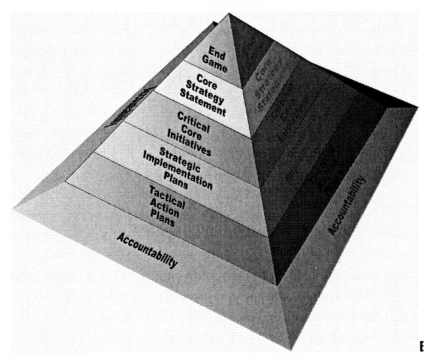

**Exhibit VIII**

## At the Core

The core strategy statement is an introductory paragraph that clearly defines the end game in understandable and measurable terms. This strategy presents an image of the character, the culture, and the values of the organization. The core strategy statement should contain a description of:

- Purpose - why the firm exists and what it seeks to accomplish

- Business - the main method or activity through which the firm tries to fulfill its purpose

- Values - the principles or beliefs that guide an organization's members as they pursue their purpose

- Specific-long term objectives

- The company's future expectations

Once the core strategy statement has been finalized, the planning committee performs strengths, weaknesses, opportunities, and threats (S.W.O.T.) analysis. A S.W.O.T. analysis means obtaining current information about the organization's strengths, weaknesses and performance that highlight critical issues the plan must address. These could include concerns such as funding issues, new program opportunities, changing regulations, or changing customer needs. The primary purpose of a SWOT analysis is to target the most important issues and uncover any critical constraints that could create roadblocks to success.

## Launching the Detailed Planning Process

Executing the detailed planning process is a major endeavor. Therefore, certain organizational elements must be in place to ensure that this phase of the process works. The primary element is a firm's readiness to begin. Does the company have the resources, manpower and willingness to commit to support this process? Typically an outside consultant handles this

best. Additionally, third party customer, vendor, and employee surveys prove revealing.

Once the readiness factors have been assessed and the preparatory research has been conducted, the company is ready to launch the detailed planning phase of the process. Start with the following:

- Create a planning committee
- Announce the process to all employees and identify the strategy team members
- Assign a project manager
- Identify specific ongoing initiatives
- Clarify roles (who does what in the process)
- Identify any additional research or outside resources required during the process

## Managing the Planning Process

To stay on track, the organization must regularly perform trend analysis in order to make good decisions. Strategic planning is never a substitute for the sound judgment of managers. Also, keep in mind that committees are not conducive to quick decision-making. They are more suited to producing feedback, ideas, and suggestions.

An executive planning committee with at least one key staff member skilled in project management can ensure that everyone involved understands and shares the same set of expectations and that the firm's energies remain focused. While the executive

team maintains responsibility for decision-making, the planning committee and the project manager control the process itself.

The project manager assigned to the executive committee helps it outline the steps and activities that must take place during the planning process. This outline specifies the tasks, outcomes, and resources required as well as the people responsible for each phase of the detailed planning process.

## Changing the End Game is Not a Crime

Strategies, goals, and objectives will come from individual inspiration, group discussion, and formal decision-making techniques. In the end however, management must agree on how to address critical issues. Gaining consensus can turn into a negotiating process and eat up considerable time and flexibility. Along the way new insights may emerge that can change the thrust of the end game. Planners should not fear a return to an earlier step in the process to take advantage of new information to create the best possible plan.

The process concludes with the production of a written plan that includes an articulated end game, identified issues and goals, and a set of strategies supported by specific action items. A planning consultant can help draft the final document and submit it for review to all key decision makers - typically the board and senior staff.

## The Benefits of Planning

The true value of a strategic plan is not in the documents it produces - it's in the process itself. Creating a plan engages employees from the bottom up - it empowers them to become effective and better-informed leaders, managers, and decision makers. It is the Lead Wolf style of management. The fundamental benefits of the planning process includes the development of the following:

- A framework and a clearly defined direction with unified support

- A clear vision and purpose owned by all employees

- Enhanced employee commitment to the firm and its goals

- A set of priorities that matches company resources

- A trend analysis that generates the confidence to take risks

- Accountability

Strategic planning is a creative process that involves looking at a longer time horizon, identifying future trends, and developing action plans based on the highest probabilities. Although it may

seem like a daunting task, it is a process that defines the direction and activities of the organization, anticipates changing trends, and maintains the competitive edge.

**SEE Appendix I for Five End Game Examples**

# Chapter VIII

# *It's not about Power and Politics; It's about Principle and Process*

## A Lesson in Leadership

An acquaintance of mine coined the phrase of this chapter in a discussion we were having regarding creating success in wholesale distribution. At the time, I perceived that to be "consultantese," another cliché to be used in the speaking arena. However, since that original perception, I have come to realize a deeper meaning in those words.

## *"It's time to stop thinking about power and politics and start applying principle and process."*

Principle and process form the baseline for all models of effective leadership. Power and politics are old school and can lead to ultimate failure. We have experienced many unfortunate examples of this kind of failure recently, including Enron, Tyco and WorldCom. Behind each of these failures stands a towering figure: a CEO or business leader who may have embraced power and politics over principle and process. Most of the CEOs of these failed companies were considered great leaders

at one time. That is scary. Remarkably, many of their qualities fit the definition of effective leadership. Leaders that cause this kind of destruction can't reach the position of power they attain without demonstrating admirable qualities. Generally, they are very intelligent individuals. Perhaps, however, there came a time when their focus shifted more to power and politics than principle and process.

Power and politics in the business world can lead to devastation if principle and process are ignored. Principle is built on integrity. Process keeps execution within the realms of ethical business practices.

When a CEO begins to believe their primary purpose in life is to instill a belief in their vision, doing everything possible to get everyone to buy into it, with a paranoid belief that those who don't rally to the cause are undermining that vision, they have lost sight of principle and process. They had lost sight of effective leadership. This practice is not only unnecessary, it is destructive. A true leader welcomes a challenge to their vision. It creates a balance, a reason to reflect upon personal values, intuition, and to make sure the vision has foundation. Effective leaders don't need 100% endorsement of their vision to carry out its execution, but what they cannot afford to give up is the right and responsibility of the executive staff to question and challenge that vision.

*Evolving Lead Wolf executives understand this.*

The National Association of Wholesalers (NAW), funded by its Distribution Research and Education Foundation (DREF), did

a series of interviews with seven of the most successful CEOs known in wholesale distribution. Listening to those interviews and reviewing the transcripts is what cleared my thought process and provided real meaning to the phrase:

*"It's time to stop thinking about power and politics and start applying principle and process."*

It validates my personal belief that effective leadership has become more servant natured and a situational style of execution that empowers employees is key to their release of discretionary energy and creativity. That's what the Lead Wolf model of leadership is all about.

## Leadership Models and the Ego Factor

As quoted earlier, effective leaders are driven by a model. A model is a tool used to predict future outcomes of current decisions. Effective leaders build their models on the sum of their experiences, knowledge and deeds, as well as their mistakes.

An emphasis on power and politics is more likely to occur if personal objectives are ego-driven rather than profit-driven, based on principles, integrity and ethics. Being ego-driven often leads to putting personal needs ahead of business needs.

**Thought Provoker**

**During his DREF interview, Steve Kaufman, former CEO of Arrow Electronics, stated that he did not invent the phrase "Servant Leadership," but he leans heavily toward that methodology.**

**"The academics tell us a leader's role is to serve those people that report to him. He or she is not a dictator but their ultimate role is to serve, to allow those people to achieve their goals. It's a style that starts by asking: What do you want to accomplish, rather than telling them what you want to accomplish. I would say that the servant leadership model is the one that I like."**

Larry Spears, CEO for Greenleaf Center for Servant Leadership said, "We are beginning to see that traditional autocratic and hierarchical modes of leadership are slowly yielding to a newer model, one that attempts to simultaneously enhance the personal growth of workers and improve the quality and caring of our many institutions through a combination of teamwork and community, personal involvement in decision making, and ethical and caring behavior." Spears is describing the concept this book is built upon. Leading the Pack utilizing the Lead Wolf model of leadership.

Putting power and politics ahead of principle and process creates failure. This ego-driven situation can lead to a death spiral which often leads to panic response management. A restructuring plan is often adopted. However, in an ego- driven

situation, this restructuring is more apt to occur from the bottom up versus the top-down.

In other words, revenue producing functions or revenue producing people may be prematurely cut. These people or functions may, at a minimum, be covering their variable expense and contributing toward fixed expense to some degree. Eliminating a revenue producing function creates a redistribution of allocated fixed cost which may now jeopardize the profitability of some other segment or division. This may create pressure to close more branches or business segments, or cut deeper into other revenue producing functions, thus creating "*The Death Spiral.*"

Focusing on principle and process indicates the right approach is to view restructuring from the top-down, including taking a serious look at corporate and/or family overhead.

---

**Thought Provoker**

"**Leadership is something which should be inferred to one by their subordinates and peers --- not bestowed upon them by their masters. This attribute comes from the heart, soul and spirit of a human being. It is difficult to define, but easy to recognize.**"

**Leonard Riggio**
**CEO Barnes and Noble**

---

## Success Culture

Wholesale distribution organizations today face tremendous challenge including consolidation, dealing with "big box" (Home Depot and Lowe's), recruitment, retention, succession and the incredibly complex set of independent relationships between highly diverse groups of people. Success is dependent upon effective leaders that create a culture, an environment that is conducive to employee retention, loyalty and a willingness to accept responsibility and be held accountable for success.

During his DREF interview, Chuck Steiner, another Lead Wolf executive and former CEO of Branch Electric, said,

*"Refinements to industry practice, refinements to operation, excellence in what you do [and] continuous improvement aren't words. They're a way of life. When you understand that they're a way of life, then the change that you have in the way you perform is beyond comprehension because you just wind up operating at a different level, and if you can find a way to capture that in the culture of your business, in the culture that you emanate to your people, then as this culture structure changes, you have an opportunity for a superior level of excellence, and that's what in the end it's all about. Excellence breeds a high level of profitability."*

Lone Wolf leaders that put power and politics ahead of principles and process will create a culture within the workplace that breeds distrust and paranoia. Most employees devote a major portion of their lives to the job. Many "live to work" instead of "working to live." They need more from their job than just a paycheck. They deserve an environment that encourages initiative and empowers them to use that initiative. They need leadership that understands listening to their employees is a prerequisite for success. Executive management has responsibility for the direction and results of the organization. The key role of the executive team is to establish and execute company strategy. The single most important determinant of

long-term success is effective leadership. Effective leaders understand communication is critical to the success model. That concept is based on principle. Every employee must understand and support the company strategy. Managing for growth and success requires that leadership focus with laser light clarity on the determined activities that are going to produce the desired results. Focus from the leadership ensures that the process necessary to achieve the predefined activities required for success are in place and operational.

## The Lead Wolf Model in Action

Lead Wolf leaders believe in principle and process. They take the time to listen, imagine and investigate numerous alternatives. With the others' involvement they forge creative solutions to difficult problems. They challenge their people to stretch, go beyond their previous boundaries and think outside the box. Lead Wolf leaders feed off their employees and allow their employees to feed off of them. They give credit where credit is due. They give recognition as a means of gaining respect. They believe individuals can make a difference. Through these methods, they learn to create new insights and possibilities. They insist upon best practice and a process that defines responsibilities, provides clarity and embraces accountability.

Lead Wolf leadership, "Leading the Pack", means creating a sense of urgency, getting mutual commitment to action. Action steps are always clearly defined, precise and backed up by a commitment to the process necessary for execution. Often, due to the personification of the leader's own personality and charisma, employees are eager to leap into action – without forethought. A successful leader recognizes this possibility and takes the necessary steps to avoid this pitfall by teaching precision in planning. They are clear and explicit. They communicate with encouraging clarity that commands ownership by everyone involved in the commitments made.

---

**Thought Provoker**

**Randy Larrimore, former CEO of United Stationers, stated in his DREF interview,**

**"I think you need to realize that the Leader, the President or CEO puts their pants on just as you do in the morning, and they make mistakes. The trick is to make fewer mistakes than the next guy. I think it's easier sometimes to apply knowledge that you've gained [from] someplace else to an industry that hasn't done some of those things. You can almost become a bit more of a hero by transferring lessons learned than trying to invent new lessons."**

---

The successful leader is constantly building advantages into his or her organization. The belief is that you don't always have to be better than your competition, but you must be different. This concept demands creativity and innovations. However, this creativity and innovation must be built into the plans and the process that support it. It must be distinctive, yet it must be manageable and predictable. This could involve anything from new technologies to market segmentation to development of new channels. It is all about improvement and finding newer and better ways of doing things. It involves cross-activity integration of process and people. Activities must be linked across the entire value chain. Understanding this concept is critical to leadership success. Yes, as I have learned to believe, it is essential that leadership understands:

> "It's not about power and politics;
> it's about principle and process."

Become a Lead Wolf and demonstrate your ability to lead employees to success in the 21st century.

## A Fictional Story Based on Fact about a Lead Wolf Vice President of Sales that embraces the Lead Wolf Model

Bill Borders stepped up onto the podium. He had just been introduced as the new Vice President of Sales for Kiechler Building Supplies. As he looked out at the fifty seven faces staring back at him, time seemed to stop and everyone was

motionless. Bills mind wandered. This wasn't a nervous reaction; it was more of a reality check.

Bill had already met most of the fifty seven faces that were now looking at him in anticipation of what he might say. In fact, he had individual casual conversation with many of those faces in the audience.

Bill had been hired by Tom Thompson, third generation President/owner of Kiechler Building Supplies just five short months ago, but he had already managed to personally visit every single one of the sixteen branches Kiechler owned. He was hired to change the direction of the company, to recapture lost market share, to rejuvenate the sales force and put Kiechler back on the growth track to become the premier building supplies distributor in the Southwest once again.

Bill was confident that he could meet the challenge that Tom Thompson had laid out before him. His personal history and knowledge of the industry gave credibility to his confidence. Challenge was no stranger to Bill Borders. Being a decorated Marine platoon sergeant combined with the street experience he gained growing up in the building supply business, provided Bill with exactly the quality of leadership necessary to tackle the issues Kiechler had been facing for the past five years. Lost market share, deteriorating competitive advantage, a culture of compassion that lost all of it's acquaintance with accountability and a lack of trust in the leadership of the company was pushing Kiechler toward the brink of disaster.

As Bill stood on that stage, facing his sales force all together for the very first time, he scanned the room looking from left to right and then right to left. As he looked into the faces of the people that held a major share of Kiechler's final destiny in their very own hands, he briefly revisited his decision to accept Tom Thompson's offer and plea to come out of retirement and help rebuild a company that had seemed to have lost it's passion, it's energy, it's sense of urgency and most importantly it's will to regain the reputation it held for over fifty years as the premier building supply distributor in the Southwest.

Bill had sold his own company located in the Northwest and moved to Southern California four years ago. He was only fifty eight years old at the time. Retirement seemed like the very thing he wanted to do. After two years of playing golf five days a week and relaxing by reading over 100 different books, boredom started setting in. He tried his hand at the consulting game for two years but didn't find the satisfaction he was looking for. Then Tom Thompson approached him with an offer. Bill's wife even encouraged him to go back to work. She believed he just wasn't quite ready for retirement and needed to conquer one more challenge before retiring for good. Bill accepted Tom's offer and they agreed on a three year contract that would take Bill to age sixty five. Bill knew with complete confidence that he could solve Kiechler's problems and recreate the success factor that had once existed at the company. Bill knew that Tom Thompson needed guidance, coaching and mentoring, but he believed that Tom was not the root cause of the problem even though he was a young forty two year old President trying to fill his father's shoes. Tom had taken over when his dad passed

away two years ago but the pathway Kiechler was on had already been laid. Bill planned on mentoring Tom as part of his obligation and commitment to the company.

Bill was confident that in three years, he would make Kiechler Building Supplies the number one distributor in the Southwest once again. He was sure that he could rekindle the passion, the commitment, the culture and ultimately the reputation Tom's grandfather began creating the day he opened the business in 1957. He knew it would be a challenge, but Bill seemed to have that unique leadership quality that made people want to follow him. He had that unique ability to get people to release the discretionary energy that is critical to success, energy that is only released if you believe in the company and you believe in your leader.

A few seconds had passed since Bill stepped onto that stage, but time was still at a standstill in Bill's mind. He scanned the room one more time. Slowly this time looking squarely into the eyes of the men and women that represented the $125 million in revenue Kiechler reported the prior year. This was a year that reflected a 20% decline in previous year's sales. As Bill looked into the eyes of his sales force, he felt he could almost feel the many different facets of the problems the company faced. The sales force before him seemed to send that message. In Bill's eyes, most of the problems were written all over the fifty seven faces that stared back at him from the classroom style setup in this conference hall.

A few faces in the crowd were even older than Bill himself with a look that cried out, "What do you know? What can you tell me? Why should I listen to you? Why should I bust my butt? I'm happy with the ways things work here. We don't need any 'Rah Rah lets all work harder speech'."

That look didn't appear just on the faces of the few in the audience that were older than Bill. He could see that look on most of the veterans in the audience that had ten or fifteen years of service with the company. Bill had seen that look before. It was a look of complacency. He liked to refer to it as the "pickup truck and boat syndrome." He actually had a salesperson at his own company confirm his theory face to face once. He recalled those words as if he had heard them yesterday as he reached down and turned on his lavaliere microphone to begin his presentation to his sales force.

"I don't need to work my butt off anymore. I paid my dues. I've been around a long time. I own my customers. I have my boat, I go fishing every weekend and my son finished college. What else is there? Life is good and a few extra bucks every year isn't worth messing up my life style."

Bill almost chuckled out loud as he recalled that conversation with the stogy old veteran of the industry that had worked for him. It took a little while, but Bill had reached that sales veteran and today he is a good friend and still the number one sales person at Bill's old company.

Bill's recollection of that conversation also reminded him that the "pickup truck and boat" syndrome is probably just a part of the problem. The faces before him seemed to confirm that suspicion. There were the eager faces of the newer sales people

willing to learn but perhaps they haven't had the opportunity. Bill knew the company "Talked the Talk" professing in their mission statement that employees are their most important asset but they failed to invest profits in training and development. Bill also saw a different look on the faces of the majority of his sales people. That look seemed to point out that they were being held captive in a culture embracing a reactive, passive order taking environment, a culture that didn't even understand demand creation, a culture so distant from accountability that reactive route mentality sales became the platform for Kiechler's market share degeneration.

Bill's microphone went live and a loud screech from the sound system brought his consciousness back to the moment. The very last thought that raced across his mind before he began to speak took him back to the biggest challenge he had ever faced in his life. For a brief moment he was back in the jungle on the outskirts of DaNang, Vietnam. He made a speech that day too, a much more important speech. He peered into the eyes of those men he had to lead also. Young men, young warriors, young marines that looked up to him as their platoon sergeant. He looked at them and told them he believed in them. He made them a promise that day. He promised he would take them back, take them back home. Twenty five of his men were in the fight of their lives that day, the day DaNang was over run. Twenty four of them came home. Bill regretted that one loss, but all his men knew that he was one of but only a few leaders that could have got them through that day. They believed in him and it paid off. Bill took them back home.

A second screech from the sound system actually startled Bill a little but before he said good morning to the fifty seven faces staring at him he mumbled to himself "piece of cake, we will make this company great once again."

Bill started his little talk by saying;

"Nowadays, salespeople must be problem solvers able to generate solutions for customers in their time of need. Therefore, we must possess a great deal of knowledge about our customers' business. We must actually define what those needs are because the customer may not know, nor take the time to explain if they do know. Customers want us to have the knowledge and intelligence to comprehend and analyze their problems before showing up at the door. Customers will listen and buy from the salesperson that finds the "pain" and takes it away."

Bill hesitated a little for effect before he continued.

"That means we need to go back to the basics. We are going to revisit sales best practices. Some of you will know exactly what we are talking about. Some of you may have forgotten it and some of you may have never known the principles upon which we are going to rebuild our sales force. In the building industry today our sales environment leans toward a more multifaceted atmosphere. Salespeople must become strategists

with a plan. This plan requires more knowledge about the business, better relationships and better solutions. Some old school salesmen may believe they know what it takes. They have the experience. They've been around a long time. They also may be wrong. The world has changed ladies and gentlemen. To recreate the competitive advantage that Kiechler enjoyed in the past we must do things differently. We can't afford to be complacent. Complacency destroys competitive advantage. As sales professionals, we can't become full of ourselves, no matter how long we've been in the field, no matter how much experience we have."

Bill's gaze sought out the veterans in the audience as he spoke those words. He continued:

"Going back to basics and revisiting best practice means we are going to be talking about targeting, goal setting, action planning and customer profiling. Targeting is the process of selecting high potential customer accounts to receive intense sales focus. Goal setting translates that high potential into achievable numeric objectives, i.e. revenue and margin growth. Action planning means we have to define the activities that are required to achieve our expected results. It's about strategizing, figuring out exactly what it is going to take to succeed at every individual account we target. That is why it is important that we understand the customer's customer and the customer's industry. Be more knowledgeable and conscious of our customer's problem. We are no longer selling a product, we are selling a solution to make their life easier, happier, better, less complicated, or more fun. By understanding the customer's business and his customers, we help them make a profit through cost reductions, improved efficiencies, increased value and increased sales. Solutions come in many forms and may have nothing to do with our products. That's okay. Look for the pain regardless of what it is and focus on the solution. Customers don't want products; they want profits - or ways to make profits. They want satisfaction, feelings of comfort, pride, praise and self-esteem. They are people just like us. Well, maybe they don't have the same crazy genetics that we have as salespeople, but they are just as smart, just as caring and have similar personal needs and feelings."

Bill paused again as he contemplated the reaction he may get to his introduction of a sales effectiveness process. A process he himself had employed at his own company. One of his first initiatives as the new Vice President of Sales was to create a team to develop and implement this process at Kiechler Building Supplies - Bill had formed a hand picked team that included two of his sales managers, an IT person and three sales representatives. Those three sales representatives were in the audience today. Bill knew rumors had been flying about what this team was up to but nothing had been officially disclosed as of this date. The team worked hard and developed a process and program that would bring Kiechler back to a level playing field with the competition. This process would give them the opportunity to rejuvenate the sales force and create the success necessary to recapture the market share they have lost over the past five years. Bill started his introduction of the new sales effectiveness program by saying,

**"There is a pill called Nexiom** that some people believe is a wonder drug. It solves several problems. It does wonders for people that have experienced distress. I wish I could pass out a pill to each and every one of us including our entire management team to create instant success. Unfortunately, there is no **"Purple Pill"** that you can buy to drug our sales team. There is no **"Purple Pill"** that will improve

effectiveness, there is no **"Purple Pill"** that will increase profit, there is no **"Purple Pill"** that will generate more revenue, there is no "Purple Pill" that will increase market share but there is a proven process that sustains continuous improvement that can help you achieve all those objectives. It's actually very simple, and not that difficult of a methodology. It's called a Sales Effectiveness Process. This is simply a structure for continuously improving sales force performance through focus, discipline and process built on a platform of accountability. We have put together a team that has helped develop such a process for our company. This team has worked very hard over the past four months developing this process built on a best practice platform."

Bill could almost feel the anxiety experienced by some of his sales people in the audience. Bill knew that by introducing the

sales effectiveness program they would all but eliminate any place for the non performers in his group to hide. He expected that about 20% of his sales force would not be able to meet the requirements of this new program. He fully expected to have to replace them. He also felt sure that he had several sales managers that may have been great salesmen at one time but just weren't cut out to be sales managers. He had reminded himself and Tom the President that compassion was an admirable quality but it was also one of the biggest weaknesses that privately held companies exhibit throughout wholesale distribution. Bill explained that we may think we are being ethical and acting with integrity by not replacing under performers that have been under performing for a long time. But in reality, we are doing a major disservice to the majority of our employees that want to step it up and recreate that sense of urgency for success that has been missing for the past five years.

Bill continued his introduction of the sales effectiveness program by using power point slides to talk about a sales force scorecard that would be introduced.

"Once we understand basic sales best practice and make sure we have trained our entire sales force, it's really about execution. Execution involves the day-to-day activities of the salesperson. For most industries, this entails both planned, proactive tasks and opportunistic, reactive events that the salesperson uncovers by doing the right things in the right place at the right time. It's critical that the progress of the tasks in the target action plans are carefully monitored to avoid surprises. Our new sales effectiveness process will circumvent the most common mistake made in distribution today, trying to manage results. We have to manage activities because it's the activities that produce results. Once the results are in, the horse is out of the barn and everything we do from that point on is reactive. That's the biggest mistake we have been making for the past five years. If we proactively manage the activities, the expected results will follow."

Bill paused again to search the faces in the crowd to get a feel for their reaction to his words. Most of the faces glowed with excitement. Some showed disdain, a look of disbelief and some had that look of; "Ya right, I'll just wait and see." Bill knew it wouldn't be easy, but he was pleased with what he saw so far. He continued;

"Sales is a profession that requires professional sales people. Every company needs aggressive, creative and resourceful salespeople to have their products specified, accepted and used by customers. Without informed and capable field salespeople, no company, including Kiechler could hope to compete in the marketplace today.

I believe that good salespeople, the kind who can help a company really grow, don't just happen to come along by chance or fate. There is no such thing as a "born salesperson," because selling ability is much more than an intangible given that a person either has or doesn't have. Granted, selling does require certain attributes in a person and some people are naturally born with these attributes and some aren't. Also, the person must be intelligent, able to grasp ideas and details easily, retain them and recall them for use whenever necessary in selling situations.

These factors and many others relating to personal and emotional characteristics are contributing elements in the makeup of the professional salesperson. However, these attributes alone do not make a sales person nor do they guarantee success. It takes more than that. A sales person must have adequate tools, resources and leadership to maximize their effectiveness. I am here to provide that leadership. I am here to take us back to the level of success this company used to enjoy. Things will change. Your President has made a commitment to me and to you that we will have the resources and the training necessary to make this happen. This new program is our first step. That is why the Sales Effectiveness Process is so vital. This is the program that provides the support and the resources to allow each and every one of you the opportunity to maximize your personal effectiveness in your individual territories. This is our chance to prove we are professionals. This is our chance to prove we can create success. This is our chance to regain our position in the market place. This is our chance to regain our pride. Our pride in our company, our pride in our leadership, our pride in each other but more importantly this is our opportunity to regain our pride in ourselves."

Bill was taken back by the noise, the applause. Unexpectedly all the people in the audience rose to their feet and cheered. It was exhilarating. Bill had planned to talk for another twenty minutes. He was going to

discuss the sales management review process. He was going to explain his hands on involvement. He wanted to talk about functional cross selling but Bill knew when he had the order. And when you have the order you need to shut up. He waited for the applause to die down and he ended his talk that day by saying,

"I believe in this company or I wouldn't be here. I believe in our President or I wouldn't be here. I believe in our ability to change the direction of this company or I wouldn't be here. But I want to tell you from the bottom of my heart that I believe in you. If I didn't, I wouldn't be here. I know that you can become the most talked about, the most feared and the most successful sales force in the building products industry that exists today. I have faith in you. I believe in you and I'll be by your side as we win this battle together. We will make it back, back to success."

Bill walked off the stage to an applause that was deafening. He had a big smile on his face as he muttered under his breath, **"Step one!"**

# Chapter IX

## *Corporate Recreational Mating*

*"WOW DENISE, THOSE TIGHT JEANS SURE LOOK GOOD. DO YOU WANT TO SELL THEM?"*

*"NO, SWEETIE, BUT YOU CAN RENT THEM FOR A LITTLE WHILE."*

Starting this chapter with that actual quote and giving other real life examples of the type of interaction that goes on in many offices today creates a self imposed need in my mind to assure you, the reader, that we will be discussing Sexual Harassment in the work place later in this chapter.

Recreational mating in the work place has been going on since organized business began. This term, Corporate Recreational Mating as used in this chapter does not pertain to simple "office dating" that goes on between two single adults that happen to work at the same place of business.

What we are going to discuss in this chapter is the type of recreational mating that has an impact on the performance of the business itself. Most of this type of recreation takes place among members of upper management and a high percentage of it is illicit. In other words, one or both of the participants are married and not to each other.

This is a situation that exists in many corporations, it's rarely reported, often ignored and in spite of the participants attempts at secrecy, it is often a well traveled rumor, if not a fact.

In their January 2003 issue, Stuff Magazine reported on a survey done with 3000 participants revealing what goes on within the office walls.

"THEY'VE TURNED BOARDROOMS INTO BEDROOMS, GIVING WHOLE NEW SPIN ON SPREADSHEETS."

## Baby Boomer Chauvinism

Before going on I should preface my remarks by admitting that I am definitely a card carrying member of the "Baby Boomers." Being more honest I have to admit that during the early years of my career, the 70's, I undoubtedly could have been classified as a male chauvinistic pig. I could have qualified as poster child for the official "Male Chauvinistic Pig" movement. However, experience has taught me a very important lesson regarding leadership and its personal relationship with employees.

I now have a much greater appreciation for the abilities, the intelligence, and the value of female employees. Today, I firmly believe women in the workplace are the most under utilized asset this country has. We have made a lot of progress in the last two decades but we have a long way to go. A few years ago I was asked to speak to a group of female business ladies called "Women of Steel." This was an organization for women working in the steel industry. Being a little intimidated, a bit scared due to my chauvinistic past I reluctantly agreed. As a result of personal research and interviews, I decided to title my presentation "Women in the Workplace."

I felt I had gained a deeper understanding and wanted to share that understanding and compassion for the challenges facing a woman of the 90's in trying to build a career in business. I knew it wasn't enough to be as good as her male counter part – they had to be better. I knew it wasn't good enough to be intelligent – they had to be smarter then their male competition. I felt guilty about the sexist pressure they faced, the remarks, the lingering eyes and the assumptions and rumors that often came as they get promoted and begin to climb the corporate ladder.

I felt guilty because I was part of that culture at one time. Too often in the 80's and 90's managers couldn't get beyond the good looks and the fact that they were dealing with a female to figure out that this person did have an intellect and really knew what she was talking about.

Added to the pressure the female faced at the office came the pressure at home being a wife and sometimes a wife and a mother. Most husbands wanted their wife working. They needed the income. However a majority of them considered their wife's employment strictly a job. They were the real bread winners. They had a career. The woman in most instances was still expected to perform the wifely duties of cooking, cleaning, taking care of the house hold and pampering her "Career Oriented" spouse. It took a special man to truly share the responsibilities of running a household. It was from this attitude that I personally observed along with the research and interviews in preparation for my speech to the "Women of Steel" that I developed a theory patterned after the text book theory called "Point of Diminishing Return." I presented this theory to the "Women of Steel." I called my theory "Point of Diminishing Ego."

## POINT OF DIMINISHING EGO

In many cases when both the husband and the wife are employed, the husband is generally making more then his spouse. He is very parochial in his attitude and considers his employment a career and his wife's employment just a second income. A job. Everything is fine on the home front as long as that mind set exists and nothing takes away from the culturist attitude of the 1980's. The home is the man's castle and he is the king. His self worth is high because he is the major bread winner. Then something happens. His wife's efforts at work start getting recognized. She gets a promotion. At first he liked it because she gets a raise. But with that promotion comes more responsibility, more time commitment and work starts coming home.

She keeps doing a great job and more recognition brings with it another promotion, another raise. All of a sudden she's

making as much money if not more then her husband. She has reached the "Point of Diminishing Ego."

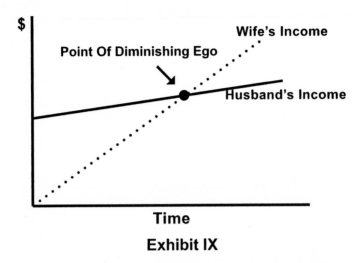

**Time**

**Exhibit IX**

Now all kinds of problems develop, including jealousy, low self esteem accusations and lack of trust. Unfortunately, in some instances the situation ends in divorce court. There are times this conflict can lead both participants to seek the understanding and comfort of someone else. This complicates the situation even further because that comfort and understanding is generally found in someone they work with.

## Survey Stats

"STUFF" magazine survey of 3000 participants revealed that 51% confessed to office affairs. Out of them, 71% slept with one to three partners other than their spouse or significant other. Sixty percent admitted to actually having sex in the office with the following locations noted.

- Bathroom ...................... 24%

- Conference Table ............22%
- Boss's Desk ................. 20%
- Parking Lot..................... 15%
- Reception Area ............... 6%
- Photo Copier .................. 6%

Other magazines have reported varying degrees of the same survey. One well read woman's magazine reported 53% of the males surveyed admitted to extra marital affairs while 23% of the women surveyed admitted the same. The office is the most likely place to meet someone since you spend more than 50% of your waking hours there. That statistic is mind boggling. It would suggest that the next time you attend a business meeting and look around the room, chances are that more than half but less than 75% of the mixed crowd is having or has had an extra marital affair.

This sounds like a chauvinistic sexist commentary. It probably is although it's not meant to be. The comments and actual quotes are not meant to give the impression that all women in the work force are having sex with their co-workers or Boss's. It is not meant to imply that most women are under the influence of the "Cleopatra Inheritance" and use their Feminine Qualities like the individual in the following quote.

*"I KNOW HOW TO USE ALL MY ASSETS," SHE REPLIED, AS SHE PLACED HER HANDS STRATEGICALLY ON HER CHEST.*

Let me state that it is an uncontested fact that the majority of females work very hard in the office and are dedicated wives. They keep their nose to the grind stone and they too are also disgusted by the minority of women that use their sexual prowess to advance their careers.

*In 2003 Florida Today* printed an article by Stephanie Green who was a Senior at Satellite high school at the time, titled, "It's Time For The Good-Old-Boy Network To Step Aside." (2003) It stated that it was time for the good-old-boys in politics to step aside and let a woman run this country. According to the declaration of sentiments, which was signed by men and women in Seneca, N.Y. in 1848, "All men and women are created equal." So if we are all created equal, how come men still tend to be narrow-minded about women becoming President of the United States?"

Stephanie states in her article, "It is the ideal time for a woman to lead our country so for those who don't believe change is a good thing and go along with the old adage, "IF IT'S NOT BROKE, DON'T FIX IT." Think again.

Stephanie believes that is a cowardly way of thinking. Change can be good and a woman can lead the country just as well as a man. This is quite an insight for a young woman still in her teens. She and every female like her is a critical element to the future success of this country. It looks like we will have at least one female candidate (Hillary Clinton) in the next presidential election with an outside chance that the Republicans could nominate a woman as well.

## Cleopatra Inheritance

The "Cleopatra Inheritance" is a force so powerful that it can topple nations. Look at the publicity our former president Bill Clinton received regarding his relationships with a number of women. Not every woman is subject to be the recipient of this phenomenon. And not every woman that does inherit this power recognize it. Most of those that do recognize it don't abuse it. But there is a minority of women that recognize this power they have over men at a very early age and begin using it. This power can bring the strongest man to his knees, fill his eyes with tears and make him do just about anything she wishes. There are a few women who have perfected this power. They have it under control and use it to advance their careers.

Women utilizing the "Cleopatra Inheritance" are very clever. They are not the "Sexy Dumb Blondes" characterized by the brunt of many of man's chauvinistic jokes.

Women who use their inheritance to advance their careers focus clearly on their objectives. They are blondes, brunettes, red heads and every other hair style imaginable. In other words,

it has nothing to do with their hair coloring. They know what they want and they go after it. Men are weak in their defense when faced with this inheritance. Its power is overwhelming and consuming. Fortunately, women who use this power are in the minority, a much smaller number than their chauvinistic counterparts of the male population in the work place.

---

**Thought Provoker**

*"Two years prior to becoming CFO she was a payroll clerk in the accounting department. She had no degree and a limited knowledge of accounting. Today she is CFO of a $500 million dollar company making a six-figure income."*

---

The success of this individual can't be traced to her academic credentials, she has none. It can't be traced to her experience, she was a payroll clerk. But it can be traced to her personal relationship with the president and her knowledge, control and use of the "Cleopatra Inheritance" factor.

---

**Thought Provoker**

**"One must understand how their actions impact not only their particular job, but the functioning of the organization as a whole. This is something like being able to see both the forest and the trees."**

**Phillip J. Carroll**
**CEO Fluor Corp**

---

Control is a very critical factor in the "Cleopatra Syndrome." Love is generally not an acceptable alternative. Love complicates

things and is rarely involved in this career enhancing experience. When the male does fall victim to this process, falls in love and may even want to leave his wife, the female panics. Love challenges her control of the situation. This is a typical response to the early warning signs from the victim that thoughts of love have entered his psychic.

Please forgive me if it sounds like I am trying to make the man the victim here. There are many more incidents where the male utilizes the power of his position to influence and intimidate the female to get what he wants as well. That's called sexual harassment which we will discuss in detail in this chapter.

## Internet Insight

The Internet provides a lot of statistics and information regarding corporate recreational mating. Much of this insight is provided by the victims who are generally hurt in the process, the other spouse.

**\*\*\*\*\*\*\*\*\***

*"Two months ago I found out that my husband had an affair with a secretary in his office. She got pregnant and had my husband's child who is now two years old. I can't forgive or forget this horrible thing. We have been married twenty years.*

*He knew from the beginning that the child was his and he never told me. His girlfriend called me and told me all about it. I can't go on in this marriage because I don't trust him."*

**\*\*\*\*\*\*\*\*\*\***

*"I'm twenty eight years old. My wife and I have been married for almost six years. We are both Christians. We don't have children. I came home from work one day to find a message that said, "I have to go away and think." I knew what was going on. It was the guy from her work. She was having an affair. I caught them in the parking lot at work kissing. She claimed it was a thank you kiss for a favor he had done. I knew that was crap. I actually tried to be friends with him. Just before she left to be with him, we all spent the weekend together boating. What a fool I was. She's with him now."*

**\*\*\*\*\*\*\*\*\*\***

## Casual Encounters

Casual encounters that sprout into full blown office romances are not uncommon given the amount of time spent at work. Offices provide a safe haven and many of the necessary components for a connection, even an illicit one. Many employers fear that workplace romances cut productivity, result in office jealousies and unnecessary distractions. They are absolutely correct. But, what do you do if it's the B.O.S.S. or other executive management personnel involved in this type of office affairs?

There's not much you can do if you want to remain employed. Executives that have affairs with married colleagues display

moronic behavior. It does affect their work and no matter how secretive they think they are, they will eventually be exposed. These executives become known as players, bottom feeders with no morals. It's a combination of the power of the Cleopatra Inheritance Syndrome and their own self indulgent egos that controls these individuals.  It may also be their power and initiative alone taking advantage of younger female employees that need their job desperately.

Things that often occur without the knowledge of the participants include them becoming the brunt of many office jokes and rumors. They may become cartoon characters and laughed at in the lunch room. Their e-mails, cell phones and other means of communication may one day prove to be there down fall no matter how careful they think they have been. Sometimes conflicts become public.

***"Are those reports ready Jennifer?"  "No, James, I was with you all night trying out most of the Kama Sutra positions."***

Public displays of bickering and arguments between these individuals, regardless of their rank in the hierarchy, are common place. This type of public arguing heightens the sensitivity of everyone in the office to what may or may not be going on. It brings to the forefront inequities in the power structure. People resent the attention, the special treatment and the fact that she or he can get away with murder while everyone else tows the line. Agreement between the two on any topic carries no validity. The conclusion is that they are a couple so they have no reason not to agree. Security leaks are the most common risk common to the company in these situations. It's amazing what everyone reveals beneath the sheets. There is no confidentiality agreement in an illicit relationship between B.O.S.S. and employee. That brings us to the concluding topic for this chapter.

## SEXUAL HARRASSMENT

With all this office romance, corporate mating and illicit relationships occurring, what constitutes sexual harassment? Sexual harassment has existed since business began. The difference today in the 21st century is that it is now recognized. It is now enforced and business managers are forced to deal with it. Title VII of the Civil Rights Act of 1964 mandated that every working person has the right to work in an environment free from harassment on the basis of sex.

Wow! What a profound statement. How does one determine the difference between unwanted sexual advances and welcomed sexual advances that later become unwanted? The answer is, it really doesn't matter. The Equal Employment Opportunities Commission (EEOC) defines sexual harassment as unwanted sexual advances, requests for sexual favors and other verbal or physical conduct of a sexual nature when:

> *A term or condition of employment is explicitly or implicitly made regarding submission to a request for sexual favor.*

> *Rejection or refusal to submit sexual favor is used as a basis for an employment decision.*

*Such conduct has the purpose or effect to interfere with an individuals work performance or creates a hostile, intimidating environment.*

There are actually two kinds of sexual harassment:

1.    Quid Pro Quo:

Where employment decisions or expectations are based on an employees willingness to grant or deny sexual favors (hiring decisions, shift schedules, salary increases etc.).

Example:

- Sexual favors demanded in exchange for promotion
- Terminating a subordinate because they ended a relationship
- Changing job performance expectations after subordinate refuses sexual advances


2.    Hostile Environment:

Where verbal or nonverbal behavior in the workplace Focuses on sexuality of a person, is unwanted, is severe or pervasive enough to affect the persons work environment.

Example:

- Off color jokes or teasing
- Comments about body parts or sex life
- Suggestive pictures or calendars or cartoons
- Suggestive e-mails or forwarded jokes and pictures
- Leering or staring
- Repeated requests for dates after being told no
- Excessive attention in the form of love letters, telephone calls or gifts
- Touching—brushing against, pats, hugs, shoulder rubs or pinches
- Assault or rape

The basis or foundation to sexual harassment is defined as being unwelcome, unwanted or unsolicited conduct that is imposed on a person who regards such conduct as offensive; that is sexual harassment. When a person communicates that the conduct is unwelcome then it becomes illegal to repeat it. This is true even if the conduct is disguised as innuendos or subtle inferences, it is unlawful.

Sexual harassment is not an expression of sexual desire. It is plainly an inappropriate use of power. Subtle infringements are the most common and the most difficult to detect and prove. Yet, they are equally damaging and just as illegal as an open forward sexual advance.

Sexual harassment that occurs during the corporate recreational mating process is a form of indirect harassment. If an equally qualified person is passed over for promotion because the B.O.S.S. is sleeping with the person he promotes then that person has been illegally discriminated against due to indirect sexual harassment. This situation occurs quite frequently but is rarely reported. Unchecked sexual harassment can also have other subtle consequences. People witnessing the harassment may feel the same loss or damage. Harassment that is ignored or denied can cause overall morale to deteriorate. Productivity will suffer and expose the organization to potential litigation.

## EEOC Guidelines

The Federal Equal Employment Opportunities Commission has issued guidelines on sexual harassment under Title VII of the 1964 Civil Rights Act. The guidelines, Section 1604.11 (29 cfr Chapter XIV, part 1604) are listed below.

Section A:
Harassment on the basis of sex is a violation of sc. 703 of Title VII. Unwelcome sexual advances, requests for sexual favors, and other verbal or physical conduct of a sexual nature constitutes sexual harassment(1) submission to such conduct is made either explicitly or implicitly a term or condition of an individuals employment, (2) submission too or rejection of such conduct by an individual is used as the basis for employment decisions affecting such individual, or (3) such conduct has the purpose or effect of unreasonably interfering with an individuals work performance or creating an intimidating, hostile, or offensive working environment.

Section B:

In determining whether alleged conduct constitutes sexual harassment, the Commission will look at the record as a whole and at the totality of circumstances, such as the nature of the sexual advances, and the context in which the alleged incidents occurred. The determination of the legality of a particular action will be made from the facts, on a case by case basis.

Section C:

Applying general Title VII principles, an employer, employment agency joint apprenticeship committee or labor organization (herein collectively referred to as employer) is responsible for its acts and those of its agents and supervisory personnel with respect to sexual harassment, regardless of whether the employer knew or should have known of their occurrence. The Commission will examine the circumstance of the particular employment relationship and the job functions performed by the individual in determining whether an individual acts in either a supervisory or agency capacity.

Section D:

With respect to conduct between fellow employees, an employer is responsible for acts of sexual harassment in the workplace where the employer, its agents or supervisory personnel know or should have known of the conduct, unless it can show that it took immediate and appropriate corrective action.

Section E:

An employer may also be responsible for the acts of non employees, with respect to sexual harassment of employees in the workplace, if the employer knows or should have known

of the conduct and fails to take immediate and appropriate corrective action. In reviewing these cases, the Commission will consider the extent of the employers control and any other legal responsibility which the employer may have with respect to the conduct of such non employee.

Section F:

Prevention is the best tool for the elimination of sexual harassment. An employer should take all steps necessary to prevent sexual harassment from occurring, such as affirmatively raising the subject, expressing strong disapproval, developing appropriate sanctions, informing employees of their right to raise and how to raise the issue of harassment under Title VII and developing methods to sensitize all concerned.

Section G:

Other related practices, where employment opportunities or benefits are granted because of an individual's submission to the employer's sexual advances or requests for sexual favors, the employer may be held liable for unlawful sex discrimination against other persons who were qualified for but denied that employment opportunity or benefit. If in doubt about any circumstance or situation, check with legal counsel.

## Handling Complaints

Handling complaints is not easy. Knowing what to say and what to do isn't taught in Management 101.  Sexual harassment isn't your ordinary everyday problem. The first thing you must do is listen intently. Assure them that you are taking them seriously because it is a serious matter. Express no opinion,

just listen and take notes. Do not be biased. Encourage them to give specific details. It is very important that you ask them specifically how they reacted, communicating the fact that this action was unacceptable.

The next step is to interview the alleged offender. He or she has the right to hear and respond to the accusations. Be sure to conduct the interview in the same, straightforward, unbiased manner you did when you talked to the person who filed the complaint. If no resolution or conclusion is made and the offender denies the behavior or has a variation of the story, you will need to go to the next step.

Inform your corporate attorney and seek his advice. With your attorney's approval, initiate an investigation and be prepared to monitor the workplace to ensure that the harassment stops. It's your responsibility to protect the person who filed the complaint. You may want to take steps to keep the two parties involved apart temporarily by reassigning one or the other until the matter is resolved.

As you conduct the investigation, be as discreet as possible; only interview individuals who may have relevant information. Enlist any organization resources that may help or support your investigation; review the appropriate records before you actually interview any employees about the incident. You may find valuable information to direct the investigation, or even bring the investigation to a conclusion. The final step in the investigative process is to interview anyone who may have information or insights on what took place.

If you conduct a thorough investigation and still don't have enough facts to draw a conclusion, you may find it appropriate to try bringing the two parties together to determine what really happened. This option should only be arranged if both parties agree to meet. This type of meeting can be very delicate and should be approached with a great deal of thought and planning.

Once you have gathered and analyzed all the information and concluded that the incident did, in fact, occur, consult your organization's policy, review the case with your legal council and take disciplinary action. Be prepared to fully explain the results of your investigation and the action that will be taken. Explain to the harasser that he or she has the right to appeal the decision to a higher level. Lead Wolf leaders recognize the devastating effect that corporate recreational mating can have on the performance of the business. More importantly, they recognize the devastating effect it can have on their employees.

# Chapter X

## *Transitional Leadership*

### Lead Wolf ---- High Impact Leadership

It's worth repeating, a Lead Wolf gets results because they are high impact leaders. They are consistent, explicit and concise and they command a presence when they walk into a room. That's what being a Lead Wolf is all about. They have enough charisma to turn the dullest moment into a high-energy event. When they move on, others want to go with them. They have a following. Their openness and honesty create a legacy which people admire and look up to. They gain commitment and foster trust.

Leveraging the Lead Wolf leadership model entails advancing their personal agenda by advancing the agenda of their management team. A good leader is not intimidated by the success of others. They encourage others to succeed and help them fulfill their wants and needs.

Leveraging the model helps determine the hidden factors in communication. Understanding inferences and assertions becomes a key component to understanding people. Leaders have high questioning and interpretation skills that allow them to drill down to real facts and issues.

Leveraging their leadership allows successful leaders to establish emotional connections, thereby diminishing fear and intimidation. This encourages enthusiasm and cooperation.

Lead Wolf leaders take the time to listen, imagine and investigate numerous alternatives. With the involvement of people, they forge creative solutions to difficult problems. They meet the challenges imposed by recessionary times. They challenge their people to stretch, go beyond their previous boundaries and think outside the box. Successful leaders feed off their people and allow their people to feed off of them. They give credit where credit is due. They give recognition as a means of gaining respect. Through these methods they learn to create new insights and possibilities. That describes the Lead Wolf model of leadership. Thai's exactly what "Leading the Pack" is really about.

Successful leadership means creating a sense of urgency and getting mutual commitment to action. Action steps are always clearly defined and precise. Often, due to the personification of the leader's own personality and charisma, employees are eager to leap into action - without forethought. Lead Wolf, high impact leaders communicate with encouraging clarity to command "buy-in" from every person involved to the commitments made.

# Leading Through a Recession

This may not be a hot topic today due to our current economic conditions but there is one guarantee in life. "Things will change." We just don't know when. However, Lead Wolf executives believe in preparation. They believe in scenario planning, strategic planning and contingency planning.

The successful leader is constantly building advantages into the organizations at a much greater rate while they are eliminating disadvantages. The belief is that you not only have to be better than your competition but you must differentiate yourself. This means taking advantage of opportunity presented by any type of economic downturn. This concept demands creativity and innovation. However, this creativity and innovation must be built into the economic contingency plan. It must be distinctive and yet it must be manageable and predictable. This could involve anything from new technologies to market segmentation to development of new channels to take advantage of the competition's weaknesses that may be accelerated due to the declining economy. It is all about improvement and finding newer and better ways of doing things. It involves cross-activity integration of processes and people. Activities must be linked across the entire value chain. Understanding the concept is critical to leadership success.

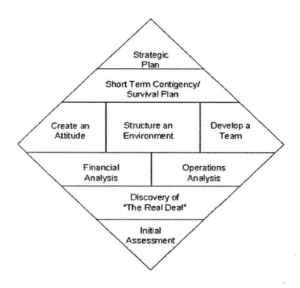

**Exhibit X**

The primary focus of most organizations facing recessionary times is improved cash flow. Everyone has heard the cliché, "cash is king." In a down economy, that becomes the most dominant issue about which leadership must be concerned. However, we must not ignore the fact that contingency planning cannot succeed in any organization without the revitalization of its people. And, revitalization of the people requires high impact leadership.

If your organization finds itself in a financial crisis due to the economic decline, then survival planning becomes essential. This requires rapid analysis, quick decisions and immediate actions. This is undertaken with a deep sense of urgency. It creates a tidal wave of shock to the culture of the organization. Once this shock subsides, strong, high impact leadership must be present to set a course, structure an environment, and

develop a team that can drive the organization back to success and profitability.

## Success

High impact leadership must be present during each phase of the turn-around process. Initial assessment, the first stage (Exhibit X), is critical since leadership must not only capture a broad overview of the company to identify all potential problem areas for further analysis, but evaluation of management competency is a critical factor. Often times, the reasons a company finds itself in financial distress can be traced directly back to the executive staff and past management practices. This becomes the platform for discovery of "The Real Deal."

There may be ownership issues. One or more of the executive staff may be at the core of the problem. This needs to be determined quickly and resolved with minimal emotion and maximum concern for the corporation's survival.

The other factors appearing in Exhibit X demand that effective leadership is demonstrated throughout the organization during the entire process. One person can't turn a company around. Revising the organization chart doesn't turn a company around. Short-term plans, strategic initiatives and restructuring alone doesn't turn a company around. Even a Lead Wolf executive cannot deal with recessionary economics alone. One person cannot create growth. One person cannot create profit alone. People are not profit, but without people, teamwork and effective leadership, there are no profits. People create success during recessionary times - people who believe, people who are

committed, people who care and people with values. You will find people with these traits in an organization that demonstrates high impact Lead Wolf Executive Leadership. The kind of leadership that inspires people to get on board, be creative and innovative. The kind of leadership that creates an atmosphere of togetherness that perpetuates an aggressive approach to achieving common objectives. The kind of leadership required to "Lead the Pack."

Wayne Gretsky, the famous hockey player coined the original phrase; "Skate to where the puck's going to be." I suppose he was trying to say that you have to anticipate the action. You must know your competition, trust your teammates and be aggressively proactive in your approach. I would add, "Arrive with an attitude." That simply means doing all those things well and doing them with the confidence that you are the best at what you do. Success breeds success and attitude is one of the primary ingredients necessary to "Lead the Pack" in business in the 21$^{st}$ century.

You and you alone are responsible for your attitude and the attitude your company reflects. You must will yourself to seek improvement in everything you do or time will catch up to you. You simply won't be able to compete. It was Mark Twain who said:

"DON'T GO AROUND SAYING THE WORLD OWES YOU A LIVING; THE WORLD OWES YOU NOTHING; IT WAS HERE FIRST."

Be a risk taker, be a maverick; avoid making a career out of procrastination and cautiousness. Those who succeed believe

in themselves. They aren't satisfied with the status quo and they are willing to take calculated risk.

Successful leaders encourage their employees to think outside the box. They empower employees to act on their own initiative. Believe in yourself; believe in your employees and their right to self-determination. Suspend disbelief and act as if your company's success is imminent.

Lead Wolf executives recognize the power of their people, especially those employees closest to the action. They encourage them to be proactive and "Skate to where the puck's going to be." They create a cultural environment that allows them to "Arrive with an attitude." An attitude of confidence, competence and the ability to demonstrate the transfer of authority that the culture created has provided them.

**"It's an attitude of winning."**

### Thought Provoker

I believe great leaders are distinguished by four characteristics;

1. They have deeply held values that guide their choices. They articulate these values clearly and share them often

2. They deal with reality. They see things as they are, not as they would wish them to be.

3. They embrace change. They see change as o[opportunity, not threat, and find creative ways to turn it to their advantage.

4. They develop other leaders, and consider the real test of their leadership to be what happens when they are no longer around.

**A.G. Lafley**
**CEO Procter and Gamble Company**

# Chapter XI

## *Leadership in a Death Spiral*

Sometimes things just happen. Maybe we lose focus and take our eyes off the ball. Maybe we don't recognize the signs. Sometimes it happens quickly due to a loss of a major customer or loss of a major product line. Sometimes it is a slow, gradual process. Market share seems to evaporate; gross margin exhibits an extended period of decline. Morale suffers, employee turnover increases, net profit declines, costs seem to get out of control and losses become imminent. Some owners, presidents and CEO's who find themselves in a situation facing these warning signs may actually contribute to the creation of "The Death Spiral" if they aren't careful.

What is "The Death Spiral" and how do you know if your company is in one?

"The Death Spiral" can be a fatal illness if not corrected immediately. This illness can be brought on by many factors including the process of building an infrastructure ("Ivory Tower") prematurely based predominantly on the self-gratifying needs of our ego. (Power and Politics instead of Principle and Process, Chapter VII) It can also be created by the circumstances mentioned in the opening paragraph. Whatever the reason, the warning signs generally appear and, if ignored long enough, red ink from losses on the P and L statement will become the megaphone that finally gets your attention.

If it becomes an infrastructure problem that doesn't have a revenue stream of sufficient magnitude to support the fixed costs it generates, then the infrastructure must be torn down and rebuilt.

Unfortunately, however, late recognition of the problem can cause the CEO or Owner to resort to a mental mode of retrenchment that should be called "Panic Response Management."

## Panic Response Management

Panic Response Management is in effect crisis restructuring. There's nothing wrong with crisis restructuring by itself. In most failing privately held companies that face restructuring it is very common to find that ownership lost sight of business objectives and put personal needs ahead of business needs; that type of situation is generally

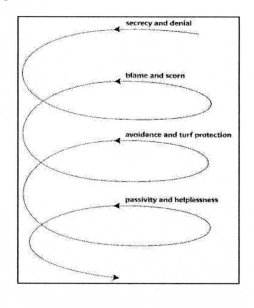

**The Death Spiral – Exhibit XI**

ego driven. This requires an honest assessment of leadership by the owners and the existing executive staff. However, in an ego driven situation, this restructuring is more apt to occur from the bottom up versus the top-down. The first instinct may be a "Reduction in Force." (RIF) Employee reduction generally represents the biggest opportunity to cut cost. Extreme caution must be exercised to avoid cutting revenue producing functions or revenue producing people. People or functions that may be at a minimum covering their variable expense and contributing to some degree toward fixed expense. Eliminating a revenue producing function creates a redistribution of allocated fixed cost which may now jeopardize the profitability of some other segment or division. This may create pressure to close more branches, business segments or cut deeper into other revenue producing functions thus creating "The Death Spiral." A RIF should be utilized to clean up the workforce, upgrade it, and eliminate non performers that should have been let go in the past. Careful analysis on employee contribution is essential when considering any type of workforce reduction.

To most of you, this may sound ridiculous or even laughable, but it does really happen. The Lead Wolf executive takes a different approach viewing restructuring from the top-down, including taking a serious look at corporate and/or family overhead. The Lead Wolf Executive begins this diagnosis by asking questions like the following.

- How is the business strategy defined?
- How is the strategy communicated to the employees?
- Define the company's competitive advantages.

- What are the strategic initiatives?
- What changes have had a significant impact on the business?
- What keeps the company from being the most efficient and effective source for customers?
- What competitive advantages does the competition have?
- What is the competency level of the executive staff?
- What volume does the top 10% of the customers represent?
- How many customers represent 80% of the revenue?
- Is account retention and growth measured?
- What is the turnover rate of the sales force?
- What is the overall corporate turnover in personnel?
- What percentage of the customers considers the company their number one supplier?
- Has the average sales per invoice increased or decreased over the past three years?
- What single thing has had the greatest impact on the company's profitability?
- What single thing has contributed the most to the decline in profits?
- How does the company compare to the industry par report?
- What metrics or industry surveys are available from the trade association?

- Does the company have a strategic plan?

- Does the company have business segment or divisional business plans?

- Does the company have or promote a culture of cost containment?

- Does the company provide functional leadership or do they dictate as a management style?

- Is there accountability within the executive staff and upper management?

- Is there accountability within the sales force?

- Which departments and individuals are competitive strengths to the organization and which are competitive weaknesses?

## The Real Deal

Get each member of your executive staff to go through this exercise for each department. When all the soul searching has been done, meet with your executive team to review the entire process and formulate "The Real Deal." What is the situation you are really facing?

Exhibits XII and XIII can be used in the initial assessment of a business that begins to struggle financially. A company scoring less than twelve points indicates that best practices are limited within the company.

# Ability: Best Practices

| Factor | Not Present 0-1 Points | Somewhat Present 2-3 Points | Employed 4-5 Points |
|---|---|---|---|
| Sales | Route sales, call reports and little else | Budgets, reviews, key account plans | SEP, targeting, pipeline mgt., coaching |
| Operations | Manual processes that are people driven | Zone picking, automated conveyor system | WMS, service-level driven purchasing, automated packing, modern facility |
| Strategy | Goals in the mind of the executive | Written documents that are shared | Actionable with formal reviews, developed by team; succession plans |
| Human Resources | No formal/informal employee programs, lack of employee awareness | Employee awareness, annual reviews, practices informal | EOC characteristics, skills assessments, performance reviews, formal hiring practices |

**Exhibit XII**

# Ability: Business Acumen

| Factor | Not Present 0-1 Points | Somewhat Present 2-3 Points | Employed 4-5 Points |
|---|---|---|---|
| Leadership | Reactive vs proactive. Lacks clear understanding of the value of people | Understands value of planning. Good people skills | Empowers, delegates, proactive. EOC philosophy. Humble, recognizes and surrounds himself with talent--benchmarks |
| Visionary | Waits for direction from B&S | Not afraid to take some risk. Has defined goals & objectives | Strategic thinker, understands both internal and external influences, has an "End Game". |
| Investor | Lacks image of excellence. Personal needs come before business needs. Minimal reinvestment in the business | Acquisition and/or some upgrades in business | Building the business is a priority. Investment in technology, modernization, operational efficiencies and people |
| Marketer | Waits for the manufacturers promotions with minimal innovation | Eager to share ideas and demonstrates creativity in employment of programs | Seeks new markets, creates one promotions, looks at all segments, creative and innovative |

**Exhibit XIII**

Effective leaders get each member of their executive team to go through a similar exercise for each department asking probing pointed questions relating to the company's inability to meet objectives. This is an exploration activity, not a bash session. It can be surprising what employees can reveal in a frank open atmosphere. The next step is to compare the organization to

industry "Best Practices." These can be obtained from National Association of Wholesalers in Washington, DC, www.naw.org. The Distribution Research and Education Foundation (DREF) funded the "Facing the Forces of Change—Transforming Your Business With Best Practices" in 1995. This publication was authored by a team of consultants and the study utilized Delphi survey methodology which included 1000 panelists comprised of 800 industry executives responding to the questions in the survey and panelist groups representing large and small distributors across all industry segments. This study created several matrixes to identify best practice of distributors performing in the high ROTA (Return On Total Assets) category (Anderson, 1995).

**The Real Deal** ----- What is the situation the company is really facing? This process starts with an assessment review. If the assessment is done by an outsider working for the owner or CEO, or the new CEO brought in to turn the company around, it is quite easy to be objective. The assessment process was discussed in detail in Chapter VI.

If the assessment is done by the owner, it is often difficult to admit to the facts. In many cases the owner of a failing organization is not an effective leader (not a Lead Wolf) and may in fact be part of the problem. If that's the case, it is highly recommended that the company hire an outside pair of eyes (consultant) to complete this assessment review. In fact, it would be wise to hire a consultant to do the actual review. Additionally, the company may want to hire a change agent to engage in the Turn-A-Round process.

Assuming the bleeding can be stopped (reduce losses and bring the company back to profitability), during the assessment process an evaluation of the executive team should also be taking place.

The following mini case study demonstrates the type of assessment necessary and the findings reported for a company in financial difficulty. This assessment became the platform to build a Turn-A-Round restructuring plan.

## Mini Case Study 111: Axitron's Survival – Turn-A-Round (A Consultant's Report)

*This assessment document is based on a detailed review of an information package provided by the executive team of Axitron. The consultants conducted a series of private interviews with all senior managers and several other key individual contributors. Findings in this document were reviewed in a late afternoon briefing with Jim and Sally Carter. It should be noted that the consulting firm conducting this assessment was selected for this work due to their knowledge of the industrial distribution industry and specific skills in turnaround restructuring.*

*It should be clearly stated that Axitron has had success servicing its markets and generated excellent sales growth from 1992 to 2002. The Denver/Salt Lake operation grew to a $13.2 million business from zero in 1984. Total company revenues tripled from 1992 to 1998, reaching $40 million. The company has a capable service and technical staff to satisfy their customers technical demands, excellent customer support, and has managed and developed solid relationships with primary vendors. However, a*

*formal evaluation of its strategic partners for long-term success may be necessary.*

*Unfortunately, Axitron did not seek help until they faced financial crisis. Revenues for 2005 are down 50%+ from the 2002 peak. The sole lending institution has indicated an unwillingness to continue providing credit to the company. The credit line in place is at its highest level of utilization (as of April 2005) and the expiration date for the credit is March 25, 2006. The company has done a "Z-score" analysis, which is a credit scoring process that evaluates financial health and bankruptcy potential, and finds that the potential of facing bankruptcy does exist. The book equity value of the company, which has always been modest relative to total assets and sales, is deteriorating rapidly and could reach zero within a few months. The company is clearly becoming an unattractive credit risk.*

*In the consultant's judgment, if the company expects to survive, stay solvent, gain and retain credit, and potentially grow out of this situation, an immediate restructuring is absolutely essential. It is doubtful the current lenders will extend the credit line for more than 3 months without a well-defined turnaround restructuring plan and any new lender or investor will require the same.*

*Axitron has been run with a relatively high level of operating expenses for several years. With the current extended downturn in the U.S. in Axitron's industry the company finds itself unprofitable, very highly leveraged, and in very clear danger of having its credit line pulled within 1-3 months. The financial woes are compounded by morale problems primarily generated*

*by a lack of sound planning. Perception of an "us vs. them culture involving family and friends vs. other employees. The company also has an overcomplicated organizational structure with redundant and under utilized people assets, and a weak sales management process contribute to the difficulty Axitron finds itself in today. The following issues were noted in our assessment and are addressed in this report:*

- Organization and leadership
- Vendor orientation/relationships
- Financial management
- Family issues in the business
- Planning, communication and execution
- Recommendations

## Organization and Leadership

*The organizational chart provided in the data package contained the names of 54 people. During the consultants visit they were told that an additional 3 full-time individuals were terminated in June, which reduces the full-time headcount to 51.*

*The organizational chart provided was created within the past two weeks and that prior to that no one had seen an organization chart for years, if ever. The consultant's recognized that if a company is very small, in a simple business, with few functions provided to customers and employees, then authority and responsibility can rest with one person, and he/she can orchestrate all activities.*

*In contrast, Axitron has 50 employees, an array of functions, several different businesses (and therefore decision-making needs), personnel guidance, development issues, job/task assignments, and customer-related activities which need to be more clearly defined for effective execution and managerial development.*

*There was a perception of a subculture within the company of "family and friends" that apparently bypasses the non-family managers/directors and takes all issues, requests, and complaints directly to the CEO. This implies either that the managers/directors who are bypassed are not worthy of the title and superficial responsibility they have (and hence are possibly in need of replacement or reassignment), or that the CEO is unwilling to delegate responsibility and trust to develop the next set of company leaders.*

*In either case, this breeds a lack of discipline in the sub-manager ranks and a lack of commitment and low morale among the managers/directors.*

*The current organizational structure is not consistent with an effective restructuring process. Ownership and governance issues are apparent. During the interview process, there was some indication of intimidation due to the amount of family presence within the business. Regardless of the position, duties or title held by family members, they are still considered part of ownership and the employees recognize and acknowledge this fact. There is a perception on the part of many employees that the ownership of the corporation has confused personal needs with the businesses needs. It is unclear within the limited scope*

*of the assessment whether or not that perception is in fact a reality. Regardless, confusion exists within the management structure as to delegation of duties, responsibilities and authority. A lack of accountability was apparent in some areas, which may be linked to this confusion. Certainly, the financial performance over the past two years indicates a lack of budgetary control and accountability.*

## Recommendations

It is obvious that Axitron's direction has been determined by "reactive" response to circumstances and trends, which have had significant impact to the decline in profitability. The issues addressed in this assessment are critical to the future survival of Axiton. The current financial crisis means that doing nothing is not an option.

The first step is to create a baseline P & L annualizing current performance and year-end estimates. This obviously will reflect a loss in the neighborhood of $1 million to $1.5 million.

Next, a new business model must be created supporting a revenue stream approximating the $15 million of anticipated 2006 sales. Profit must be planned first. By expecting a minimal profit that equals a 1% return on sales added to the reflected loss in the baseline P & L; the expected gap between loss and profitability is identified.

The third step is to identify the gap closures necessary; this is done by creating three budget/forecasts. A realistic budget based on the 1% return on sales example which recognizes

the $15 million dollar revenue stream; a catastrophic budget recognizing an approximate 10% decline in revenue from the realistic budget and an optimistic budget recognizing an approximate 10% increase over the realistic budget.

Each of these budgets will identify the profit/loss gap closure necessary to meet expectations of profitability.

- Realistic produces a 1% ROS
- Optimistic produces a 1.5% ROS
- Catastrophic provides a break even

## A Cure Can Be Found for "The Death Spiral

If the problem happens to lie within the executive staff and you own the company, don't languish in self-pity. Don't immerse yourself in the delusion that you're going to wake up tomorrow, look in the mirror, and see the "Jack Welch" of the distribution industry staring back at you. Be smart enough to swallow your pride and ask for help.

## Understanding the purpose to be served

The executive team must answer the question, what is the end game, the vision? The answer must be data and goal specific. Becoming profitable is an unacceptable response. All contributing factors to the lack of success must be identified. Determine exactly what needs to be done and what the objectives are. A common understanding of and a universal commitment to the objectives is essential. This commitment must come from not only the executive staff but from every employee within the organization. Failure to be data and goal specific often leads to disruption. You end up working on something that should have just been scrapped in the beginning. This creates wasted effort and doesn't produce results. It doesn't make sense to spend $6000 to fix a car that's only worth $2000 in tip top shape. Holding on to obsolete myths or beliefs only blocks progress. Hanging on to old Joe who has been there fifteen years just because he's a nice guy is not acceptable if in fact he really retired five years ago and just shows up to collect his paycheck.

## People

The President, CEO, Owner, Executive Team or Turn-A-Round Specialist alone is not going to solve the problems to make the company profitable. The employees are the people with the power to "Stop the Bleeding" and return to profitability. The Lead Wolf responsibility is to restructure the organization by taking out as much unnecessary cost as possible, making sure the company has the right number of people watching the right areas and that they are of the highest competency level available under the circumstances. At the same time creating an attitude that is conducive to success is important. Lastly, a major responsibility lies in restructuring the environment and providing the tools necessary to accomplish the objectives.

---

**Thought Provoker**

During a DREF (Distribution Research Education Foundation) interview, Steve Kaufman, CEO Arrow Electronics (2003) stated:

"A distributor has no really hard assets that distinguish them. A manufacturer may have a patent portfolio that gives them enormous knowledge and protection, and a platform to leverage off of. They might have a phenomenal R and D labs, even if the don't have patents, but terrific product development expertise. They might have world-class factories, world-class technology all of which are hard assets that are always there, and they leverage it. Distribution has none of those things. A distributor has nothing more than their people. Their only asset is their people. And so unlike manufacturers, the major asset walks home every night at six, seven or eight o'clock, and the question is, "Does the asset walk back in the next morning?" Patents don't have feet, development labs don't have feet, and factories don't have feet. So you come back the next day and it's still there. In distribution, your people are your business. And if they don't come back, you have nothing."

---

## Criteria

The criteria are really a result of determining what "The Real Deal" is. Once that is determined a solid foundation on which to build the restructuring plan can be identified utilizing best practice success drivers. What needs to be fixed, improved,

corrected or avoided to achieve optimum results? Defining the criteria for optimum resolution clearly is important as people often migrate to acceptable minimum actions and never ask what the ideal resolution should be. This is especially true if past performance and culture has been created under mushroom management tactics (keep them in the dark and feed them crap) and lack of communication in a fearful autocratic environment. This destroys morale creating a rapid increase in employee turnover. Collins in his book "Good to Great" says that effective leaders, before even establishing vision or strategy first make sure they have the right people on the bus, the wrong people off the bus and the right people in the right seats. Then they figure out where to drive it. Collins says, "People are not your most important asset. The RIGHT people are your most important asset" (2001).

Getting the right people in the right seats is part of establishing the criteria, "It's like holding a dove. If you squeeze it too tight you'll kill it. If you don't hold it tightly enough it will fly away," (Tommy Lasorda former Los Angeles Dodgers, Manager on effective leadership.)

*If a company finds itself in the crisis stage of decline, chances are the current PRESIDENT and his executive staff may be a major part of the problem if not THE problem.*

---

**Thought Provoker**

**During his DREF interview, Chuck Steiner (2003) said:**

"Refinements to industry practice, refinements to operation, excellence in what you do, continuous improvement aren't words. They're a way of life. When you understand that they're a way of life, then the change that you have in the way you perform is beyond comprehension because you just wind up operating at a different level, and if you can find a way to capture that in the culture of your business, in the culture that you emanate to your people, then as this culture structure changes, you have an opportunity for a superior level of performance. Excellence, and that's what in the end it's all about. Excellence breeds a high level of profitability."

---

## Formulating the restructuring process

This is not the plan. This is discussion of the process. The purpose is to draw on the experience, knowledge and judgment of the best-informed people within the new organization. If the organization has been run by the "King of the Mushroom Managers" (a Lone Wolf leader that refuses to share information and has weak communication skills), chances are the executive staff has no clue as to what's on the minds of the employees. This makes it even more important that past paranoia and distrust is laid to rest.

A template with selected events sequenced with communication to the employee being the primary objective is necessary.

Communication is not simply an announcement of the plan. Set up the process. Who's going to be involved? How will decisions be made? Who is on the restructuring/implementation team? A thorough risk analysis of employee acceptance and reaction should be considered. Never lose sight of the fact that you

**Profit is not a devious bad thing!**

must strive for excellence and people are your most precious asset, even more so in a failing or struggling organization. Most companies in the beginning of decline have people issues that are not recognized, denied or ignored causing the loss of trust and support.

Lead Wolf executives learned a long time ago that "profit is not a dirty word." Although it is essential for survival of the organization it must take its place of importance behind the employees because they hold the power to create profit or kill it. People can also save the business from many predators including the incompetence of upper management, dysfunctional family management, and apathetic foreign ownership.

---

**Thought Provoker**

*In his DREF interview Jim Warren, Cameron and Barkley (2003) stated:*

*"I learned the hard way, change really occurs more easily when everybody sees the need for it. The things the business gurus have told us for years, that I think hold true today is that you must try to manage the business, good times or bad times, like it's bad times. You have to make sure you make good decisions and then you have to make sure your team is totally committed to those decisions. It doesn't always have to be a consensus, everybody doesn't have to be totally sold on an idea, but they have to be willing to support it if you're going to be successful with it."*

---

Lone Wolf leaders that put profit ahead of their employees will create a culture within the workplace that breeds distrust and paranoia. Most employees devote a major portion of their lives to the job. Many "live to work" instead of "working to live. " They need more from their job than just a paycheck. They deserve an environment that encourages initiative and empowers them to use that initiative. They need leadership that understands that listening to the employees is a prerequisite for success. Executive management has responsibility for the direction and results of the organization. The key role of the executive team is to establish and execute company strategy. Effective leaders understand that communication is critical to the success model. Every employee must understand and support the strategy, especially in a Turn-A-Round situation. In any restructuring,

Turn-A-Round or even managing for growth mode, you must focus on the determined activities that are going to produce the desired results.

---

**Thought Provoker**

**During his DREF interview, Steve Kaufman, CEO Arrow Electronics, (2003) said:**

*"Good judgment comes from experience, and experience comes from bad judgment. And life is a series—or a managerial life is a series of building your skill and your judgment on the back of the mistakes you've made. If you have the self-discipline, and the ego control to stop and look at the mistake, admit it was a mistake, and figure out why you made it, what did you see that caused you to make these decisions so that you can then build that in, and next time you can say, "Aaah, that looks like this other time. And so let's try it differently. A phrase I love is, learn from the mistakes of others. You'll never live long enough to make them all yourself."*

---

Most organizational decisions are not made in a logical, rational manner. This is especially true if the organization is struggling for survival. Decisions often do not begin with careful analysis of the problem followed by systematic alternative solutions and finally execution. An organization may find that the decision process is characterized by conflict, coalition building, intuition and hunch. Lack of respect and distrust of the company just complicate this process pushing it closer toward the brink of disaster. Organizations must act with speed, staying in touch

with both the internal and external environments that affect their ability to meet objectives (Daft, 2001).

When a company feels the pressures of declining profits, lost market share, increased turnover and low employee morale, these are warning signs that obviously suggest trouble. What are some of the other warning signs?

- *Inability to take advantage of discounts*
- *Pressure from the bank*
- *Being put on C.O.D. or credit hold by our suppliers*
- *Credit line at its maximum for extended period*
- *Receivables aging increased*
- *Increased ageing of your payables*
- *Increased inventory and a lower turn rate*

*Now is the time for a gut wrenching reality check. What is really wrong with the business? Industrial distribution is not rocket science but it is amazing how easy it can begin to fail.*

The Turn-A-Round success of an organization in financial trouble is based upon its ability to manage the pressures in a fundamental way to not only maintain an excellent level of service to it's customers but to also provide an acceptable level of profit in doing so. Leadership must be able to lead people in such a way that their efforts automatically provide success in finance and operations that create profit. These efforts are greatly influenced by the ability to:

- Raise prices - sell higher

- Lower-cost

- Increase efficiencies

- Create continuous improvement

- Improve cash to cash cycling - reduced receivables aging, lower inventory, increased turn rates, extended terms from suppliers

These five factors can only be successful if people are energized, motivated and empowered to get the job done. Of course they must have a clear understanding of the objectives and vision of the company. This is especially challenging in a turn a round situation.

Management must figure out how to get more active involvement and creativity out of their employees. Questioning of the status quo and the generation of new ideas is a mandate of success. That success depends on a superior level of performance, a level that requires deep commitment.

---

**Thought Provoker**

**"My path came over time; it was not an epiphany or revelation. It was a slow maturing as a leader, realizing that people respond best to those that treat them with dignity and respect rather than by command and control."**

**James H. Blanchard**
**CEO Synovus**

---

# Chapter XII

## *Stop the Bleeding -- Creating a Turn Around Plan*

When profits are declining and the business is failing, leadership must discover truths independently, especially if they are new to the situation. Rumors must be filtered and the problems and solutions are not always obvious. When a company begins to bleed red ink, (becomes unprofitable) the board of directors and the finance community get nervous and may lose faith in the President's ability to deliver on promises. The company may find itself in a position that results in;

- *Declining sales*
- *Forced price concessions*
- *Shrinking margins*
- *Excessive fixed overhead expenses*
- *Poor PPR (Personal Productivity Ratios)*
- *Increased inventory*
- *Increased aging on receivables*

- *Shrinking profits—or—even losses*

- *Reduced cash flow*

Once an assessment of the business is complete (Chapter VI) and the reality of the situation is apparent, it's now crunch time. Determining how to "Stop the Bleeding" under the conditions that exist is critical. It's time to tear the Profit and Loss statement apart to determine exactly how to become profitable. In an unprofitable—Turn-A-Round – situation, pressure from the bank increases monthly. It's time to "Stop the Bleeding" and develop a plan to achieve the necessary outcome; that outcome is the development of multiple budgets that can be presented to the bank in an effort to keep their continued support until you can make the business profitable.

## Turbulent Economic Change

|  | Getting Worse | Stable | Improve |
|---|---|---|---|
| **Profitable But Off Plan** | NPCR Build Contingency Plan | Build Contingency Plan | Stay the Course |
| **No Profit But Positive Cash Flow** | NPCR and RIF Builds Survival Plan | NPCR Build Survival Plan | Build Contingency Plan |
| **No Profit Negative Cash Flow Reduction of Equity** | Turnaround Restructuring Plan | | |

Economic Difficulty (vertical axis)

Future Trends (horizontal axis)

**Exhibit XIV**  ©E. Johnson CEO Strategist, 2001

NCPR = Non Payroll Cost Reduction, RIF = Reduction in Force

The Economic Turbulence chart, Exhibit XIV, can provide the starting point for developing the leadership strategy to "Stop the Bleeding." Examine the profit and loss statement, perform a trend analysis and determine where the company is categorized in this chart.

## Multiple Budgets

The platform for the Turn-A-Round plan is the multiple budget process. This budgeting process is a survival action planning process and should not be taken lightly. It should not be entered into with a haphazard approach. Objectives include:

- *Gross margin improvement*
- *Increased market share*
- *Decreased overhead*
- *Cost containment*
- *Stable customer service*
- *Supply chain management*

Three budgets need to be developed for presentation. They are:

- Optimistic:      sales growth,10%      return on sales:1.8%
- Realistic:       sales growth, 5%      return on sales, 1%
- Catastrophic     sales decline, 5 %    return on sales, 0
                                         (Break Even)

As mentioned, the three budgets that are necessary are called "The Catastrophic Budget", "The Realistic Budget," and "The Optimistic Budget."

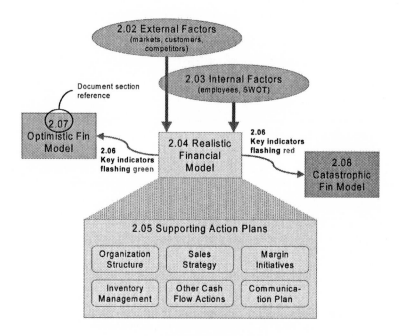

**Exhibit XV**

The percentage of growth, decline and return on sales are used for <u>example purposes only</u>. They will vary according to each individual situation. These numbers are modest in themselves but considering the fact that the company has been losing money, they can be considered aggressive. These examples will be discussed in more detail later. Most businesses are not complex.

Simplistically, to generate a profit from a losing situation you must:

- *Increase gross profit*

- *Reduce costs*

Leadership must be able to demonstrate credibility and believability in the business plan. Again, said in different terms, increasing profit requires:

- *Selling higher*
- *Buying lower*
- *Exercising cost containment*

Cost reduction must be addressed first because it has the quickest return. Head count, a reduction in force is the quickest way to take cost out of the organization. However, leadership must be aware of the "Death Spiral." (Chapter XII) Extreme care is necessary to avoid cutting revenue producing functions at the expense of gross margin, market share or service to key customers or customers that are paying for that service. Some business may be lost from small customers. If these are the kind of customers that increase service costs without paying for them, then that is a good thing. Revenue producers should be the last place to look when considering head count reduction.

## Data Gathering Method

The first place to look, even before analyzing administrative support and warehousing functions is the "Ivory Tower." In other words, look at the highly paid upper management structure. Perhaps jobs and functions can be consolidated. Initiating an executive pay cut that can be recouped, as a bonus when the company becomes profitable again may be an option.

---

**Thought Provoker**

Randy Larrimore (2003) stated during his DREF interview,

"I think the first thing that...I would advise anyone is to really try to understand the end user, as I mentioned earlier. That was something that I felt was a very valuable lesson. I learned it when I was at Harvard Business School. You really must understand the needs, and desires of the ultimate consumer, or you'll go the way of the buggy whip. You have to keep changing to meet those needs. You just can't win by selling what you make. You have to make what somebody wants to buy, and that's a lesson that most people don't know and understand. You always need to keep re-venting yourselves."

---

## Sales Force Reduction

When faced with the situation of a reduction in head count, view this as an opportunity to upgrade the sales force and eliminate any problems that should have been addressed months or years ago. The following question asked about every employee is a good reality check. "If Sally or John Doe would hand in their resignation tomorrow, what would you do?"

The answer?

1. Don't Know - DK

2. Pull out all stops to keep that individual because he or she is quantifiably, one of your top producers - a superstar.

3. Try to talk to the individual out of resigning because he or she does a decent job and improves every quarter.

4. Shake the individuals hand courteously, say you're sorry to see that person leave and escort that person to the door with no remorse.

5. Wish him or her luck; escort him or her to the door and then scream Hallelujah because he or she is a problem that you have been avoiding dealing with for some time.

If, combined with the input of sales management, there are more than a few DK's, management hasn't done a good job. If there are a lot of 4's and 5's this is the time to cut them loose. Territory consolidations may be possible without losing revenue. At the very least opportunity for upgrades and probably revenue growth may be possible. It is extremely important, other than 4's and 5's, that the lifeblood of the organization doesn't hemorrhage by arbitrarily cutting revenue or gross margin producing salespeople as a cost reduction method; that's not to say there should be absolutely no reduction in sales force. There aren't many organizations that couldn't do

some trimming without impacting revenue and gross margin production. However, it must be done with the careful precision of a surgeon. The potential downside risk must be analyzed. Once a decision is made, the trigger must be pulled.

Basically, four areas must be attacked in a restructuring "Turn-A-Round " situation to create profitability.

- *Margin improvement*
- *Reduction in force*
- *Death by a thousand cuts*
- *Change Management*

Reduction in force has already been addressed as having the most immediate impact on the bottom line. When doing a reduction in force, consolidations and branch closures must be considered and analyzed as to their contribution toward fixed costs. Of course there are other factors to consider depending upon the company's specific business, product line, customer base, etc. How will suppliers react to specific branch closures? Will consolidations jeopardize line retention?

## Death by a Thousand Cuts

Death by a Thousand Cuts is nothing more than a detailed line by line analysis of the profit loss statement and the general ledger. Exactly what are the costs that make up each expense category. The following is a list of examples of cost cuts that should be obvious. These examples are not fictitious as they come from real life Turn-A-Round case history.

- *Consulting fees to a family member for services that don't exist*

- *A 13 year old owner's daughter on the payroll for $25,000 per year to do a quarterly newsletter on her home computer*

- *The owner's housekeeper*

- *The owner's landscaper*

- *Leased vehicles for family members that are not employed at the company*

- *Large expenditures for jewelry and trips for the President's girlfriend*

- *Excessive conference expenditures that are really personal vacations*

- *Trips for friends and relatives not on the payroll*

- *Assets listed on the books that don't exist or are personal items located off the premises*

- *Rent or lease payments on condos or apartments in cities that have no justification from a business point of view. Rendezvous points for play days*

- *Airplanes, charters, boats*

- *Excessive implementation costs for new systems*

- *Excessive bonuses*

- *Excessive executive salaries*

- *Excessive corporate overhead costs -- glitz. Things such as, expensive artwork, multiple club memberships, oriental carpeting and general expensive décor*

Of course, the owner of any privately held company has the right to spend company money anyway they like within the parameters of the law. This statement should be qualified by adding "if they are profitable"--because whether they are the owner or just "the person in charge" (CEO, President), an implicit obligation exists to the employees of the company. Employees depend on ownership/leadership to keep the company prosperous. Their livelihood depends on it. When looking at cost reductions in general, trimming the corporate fat first is essential. Often times, owners and CEOs get so caught up in image and ego enhancement that trimming the corporate fat alone is enough to get to break even financially.

---

**Thought Provoker**

**Randy Larrimore (2003) stated during his DREF interview,**

**"I believe strongly that employees don't come to work just for a paycheck, they come to work for personal satisfaction, for personal enrichment. If you are the leader how do you relate to the people below you? How do you get them to follow you?"**

---

The next arena of Interest when analyzing what it is going to take to "Stop the Bleeding" is taking a look at the assets. This is not about the assets that are essential to support the business. This is about trimming the fat.

Other areas to consider:

## Real Estate

Is there a lot of equity in real estate that can be sold to generate cash that can be replaced at a much lower cost? Is lease vs. own an option at the same or lower cost?

## Other assets

Depending upon the type of business, there may be items that aren't necessary to the survival of the business. Things such as, condominiums, hunting lodge or other unnecessary executive perks need to be examined closely. Does the owner really need to drive a $100,000 Mercedes?

## Activity Based Costing

Consider doing an activity based costing analysis on the entire account base. There are plenty of instruction manuals published on how to do this. It is likely that you will find some surprises. Consider implementing a "Margin Hold" system that forces management approval on orders entered below established minimum margin levels.

## Margin Improvement

With the competitive pressures of today's market, margin improvement is your most challenging objective. As mentioned earlier the formula is easy.

- Buy lower

- Sell higher

- Control Costs

However, it does get just a little more complex than that. The first area to attack is pricing. More often than not salespeople get in a rut when it comes to managing pricing. The attitude of "don't rock the boat", "don't fix it if it ain't broke", can often generate huge profit leaks. If the company utilizes matrix pricing, look at it carefully. Is it updated and reviewed often? Is it being applied correctly? Do the sales people truly understand how to use it? Review all contract pricing. Establish review and update procedures for contract pricing. Invariably a number of customers may be getting the advantage of contract pricing that don't fit the criteria that had been previously established. Implement service level pricing to recoup the cost of servicing the demands of smaller customers for non stock items, rush orders, order changes, restocking fees, conversions and other extras often supplied but seldom paid for. Pricing management is a key best practice.

Distribution is a competitive business. Benfield and Baynard (2004) suggest the following when attacking the pricing system;

- *Review recent pricing decisions. Were they done with current operational costs in mind?*

- *Are employees aware of relevant costs in the pricing decision? Do you have a documented pricing process? Do your sales people understand the concept of shrinking margins. Do any of your sales people have mental margin caps?*

The buy side of the equation also offers numerous opportunities for margin improvements. Approach all company vendors. Don't be afraid to demand cost reductions. Customers certainly aren't embarrassed to ask. Review the entire purchasing organization. Are the buyers true buyers or are they simply order schedulers? Establish specific inventory reduction goals, turn-rate increases and fill rate improvement. Create an incentive based on the critical success factors on the buy side. Factors such as, margin improvement, inventory reduction and inventory turn rates. Include any others specific to your initiatives for profitability.

Try to take advantage of any "itchy-scratchy" opportunities. These are opportunities where the company is buying a product from someone that uses the types of products you distribute. This should enable you to increase sales. The academic term is "reciprocity."

The following is a checklist to review when considering margin improvement objectives.

- *Does the company have an established pricing policy?*
- *Does the company pricing policies consider market segmentation, risk, service levels and value added?*
- *Is the company counter sales/will call priced according to margin objectives?*
- *Does the company have well trained buyers and do they negotiate?*

- *Is the company purchasing/inventory control department managing the inventory well? Are they using the correct volume discount and item analysis?*

- *How does the company measure the company fill rate? Does the company benchmark it to the company competition?*

- *Does the company have a system to review and evaluate the company RGA's? (Return Goods Authorization)*

- *Does the company charge for restocking?*

- *Is the company getting the optimum discounts from the company supplier and are the company keeping the discounts as profit?*

- *Has the company done a supplier profitability analysis?*

- *Are the company customers profitable?*

- *Does the company have significant supplier error?*

- *Does the company have a vendor returns program and does the company manage it well?*

- *Does the company track on time delivery?*

- *Is the company selling the right products to the right customers?*

- *Does the company have an outcall program?*

- *Does the company inside sales force understand the concept of up selling?*

- *Is the company warehouse operating efficiently?*

- *Does the company have a freight recovery program or does the company fold under pressure and give it all away?*

- *Does the company rank and evaluate the company customers by gross margin dollars and gross margin percentages?*

- *Does the company have an incentive program that is tied to gross margin growth both in dollars and percentages?*

## On the Sales Side

Ultimately to create margin improvement, the entire sales team must have good judgment of market potential as it relates to margin improvement. They must be self disciplined and make intelligent decisions based on fact. Each territory manager must develop his own plan for profit improvement and be flexible on the implementation of that plan. The manager must be action oriented and customer driven and yet be extremely conscious of profitability objectives.

Results must be measured against the plan. Trend lines need to be established both on revenue and profit growth. They must be able to see the rewards for their efforts. They must accept responsibility and accountability for improved profitability and achievement of established objectives. They need to understand activity based costing.

## Sales Best Practice

Sales best practices are defined as those activities that create results. It means maximizing growth, maximizing profitability and increasing market share. It is a set of techniques used by upper quartile performers that help them realize significant improvements in reaching their predetermined measurable goals. Creativity and innovation are the essence but models of excellence based on best practice must adapt to the company's individual needs and circumstances. Most of these practices are only effective if they are process based providing focus, process and the discipline to carry them out supported by effective leadership. Accountability must be built into the practice. Informal lip service compliance is not best practice. Five sales best practices (Strategic Alignment, Segmentation, Creating Competitive Advantage, Coaching and Mentoring and The Score Card) are the key best practices that drive upper quartile performance in outside sales.

1. Strategic Alignment with corporate objectives. Sales strategy must be in alignment with overall corporate objectives regarding markets, products, strategic account management and other objectives. Focus must be on what is important to drive resource alignment and bridge the operational, management sales gap that is often present in distribution.

2. Segmentation is a best practice that can include markets, product lines and customers based on service output demands. Wholesale distributors must create and use formal methods to gather customer feedback and improve communication. The highest statistical reliability of all the 186 distribution best practices reported by NAW was the one that said Best Practice companies have a source of information about what customers think of them that does not come from their sales people. Not all customers and markets are created equal. Not all customers create value.

3. Creating Competitive Advantage—Targeting-- Goal Setting-- Action Planning--Targeting is the process of selecting high potential customer accounts to receive intense sales focus. Goal setting translates that high potential into an achievable numeric objective, i.e. revenue growth. The primary purpose of targeting and goal setting is to keep Account Managers focused on the company's strategic objectives, which center on growth and profitability. Target accounts or target markets require careful thought and substantial effort. An annual sales goal is established, and detailed action plans must be created for each of these targets. For most Account Managers, these targets will contribute a substantial portion of total territory sales and profit growth. This "big effort for big reward" means that the number of target accounts must be limited, and that sufficient time is allotted to succeed with each one.

An account action plan ensures that the Account Manager is proactively pursuing sales growth and that there is a solid basis for expecting account goals to be met. By monitoring these action plans, both the Sales Manager and Account Manager can manage activities rather than waiting for results.

4. Coaching and Mentoring—Enabling people to make a difference begins with coaching and mentoring. Of course responsibility must come with authority to accomplish the tasks at hand. Coaching and mentoring is not about holding the sales persons feet to the fire. It is about continuous improvements by offering

guidance, assistance and resources to help the sales person reach their objectives.

## The Adaptive Feedback Loop

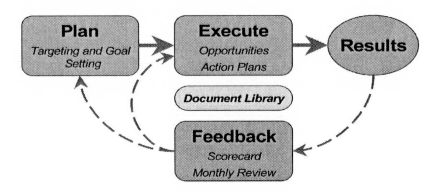

**Exhibit XVI**

The coaching and mentoring process is the cornerstone of Sales Best Practices. During regularly scheduled territory reviews, critical performance issues are discussed. It is the sales manager's/branch manager's job not to simply participate in this process, but to use these review opportunities to coach, counsel, and correct issues regarding performance. If conducted properly, the regular review process will become an effective tool in improving both the Sales Manager's and Account Manager's performance. These sessions are not intended to be disciplinary in nature but constructive sessions to drive overall performance improvement. The purpose of the review is to acknowledge and maintain good performance, as well as improve performance.

5. The Scorecard and Key Performance Indicators—All sales people like to know how they are doing. Scorecard development that focuses on territory and strategic objectives measured by specific performance indicators drives sales performance improvement. Best practice efforts require buy-in across sales and management as they consume time and talent. Resources must not be spread too thin due to a lack of commitment on management's part or a lack of buy-in throughout the organization. Initiating best practice should be done in a disciplined manner that addresses the most critical needs.

Successful leaders take the time to listen, imagine and investigate numerous alternatives. With the involvement of people they forge creative solutions to difficult problems. They challenge their people to stretch, go beyond their previous boundaries and think outside the box. Successful leaders feed off their people and allow their people to feed off of them. They give credit where credit is due. They give recognition as a means of gaining respect. They believe individuals can make a difference. Through these methods they learn to create new insights and possibilities.

Successful leadership demonstrated by Lead Wolves means creating a sense of urgency, getting mutual commitment to action. Action steps are always clearly defined and precise. Often, due to the personification of the leader's own personality and charisma, employees are eager for improved results. A Lead Wolf executive communicates with encouraging clarity that

commands ownership by everyone involved in the commitments made.

The successful leader is constantly building advantages into the organizations. The belief is that you don't always have to be better than your competition but you must be different. This concept demands creativity and innovations. However, this creativity and innovation must be built into the strategic plan. It must be distinctive and yet it must be manageable and predictable. This could involve anything from new technologies to market segmentation to development of new channels. It is all about improvement and finding newer and better ways of doing things.

This book deals with leadership in both highly successful performance in wholesale distribution and Turn-A-Round restructuring due to poor performance and poor results. Fixing the problem requires high impact transitional leadership to identify and eliminate the factors that led the company to the brink of financial disaster. Creating success and keeping the company in the upper quartile of performance requires the same kind of high impact leadership although it is applied differently.

---

**Thought Provoker**

Chuck Steiner, CEO Branch Electric, (2003) stated during a DREF interview,

"Excellence in what you do, continuous improvement aren't words. They're a way of life. When you understand that they're a way of life, then the change that you have in the way you perform is beyond comprehension because you just wind up operating at a different level, and if you can find a way to capture that in the culture of your business, in the culture that you emanate to your people, then as this culture structure changes, you have an opportunity for a superior level of performance. Excellence, and that's what in the end it's all about. Excellence breeds a high level of profitability."

---

## On the Buy Side

On the buy side of the equation, the company must be able to determine which of your suppliers enhance your margin opportunities and which suppliers detract from it. Add up all the things that each supplier does to help you increase profitability.

## Supplier Margin Contribution Enhancement

What is the company's discount structure with suppliers and how does it rank in your competitive analysis? Is the company getting the same discount or better than your competition? What are the total gross margin dollars earned by supplier? Rank suppliers accordingly to be used as a weight factor. Apply

a 1 to the lowest ranking, a 10 to the highest and an appropriate number for those in between.

Group the suppliers into dollar categories to minimize the number of rankings. If there are one hundred suppliers, apply the 80/20 rule and rank the top ten, the middle grouping and the bottom ten. Apply any form of this scale that makes sense  to your specific circumstance. The objective of this exercise is to simply determine if your suppliers are making a genuine effort to enhance your profitability.

Include cash discounts, rebates, co-op advertising, special terms and any other special incentives offered. Quantify in dollars all the enhancements each supplier offers.

## Supplier Margin Detraction

Quantify each and every issue that contributes negatively to profit enhancement. Issues to be considered are excessive inventory carrying costs due to extended lead times, late shipments, missed deliveries, inability to direct ship, excessive conversion costs, rework, packaging issues, lack of or restrictive return policy and the general level of co-operation and willingness to keep you competitive in the market. Some of these issues are easily quantifiable. Others may require an arbitrary assigned dollar figure based strictly on gut feeling. What is the real cost of a lost order, a late shipment etc.? Guesstimates are okay as

long as you are consistent in your application. Total all those negative costs to determine Supplier Margin Detraction.

## Common Margin Detractors

| |
|---|
| *Short shipments/wrong counts* |
| *Missed promise date* |
| *Damaged goods* |
| *Partial shipment* |
| *Lost back order* |
| *Incorrect technical advise* |
| *Pricing errors* |
| *Wrong or no part number* |
| *No packing slip* |
| *Illegible documents* |
| *No PO number* |
| *Duplicate shipments* |
| *Wrong PO number* |
| *Poor customer service/response* |
| *Faulty products* |
| *Difficult claim procedures* |

| |
|---|
| *Shipment to wrong location* |
| *Faulty products* |
| *Difficult claim procedures* |
| *Shipment to wrong location* |
| *Non responsive to emergency requests* |

## Supplier Profitability Ratio

Determination of The Margin Enhancement Rating and The Margin Detraction Rating is necessary to create a Supplier Profitability Ratio using the following formula.

| | |
|---|---|
| SR= | Supplier Rating |
| SPR= | Supplier Profitability Ratio |
| MC= | Margin Contribution |

**SUPPLIER PROFITABILITY RATIO**

$$\frac{1000}{\text{ME-MD}} \times SR \times 100 = SPR$$

Example:

| | |
|---|---|
| Margin Enhancement | = $230,000.00 |
| Margin Detraction | = $110,000.00 |
| Supplier Rating | =8 |
| $\frac{1000 \times 8}{\$230k - \$110k}$ | = .066 X 100 = 6.6 |

**Exhibit XVII**   ©E. Johnson, 2002

This formula is by no means scientifically accurate. In fact, it is an arbitrary conception designed specifically for the exercise and not the result. The rating itself is not of significance here.

What is significant is the exercise itself. It forces the company to take a serious look at true vendor performance. List vendors by their profitability ratios. This should be an eye opening exercise. Take this information and use it in discussions and negotiations with vendors. Be careful not to reveal all the details of the rating as it can be easily challenged due to the intangible assignment of various factors. However, it can be invaluable in discussing many supplier issues contributing to margin detraction.

## Cash Rules

The primary focus of any turn around effort is improved cash flow. Everyone has heard the cliché, "cash is king." In a turn around situation that becomes the most dominate statement about which leadership must be concerned. Mcguinnes in his book "Cash Rules" lists several cash drivers that impact cash flow.

a) Sales growth—The most basic cash contributor measured as the percent of change in sales volume from the previous period. Of course a sales decline consumes cash. Sales growth is a key performance indicator on how the business is doing.

b) Gross profit—This is the money left over after you cover the direct cost of goods sold. This is what covers the expenses and pays the bills. As gross profit increases cash will increase based on collections.

c) Accounts receivables, payables and inventory—These are manageable items that have a direct impact on

cash. Reducing inventory, reducing receivables and extending payment terms can increase cash flow.

d) Capital expenditures—Purchasing equipment or other assets can delete cash even if the purchases are financed. Cash down payments, related costs, monthly payments and interest will impact cash flow. Of course this does not mean that you stop all capitol expenditures. The key is determining the return on investment (ROI) and the long-term impact on cash flow, which could be positive by an increase in sales or better efficiencies.

These cash drivers provide an essential paradigm for business survival and long term strategic thinking.

It became apparent during research for this book that we must not ignore the fact that restructuring cannot succeed in any organization without the revitalization of its people. And, revitalization of the people requires high impact leadership. Turn around and restructuring is an intensive short-term intervention. Revitalization is the key to long-term success for the organization.

## Turn-A-Round Restructuring

A company finding itself in a turn around situation due to financial distress requires rapid analysis, quick decisions and immediate actions. This is undertaken with a deep sense of urgency. This creates a tidal wave of shock to the culture of the organization. Once this shock subsides, strong high impact leadership must be present to set a course, structure an

environment and develop a team that can drive the organization back to success and profitability.

Most companies that become financially troubled demonstrate a weakness in leadership. This weakness or lack of effective leadership may be a result of the CEO's qualifications for being the leader of the organization not extending beyond his DNA (family member). This weakness in Leadership may extend throughout the executive team if one or several were appointed simply because they were members of the lucky sperm club including the CEO himself.

McClelland (2004), a recognized leadership guru, states that 99% of the reason companies fail are due to a lack of effective leadership. He goes on to state that this failure is not due to the economy, not due to the competition and not because of market share. Failure is due to the leader not having a vision and dealing with those issues in the strategic planning process.

## Participative Leadership

McLagan and Nel (1995) state that leadership is about breaking new ground, going beyond the known and creating the future. They talk about new governance requiring effective leadership to create a future. This is exactly what restructuring a financially troubled company is all about, recreating a new future. This requires

immobilizing an existing culture long enough to introduce the organization to change. This change is often traumatic because people's lively hoods are at stake. This requires a specific type of leadership that has a compassion for the whole of the organization as opposed to individualistic compassion.

## Restructuring – Integrity and the Bottom Line

Restructuring and creating a Turn-A-Round plan for a failing organization almost exclusively means a reduction of the work force. Additional difficult decisions often occur when dealing with family members that may not be contributing to an extent that they are earning the income that they are being paid. The moral questions that challenge the leader's integrity are simplistic although the answers can be complex.

"Where should the expense reduction occur with regard to head counts?"

"Do we start at the top or the bottom of the employee food chain?"

Frank Sonneberg and Beverly Goldberg point out in Ken Shelton's book, Integrity at Work , (1998) that way too many people believe there is no correlation between integrity and bottom line performance. Wrong. Integrity and performance are not polar opposites. They go on to state that if people believe the organization is fair, they are willing to give of themselves.

This becomes a critical leadership issue. The leader has an obligation to create profitability. This can often mean innocent people get hurt. Personal experience in this arena has formulated this writer's theory that it is absolutely essential that reduction in force must start at the top of the organization, not at the bottom. If this concept is followed an effective Lead Wolf leader can face his innermost doubt with integrity due to the fairness used in making the most difficult people decisions. The formula is simple:

- Base decisions on competency and performance
- Trim corporate excess first
- Use the situation as an opportunity to eliminate under performing employees that should have been let go when the company was profitable
- Upgrade the workforce
- Cut revenue providing positions last if at all

## Employee Financial Impact

"People aren't profits but without people there can be no profit", Kelso. This quote says it all and supports Becker, Huselid and Ulrich's opinion (2001). These authors state that in addition to grasping the importance of fixed, variable and sunk costs; effective leadership must understand the financial impact of employee performance in identifying cost/benefit categories and estimates. At its core, determining the return on investment in people entails comprehending the relative impact of high and low performance employees.

It is this writer's personal experience in Turn-A-Round (T.A.R.) restructuring that can validate the statement that determining employee competence and contribution with respect to return on investment is absolutely critical to the T.A.R. plan. It is specifically critical when analyzing the reduction in force initiative.

Pearce and Robinson (2000) point out key questions relevant to the restructuring process.

- What is the best way to organize the company?
- Where should leadership come from?
- What values should guide us?
- What should this organization and its people be like?

Pierce and Robinson point to these questions as fundamental issues of leadership in the restructuring process. Downsizing, restructuring, reengineering, outsourcing and empowerment are all emblazoned in our minds as a result of the extraordinary speed with which companies worldwide have incorporated them in response to global pressures.

## Creating the Turn-A-Round Plan

Now let's get to the meat of Turn-A-Round restructuring. Analysis of the Profit and Loss statement has been completed. Establishment of the magnitude of the reduction in force required is complete. The exercise, "Death by a 1000 Cuts," (cost containment) is complete. Additionally, a margin improvement plan has been developed. The next step is to create and implement the company Restructuring Turn-A-Round plan.

Again, communication is the key. It is imperative to act swiftly enough and boldly enough to immobilize the old culture to allow the new executive team to create a culture shift that lends itself to leadership, communication, accountability and most importantly profitability.

---

**Thought Provoker**

*John Woodhouse, CEO Sysco Systems (2003) stated in his DREF interview,*

*"The first thing, I'd really look to make sure that they had the financial controls. That they really knew what was going on because there are a lot of distributors out there that don't have those financial controls. This is not a financial business. It's a sales and marketing business. I'd make sure that there was a really competent, above average financial individual shoulder-to-shoulder to me as the CEO. because more failures take place there than anyplace else."*

---

## Multiple Budgets

As mentioned earlier in this chapter, the platform for the Turn-A-Round plan is the multiple budget process. This budgeting process is a survival action plan and should not be taken lightly. It should not be entered into with a haphazard approach. Objectives include all the issues we've discussed previously.

- *Gross margin improvement*
- *Increased market share*
- *Decreased overhead*

- *Cost containment*

- *Stable customer service*

- *Supply chain management*

This is important enough to repeat. The three budgets that are necessary in a Turn-A-Round restructuring are called "The Catastrophic Budget", "The Realistic Budget," and "The Optimistic Budget."

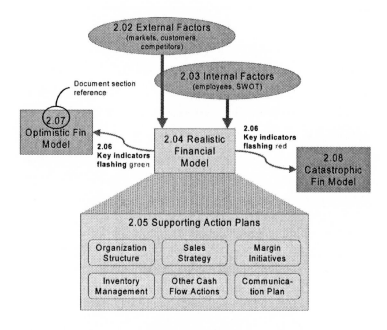

**Exhibit XVIII**

## Creating the budgets

## Step #1    The Sales Forecast

All budgets generally start with a sales forecast. Request from the Vice President of sales a new, realistic forecast. The V.P. of Sales needs to be intimately involved in this process.

Chances are the new realistic forecast received from the sales force is going to be highly optimistic. It is by nature difficult for any salesperson to forecast anything other than solid growth regardless of conditions. This is especially true if their incentive is based on revenue growth. The Chief Financial Officer (CFO) takes that forecast and using historical percentages creates a proforma (a projected Profit and Loss statement based on the forecast). Unless the sales force is unique and turned in a forecast showing no growth or a revenue decline, this forecast and proforma becomes a basis for the "Optimistic Budget." This budget includes all past sins prior to incorporating any of the Turn-A-Round initiatives and adjustments.

## Step # 2   The Proformas

The next step is to take the current year's actual performance and extend it through year end and determine the profitability or the extent of loss expected. Additionally, take the prior year's actual Profit and Loss statement and post it openly in the "War Room." The "War Room" is a convenient, confidential place for the Turn-A-Round team to meet regularly and develop the plan. It's called a war room because there can be a lot of blood shedding involved in a situation where the company has lost money consistently.

Usually in these types of situations it isn't just a one year anomaly. Create a proforma (projected Profit and Loss statement) for a realistic forecast and a catastrophic forecast utilizing the same process used for the optimistic forecast. These three proforma's become the platforms to build  three new budgets on. "The Optimistic," The Realistic," and "The Catastrophic" budgets. If

it is the first half of the year, use last years actual numbers as a basis for determining your three new budgets. If it is the latter half of the current year and year end results can be accurately predicted without the impact of any of the changes discussed in the assessment process then that proforma becomes the basis point.

## Catastrophic Budget

In calculating the necessary expense reduction and margin improvement the catastrophic budget takes the platform year proforma revenue and reduces it by 5%. This may vary according to individual circumstance which may dictate a 10% reduction or more. The idea is to demonstrate credibility in recognition of the possibility that conditions can become worse than anticipated. In that event, the company is prepared to remain at least at break even if initiating the catastrophic budget is necessary. The budgeted revenue becomes a reduced number, in this case a minus 5%, from the platform year (based on economic predictions.

Utilizing historical data and percentages, calculate the gross profit dollars. Take the platform year's budgeted total expense (without any restructuring adjustment) and subtract it from the gross profit dollars. This shows you the resulting profit or most likely your resulting pre tax loss.

Starting with the Catastrophic budget, the objective is to break even at that level of revenue. Consequently, a profit is not expected to be added to the pretax loss to determine your total shortfall (see example).

## Example: Catastrophic Table 1A

| Sales Revenue | | 5% Decline | $41,000,000.00 |
|---|---|---|---|
| Gross Profit | | 27% | 11,070,000.00 |
| Platform year Expense | | | 13,000,000.00 |
| Resulting profits | | <loss> | -$1,930,000.00 |
| Necessary profit | Break Even | 0% ROS | 0 |
| Necessary expense reduction | | | $1,930,000.00 |

Gap closure needed          $ 1,930,000.00

**There could be a slight reduction in variable expense due to reduction in sales, but for the purpose of this exercise it isn't significant enough to include in the calculations.**

This exercise now indicates exactly how much cost reduction and/or margin improvement is required to reach break even.

## Optimistic Budget

This same exercise applies to the realistic and optimistic budgets. If the company has been bleeding red ink as a company, it is highly unlikely that anyone is going to believe revenue can increase by 15% or more. So, regardless of what the company's optimistic sales force has forecasted, it is recommended that the optimistic budget shows no more than a maximum revenue growth of 10%. Additionally, the maximum Return on Sales (ROS) forecasted should not exceed 2%. Consider these important factors.

- The company has been in a loss situation.

- These budgets should be prepared with the understanding that they may be presented to your financial partner (the bank).
- They must be believable and demonstrate credibility.

## Example: Optimistic Table 1B

| Sales Revenue | 10% Increase | $47,000,000.00 |
|---|---|---|
| Gross Profit | 27% | 12,825,000.00 |
| Platform year Expense | | 13,000,000.00 |
| Resulting profits | <loss> | -$175,000.00 |
| Necessary profit | 1.8% ROS | 846,000.00 |
| Needed expense reduction/ margin improvement | | $1,021,000.00 |

Gap closure needed       $1,021,000.00

## Realistic Budget

The realistic budget can show a modest revenue increase but again revenue growth should be limited to a maximum of 5% with only an expected 1% **ROS  (Return on Sales)**

## Example: Realistic Table 1C

| Sales Revenue | 5% Increase | $45,000,000.00 |
|---|---|---|
| Gross Profit | 27% | 12,150,000.00 |
| Platform year Expense | | 13,000,000.00 |
| Resulting profits | <loss> | -$850,000.00 |
| Necessary profit | 1.0% ROS | 450,000.00 |
| Needed expense reduction/ margin improvement | | $1,300,000.00 |

Gap closure needed       $1,300,000.00

The end result is the calculation of the net combination of expense reduction and/or margin improvement necessary to achieve the objective of each specific budget. Focus must now be on the realistic budget. Of course any or all of these numbers or percentages can be adjusted according to specific circumstances.

The objective in making a presentation to the bank should be to demonstrate that the company will end the next year with an achievement somewhere between the realistic budget and the optimistic budget. If the presentation is done well, backed up by facts with definitive initiatives and action plans, the bank will probably believe that the company will end the next year somewhere between the realistic budget and the catastrophic budget. This is  okay because that means the bleeding has stopped and the company will end the year with a profit.

## Step #3   Baseline Extraordinary Expense

The next step is to baseline any extraordinary expense that occurred in the platform/prior year that will not repeat itself. Additionally any unusual expected expense that will occur in the budgeted year should be recorded.

| Line item | Decrease from prior year | Increase from prior year |
|---|---|---|
| Legal | | $ 50,000.00 |
| Interest | | $100,000.00*** |
| Executive salaries | <$ 50,000.00> | |
| New systems start up | <$100,000.00> | |
| Head hunter fees | <$ 50,000.00> | |
| Wage increase | <$100,000.00> | |
| | <$300,000.00> | $150,000.00 |
| Net change | <$150,000.00> | |

**Table 1D:**   Baseline Extraordinary Expense

**Chances are that the bank has become nervous due to the red ink and interest rates will increase.

## Step #4   Closing The Gap

Now it's time to close the gap and create the actual Turn-A-Round plan. Of course every department is expected to develop their own business plan outlining specific initiatives that are in alignment with the overall T.A.R. plan. This plan should list detailed strategic initiatives, action plans, critical constraints, milestones and key management indicators to be used in the accountability process. The three methods previously mentioned that are used to "close the gap" are:

- *Margin improvement*
- *Reduction in force*
- *Cost containment (death by a 1000 cuts)*

Each budget should be categorized to reflect how the "Gap" (deficit) is to be closed.

## Margin Improvement Table 1E

|  | Buy Better | Itchy Scratchy | Sell Higher | Total |
|---|---|---|---|---|
| Optimistic | $150,000.00 | $100,000.00 | $100,000.00 | $350,000.00 |
| Realistic | $85,000.00 | $80,000.00 | $200,000.00 | $365,000.00 |
| Catastrophic | -------0------- | -------0------- | -------0------- | -------0------- |

# Reduction in Force Table 1F

|  | Head count reduction | Department or division | Total net savings |
|---|---|---|---|
| Optimistic | 10 | 2-sales; 2-admin; 6-ops | $400,000 |
| Realistic | 10 | Same as above | $600,000 |
| Catastrophic | 26 | 5-sales; 2-admin; 18-ops; 1-executive | $1,055,000 |

# Cost Containment – (Death by 1000 Cuts) Table 1G

| Expense Category | Optimistic | Realistic | Catastrophic |
|---|---|---|---|
| Accounts receivable reduction-interest | $50,000 | $50,000 | $50,000 |
| Inventory reduction-interest | | $37,000 | $37,000 |
| Carrying costs | | $120,000 | $120,000 |
| Country club dues | | $13,000 | $13,000 |
| Daughters news letter | | $25,000 | $25,000 |
| Executive pay cut | | | $80,000 |
| Management pay cut | | | $100,000 |
| Overtime | $ 50,000 | $120,000 | $180,000 |
| Conventions | $ 10,000 | $ 20,000 | $20,000 |
| Transportation | | $ 50,000 | $100,000 |
| Total | $200,000 | $435,000 | $725,000 |

# Summary of Gap Closures Table 1H

| Expense Category | Optimistic | Realistic | Catastrophic |
|---|---|---|---|
| Reduction in force | $400,000 | $400,000 | $1,055,000 |
| Cost containment | $200,000 | $435,000 | $725,000 |
| Margin improvement | $350,000 | $365,000 | $0 |
| Nonrecurring extraordinary expense | $150,000 | $150,000 | $150,000 |
| Totals | $1,100,000 | $1,350,000 | $1,930,000 |

## Operational Strategy
## Red Light—Yellow Light—Green Light

It's difficult to determine when to initiate further cost reductions, when to relax and when to be on guard. In a Turn-A-Round situation, it's important to  act and react quickly. Observation of key performance indicators (KPI's) guide your reactions.. Interpretation and understanding of these measurement tools is critical. These indicators may include among others:

## Key Performance Indicators    Table 1I

| Indicator | Owner | Actions required |
|---|---|---|
| Forecast vs. actual sales | | Target initiatives |
| Cash to cash cycle | | Expense control and collections |
| Net income vs. forecast (1.3% ROS target) | | Trend line |
| Gross margin percentage | | Monitor pricing |
| Gross margin dollars | | Monitor pricing |
| Sales per employee | | Evaluate territories and Personnel |
| Gross margin per employee | | "          "          " |
| DSO—accounts receivable | | Collections |
| Payables ageing trend line | | Seek extended terms |
| External factors- --Interest rates, Manufacturing backlogs, Purchase managers index, | | React to market conditions with sales initiatives |
| Book to bill ratio | | Establish baseline |
| Headcount | | Establish PPR-- productivity |

| | | |
|---|---|---|
| Quote creation rate | | Confirm consistent process for capturing quote activity and establish baseline. |
| Quote kill rate | | See above. |
| Customer market feedback (informal) | | React as necessary |
| Information from vendors | | Determine what market metrics. |
| NAPM index | | Market awareness |

---

**Thought Provoker**

Chuck Steiner, CEO Branch Electric, (2003) stated during a DREF interview,

"Refinements to industry practice, refinements to operation, excellence in what you do, continuous improvement aren't words. They're a way of life. When you understand that they're a way of life, then the change that you have in the way you perform is beyond comprehension because you just wind up operating at a different level, and if you can find a way to capture that in the culture of your business, in the culture that you emanate to your people, then as this culture structure changes, you have an opportunity for a superior level of performance."

The red light, yellow light, green light scenario establishes what mode the company should be operating in based on the key performance indicators established.

**RED LIGHT: Catastrophic Plan**
**YELLOW LIGHT: Realistic Plan**
**GREEN LIGHT: Optimistic Plan**

*Note: It is possible due to specific circumstance and your position on the Economic Turbulence Chart that you may have to launch your TAR plan under the Red Light Catastrophic Plan.*

In a Turn-A-Round situation the realistic plan is automatically implemented in a precautionary status, the Yellow Light mode. Determining when or if the mode changes to red or green is supported by tracking your indicators.

## Key Performance Indicators—Green Light  Table 2A

| Indicator | Situation | Action |
|---|---|---|
| Cash Flow | Positive Cash Flow | Manage To Plan |
| Operating Profit | Profit To Budget | Manage To Plan |
| Internal Indicators | Positive Trend | Manage To Plan |
| External Indicators | Positive Trend | Manage To Plan |

## Key Performance Indicators—Yellow Light  Table 3A

| Indicator | Situation | Action |
|---|---|---|
| Cash Flow | Trend Flat | Stretch Payment Cycles |
| Operating Profit | Meeting Plan | Increase Turns |
| Internal Indicators | Trend Down | Review All Staff Replacements |
| External Indicators | Loss Of Contract | No Pay Increase Reduce TandE |

## Key Performance Indicators—Red Light   Table 4A

| Indicator | Situation | Action |
|-----------|-----------|--------|
| Cash Flow | Decreasing | Executive Pay Cuts |
| Operating Profit | Not Making Plan | Manager Pay Cuts |
| Internal Indicators | Indicators Down | Planned Head Count Reduction |
| External Indicators | Indicators Down | Crisis Cost Containment |

## Key Performance Indicators: Green Light, Yellow Light, and Red Light

## Creating Change

It is imperative that a giant shock wave is initiated that will immobilize the old culture instead of a lingering multitude of many small shock waves that do nothing more than upset the entire company creating paranoia and distrust. This means that major changes in the work force are done as one big change and not a multitude of many. Get it done quickly, move on and be prepared to sell the Turn-A-Round plan to the rest of the company. That presentation may be even tougher and just as critical as the presentation to the bank.

---

**Thought Provoker**

*Steve Kaufman, CEO Arrow Electronics, (2003) stated in a DREF interview,*

*"The leader has to be an agent of change. Most people in most organizations prefer not to change. As an individual person, I don't like to change. Change is hard work. You know, it's scary. You don't know how it's going to come out. You have to learn new and different things. One of the roles of leadership is to cause change, to create change, to force change, to instigate change. And so I would tell anybody in a senior position in management, particularly in distribution that you have to be—not just willing to change, not just open to change, but you have to go looking for change. If you don't do that, then you're not doing a service to your organization."*

---

**It All Starts With Leadership and Communication**

Next to Leadership and people, communication is the most critical element to success whether the company is in a growth mode or facing a Turn-A-Round situation. However, in a Turn-A-Round situation, failure to communicate has much greater consequences. Failure to communicate could ensure absolute failure. Communication is essential to developing trust. Trust is necessary to get people to reach down deep inside and give everything they have under the most difficult circumstances.

The reason people follow any leader, especially in the business world, is due to trust. The only way to develop trust is through communication, talking to people with respect to gain their respect. Their respect is a key ingredient to developing trust. Trust is gained when people think the company cares about their welfare and recognizes the role they play in creating a profit. People have to think that the company not only cares about their problems but that the company will make every effort to solve them. This is an especially difficult task in a Turn-A-Round situation when jobs have been eliminated. This is one of the reasons that it is critical to act quickly and swiftly when implementing the restructuring plan. It is not only important to create a big enough shock wave to immobilize the old culture, but the survivors must be convinced that they are the keepers and you will all succeed together. Leaders are respected for discipline. Survivors will recognize, if their respect has been gained, that terminating people is part of the job, a sacrifice of part to protect the whole. Removing non-contributors and disruptions due to poor performance is in fact to their benefit.

WARNING---Do not under any circumstances keep an employee that is obviously a non-performer due to politics, tenure or relationship with the owner or anyone on the executive staff. This can countermand every honest effort and sincere communication made. It also sends a message of dishonesty.

Employees want to take pride in their leaders. They are eager to give their trust but demonstrating the kind of character as a leader that deserves that trust can not be over emphasized.

Don't let the employees down. Character is built around a true concern for the people within the organization. It is based on fairness and consistency.

## Delivering the Message

The very first step required after a restructuring process is mass communication. It is difficult, as President or CEO to get out in the field and talk to every employee face to face unless the company is small with less than 100 employees. However, that should be a priority during the course of the year. An acceptable alternative to reach every employee is teleconferencing. However, most companies are not set up for that process. A second alternative is the production of a video tape presentation to every employee simultaneously. Mandatory viewing of every employee at a pre-selected time is essential. The video should send a positive message addressing the following issues.

- Reasons behind restructuring
- Future objectives
- Commitment to success
- Discussion of survivors and honesty of future actions
- Motivational teamwork discussion
- Framework for future communications
- Discussion of trust and values
- Answering questions posed by employees (at least 30 pre-selected questions and others asked by panel of employees)

Before creating the video, it is necessary to solicit ahead of time questions to be asked by employees. These questions are the heart of what's now on the employee's mind. Do not duck the tough ones. The employees will know and will lose respect and trust. Face the issues head on with honesty. Supervisors can generate these questions from the employees company wide and submit them for review. Every question does not have to be addressed, but the most relevant to the employees must not be ignored. The answers need to be rehearsed ahead of time. The President facilitates this Q and A session but can direct different members of his executive staff to provide the answers on video tape.

A hand picked group of line employees should be selected to ask these questions of the executive staff on tape. The tape can be edited to insure a positive message. However, honesty and integrity must be preserved. This is only the first step. Answers must be open, honest, sincere and complete. This is the very first opportunity since the restructuring announcement to demonstrate leadership, respect and trust.

It is especially important that the message is consistent throughout the management team. As important is the demonstration of respect, trust and leadership. However, no one factor plays a more precious role in building and preserving that trust amongst the employees, than communication. It is a make or break issue.

It is important for the President to know what the CFO and the rest of the executive team are doing and what they intend to do under every circumstance. This sounds like micro management but in a crisis driven situation it is called effective communication. Once those determinations are made, the employees deserve to know what is planned. After all, they are expected to execute with precision. People need a keen sense of trust and a feeling of being part of the plan. The communication network should connect all employees. Everyone needs to be a part of the overall plan. Miscommunication, rumors and garbled messages cause conflict and distrust. Don't settle for second-rate communication, it's too critical to success. Avoiding informing all employees, specifically on matters that affect their lives, is like playing with fire. This kind of action breeds resentment, mistrust and paranoia.

We all communicate daily. We practice communicating daily, yet experience confirms that we fail to communicate effectively most of the time. Add to that obstacle the fact that the company is undergoing a restructuring process and the challenge of communicating effectively seems overwhelming.

Difficulty in communication is enhanced when there is a crisis situation or adversity of some nature. A restructuring certainly qualifies under those guidelines. In normal times communication is difficult in itself due to individual psyche and individual agendas.

Listening skills are especially important. Proof of effective listening is in the resulting actions. Listening should dominate interaction with the employees. Distractions need to be removed. Trust must be developed. A sincere desire to understand is important. Individual needs must be considered. Sustaining an open mind and compassion are essential.

## Not a Cake Walk

Leading the restructuring process is not a cakewalk. Determination of employee loyalty, willingness and competency is mandatory. An understanding of what can really be asked of employees during these times is imperative. Be careful of misplaced or misdirected loyalty. Misdirected or false loyalty can become an issue. Maximum loyalty from employees during this restructuring is key to succeeding with the Turn-A Round plan. Trust, loyalty and the need for a high commitment to the company are equally important.

A willingness to hang tough and commitment demonstrated by the leader will enhance commitment by the employees. Commitment is self-nourishing and it gives meaning to work. Employees will look to the leader first to measure levels of commitment. Employees want to take the leaders pulse. Employees want to believe. Employees need a leader they can follow. It's imperative that the leader shows no signs of weakness and does not let them down. This goes for the entire executive staff.

Employee commitment will soar if the entire executive staff demonstrates a passion for success. Excitement breeds excitement. Success breeds success, the more consuming the desire to fix things, the more leadership is demonstrated and this draws support from the employees. The President, as the leader and the executive staff set the stage. If the company fails, chances are the leader did not set the proper environment for success. Create an attitude, Structure an environment, Develop a team (Chapter XIII).

*A Lead Wolf executives intensity, focus, drive and dedication along with these same attributes from the executive staff are the determinants of the level of commitment provided by the employees*.

Commitment won't survive if leadership doesn't exist. The leader must be proactive and publicly demonstrate leadership, confidence and commitment. The Lead Wolf model of leadership during transition is difficult and challenging. However, Rosevelt reminds us:

"If you lead through fear and authority you will have little to respect; but if you lead through confidence, commitment and respect you will have little to fear." (Roosevelt)

It is important to deliver a message of renewed life to the employees. Come up with an acronym that reflects the new strategy, "A new Vehicle for Success," "The New XYZ Company Way", anything that can be referred to over and over again to communicate progress and success.

Restructuring in a Turn-A-Round situation is not an every day occurrence. Although reengineering and restructuring occur frequently, as continuous improvement initiatives, Turn-A-Round restructuring is a matter of survival. It has its own unique set of challenges. Failure should not be an option. Failure means lost jobs, lost income, lost retirement and it can devastate many lives. Creating a Turn-A-Round plan is a big challenge and it carries with it an even bigger responsibility. It must be taken seriously with intense commitment and passion.

# Chapter XIII

# *Transitional Restructuring Leadership*

## The Non-Financial Steps in Restructuring

There are three basic steps in developing a Turn-A-Round plan to be successful beyond obvious financial cost reduction initiatives. These steps involve a Lead Wolf style of leadership and become the cornerstone for the plan. These steps will determine success or failure.

1. **Create an attitude**

2. **Structure an environment**

3. **Develop a team**

## Create an Attitude, Structure an Environment and Develop a Team

## I.    Create an Attitude

Employee attitude is critical to the execution of the Turn-A-Round plan. Rebuilding employee confidence in a failing company is difficult at best but not impossible. Swift, quick financial moves done all at once including reduction in force shocks and immobilizes the existing culture long enough to introduce change. Communication becomes a critical first step. Secrets are not acceptable because the most important part of employee attitude involves gaining their respect. Gaining their respect requires giving them respect and that involves communication. Telling every employee the truth is the only option.

---

**Thought Provoker**

**"Set up a third party hot line to answer all employee concerns confidentially."**

---

Start the human due diligence process. Human due diligence answers the question "Do we have, and can we retain the psychological capacity to successfully create a winning and cooperative attitude amongst our employees?" Conducted properly, this assessment, this touching the pulse of the employees, will identify the assets and liabilities that exist within the people organization. Capitalize on the assets and deal swiftly with the liabilities. Hopefully, if the initial restructuring process was done properly, the liabilities will be minimal. The dead wood and under performers should now be gone and the employees that survive the RIF (reduction in force) should all be winners.

Creating an attitude means getting your employees to work **with you**. Accomplish that and the road to recovery is much smoother. If the employees only work for you, they will tend to do only what is asked of them. Sometimes only enough to stay

under the radar screen. They will demonstrate no initiative and take no risk. The company can't afford that.

## 2. Structure An Environment

Creating the right attitude is paramount to structuring the proper environment. Getting employees to work with you and join in the search for better ideas, new methodology and higher profitability will transform the company from passive individualists to intelligent action takers and change agents.

The company needs "Risk Takers and Mavericks." Identify every employee in that category and empower them to go out and get the job done. So what if they bend the rules sometimes. As long as they don't break the law, violate corporate core values or embarrass the company, "Turn Them Loose." In a Turn-A-Round restructuring environment the company has everything to gain and nothing to lose. The employees will see this demonstration of trust and empowerment. Word will travel fast. Promote that concept. Send a monthly memo to everyone praising individuality that results in improvements. Title the memo, "OFF the CUFF" for it's informal straight talking honest feedback from the top. Reward and recognize the risk takers. Commend the change agents. Then align both management and the employees behind the new vision. Support this new environment by sharing the vision, departmental goals and strategic initiatives. Publish the minutes to every executive meeting that is held. Hold nothing back short of personnel issues. Be proud and announce the fact that there will no longer be secrets held under close cover behind the doors of the executive staff.

---

**Thought Provoker**

**Ethics breeds trust.**

**"It is critically important to do the right thing – to commit to conducting yourself with the highest standards of ethics and integrity. It will inspire people's confidence and trust in you. And people, as a result, will help you in ways that you would never expect, and maybe never even know about it. They will go to great lengths to help you accomplish your goals. They will solve problems on your behalf. They will come to your defense when you are in trouble, which will happen from time to time. If you work for them, they will promote you."**

**Raymond V. Gilmartin**
**CEO Merck and Co.**

---

Educate managers and supervisors for their new role in this new environment. Do not tolerate deception or deviation from attitude or the new structure. Teach them to be coaches, mentors and transmitters of directions. Educate line employees to make them know they are part of the plan, part of the new way. Teach them new skills for self-management, planning, team building, goal setting, risk taking, conflict resolution and negotiating. Show them you care. That's all part of structuring an environment.

The "New Way" is the new corporate vision. It's a mental picture of what the company is all about, where the company wants to go and how the company is going to get there. This is the vision of the company. It does not reflect the personal idiosyncrasy of

the CEO. It has a broad base of support and buy-in from the employees.

Communication is also a key in creating an environment that encourages retention of the remaining workforce that has been selected to become part of the Turn-A-Round plan. Respect, belief in employees, empowerment and involvement are key factors that get buy-in. Effective leadership and respect must be demonstrated at every level in the organization.

The initial financial restructuring process must create enough shock to immobilize the old culture at least temporarily. Leadership can then seize control of the energy level left within the company so that it cannot perpetuate the old culture. Any clouds of secrecy must be removed. This requires open sharing of information. Copies of staff meeting minutes, sales meetings minutes, purchasing workshops and all other meaningful meetings need to be shared with all employees short of confidential personnel issues.

Culture is a powerful management tool and it is a key part of structuring an environment toward becoming "Employer of Choice" (EOC). Effective leadership drives the organizations culture by communicating vision, beliefs and values. It should be noted however that a company's culture is not easy to manipulate or change. It's like trying to turn a large aircraft carrier, a slow process under normal circumstances. Cultures evolve over time. You cannot buy a new culture in a box and install it. Consequently, to speed up the introduction of change and to create a new culture, as mentioned, I submit that it is absolutely necessary to immobilize the old culture by introducing restructuring change in one major initiative in the shortest time cycle possible. This is especially true of the reduction in force initiative, which is likely to be a major part of the initial financial restructuring plan. It becomes a critical painful but necessary event for the survival of the organization as a whole. This critical painful event (CPE) will immobilize the old culture to allow the introduction of change, the restructuring Turn-A-Round plan upon which the new culture begins to emerge.

## 3.    Develop The Team

Trust people to act and their initiative, their creativity and their intellect will surprise you.  It may even seem like magic. It releases the discretionary energy we discussed previously. Empowerment provides the freedom to act and it demonstrates trust and belief in the ability of your employees.

- Share information and help employees understand objectives and issues

- View mistakes as an investment and learning opportunity

- Promote the entrepreneurial attitude, help employees act as owners

- Build trust

- Gain respect through clarification of:

    - The big picture and current objectives

    - Define the "rules of engagement within the company

    - Define values

- Educate and train

- Promote accountability throughout the entire company

- Provide support, encouragement and direction

- Recognize there will be mistakes and obstacles-they only build on competence through the learning process

Creating a proper attitude and boosting moral are essential to any type of team development. This concept must be all encompassing throughout the organization. It cannot be isolated to sales and purchasing alone. Communication and involvement in the Turn-A-Round process will set the stage for team development and assignment of Turn-A-Round initiatives.

Change is what Turn-A-Round restructuring is all about and leadership becomes the driving force. We often don't give employees enough credit for their intellectual capacity. Employees aren't stupid and even though they might not see the profit and loss statement, most employees know when a company is in trouble. There are many signs the employees recognize that have nothing to do with the financials. .Employees want leadership that can align internal and external realities to make the company successful. They expect leadership in a Turn-A-Round situation that can guide them through the uncharted and threatening world of the unfamiliar.

# Discretionary Energy

**Thought Provoker**

*Randy Larrimore, CEO United Stationers, (2003) stated,*

*"We believe at United that having strong values and treating people with respect makes people more productive. We think that people can come to work and do their job from 8 to 5 and go home. Everyday associates come to work with discretionary energy that they could elect or not elect to use. We try to get people to give us that discretional energy. It's really the difference between the actual and the potential performance of the employee, and therefore of the entire organization If we can get employees involved in the business, invested in their work, they'll work harder, smarter, come on time, probably stay later when needed, and take pride at what United is and does."*

Mandating new rules, stipulations, threats and unreasonable demands does not promote unity or trust. It is destructive to the kind of attitude required to succeed. Employee consideration and input is absolutely essential to structuring a new environment. The company needs employee support, trust and respect. But, the company must give before they receive. The leader must know when to lead and when to listen before acting. Empowering the employees allows them to use their own initiative, their own creativity and figure out things you'd never imagine they could accomplish.

Change is tough in itself. Add the fact that a restructuring change is even more threatening and creates an enormous amount of resentment and fear. It is scary and disruptive, often times leading to rebellion. This is why it is so important to communicate well and build the proper attitude within the company's core group of employees. Developing a team that breeds success and promotes openness, honesty and trust is an essential ingredient to successfully executing a Turn-A-Round plan.

Initiatives should be simplistic, realistic and achievable. The initiatives should be phased so that early successes will come and be recognized. Complexity has no place. If the employees don't understand, no amount of effort will allow them to reach the desired results. Learn to listen to the employees. Nothing is more frustrating to an employee than a supervisor who will not listen to a solution to a problem that is so obvious the supervisor should have acted independently long ago.

## Employees: The Most Precious Asset

Developing a team is not that difficult if employee development is a priority.

Every employee wants to feel that they have a voice and can be heard. They want to know that management knows they exist and what their contribution is. They want the satisfaction of doing a good job. They want to prove their talent to achieve the desired results. If they are challenged they will become self-motivated.

People enjoy other people. They derive satisfaction from interaction with their peers. Recognition is icing on the cake. Employees find the social aspect of the work place rewarding if the environment is positive and conducive to success. Make coming to work enjoyable for your employees. Create ways to challenge as well as entertain the employees. Provide the opportunity for social interaction. There are a number of ways to do this from a once a week company sponsored lunch to monthly breakfast sessions with the president to talk about current issues and new events.

Recognition and praise raises self-esteem. Positive feedback and ample communication allow employees gratification and a newfound confidence in the organization. Employees need to feel some sense of power. Most employees derive satisfaction by having an influence over some thing or someone. Leadership is an inborn trait to some degree in every human being. Some more than others. Allow the employees the opportunity to demonstrate leadership in some form or fashion. Create work teams, committees and projects that motivate by presenting the opportunity to make decisions and be a part of the overall process of turning the company around.

---

**Thought Provoker**

**"The only CEO that walks on water is one that has a talented team of executives holding their breath under the water in order to hold him/her up."**

**Jack M. Greenberg**
**CEO McDonalds Corp**

---

Allow the employees to take risks and demonstrate initiative. Empowerment is a trait used by most effective leaders. The rewards are far greater than the risk. Give them some independence in choosing their work schedules or other factors that won't affect overall objectives.

A common mistake some executives make is demonstrating insensitivity by making a big expenditure for some asset right after restructuring and terminating a number of employees. This is a major mistake. It is by far the worst message that could be sent.

---

**Thought Provoker**

"A personal experience I witnessed involved a president of a corporation that had just restructured, terminating one hundred and eighty seven employees, who then remodeled the executive conference room spending over $50,000 which included a wall mounted big screen TV and remote control curtains. Obviously that disrupted any attempt at creating the proper attitude, not to mention the environment of distrust and animosity it created."

---

Employees must take ownership in the restructuring plan. Acknowledge their presence, their contributions and praise them at every opportunity. But, be sincere. Jack Welch had a favorite method of sending personal handwritten notes to employees that demonstrated some form of success. Sincerity is a must. Handing out praise indiscriminately is not better than no praise at all. If praise is delivered the wrong way or for the wrong reason at the wrong time it can do a lot of harm. Praise and the reason for it must be specific. Praise to employees for just achieving their normal expected performance becomes meaningless and will not motivate. Additionally, when they do something outstanding, praise becomes meaningless. Lastly, don't think that telling an employee that he has done a good job on twelve different occasions is a substitute for some other type or reward. Specifically a monetary reward and recognition of some type is essential for the outstanding performer even in tough times including a Turn-A Round situation.

The employee issue cannot be emphasized enough. Tough times weigh heavy on employees. They know when a company is not performing without seeing the profit and loss statement. The good ones start to abandon ship and seek employment elsewhere. Add restructuring and employee terminations to the formula and keeping good employees becomes the most life threatening issue the company is likely to face in a Turn-A-Round situation.

Losing good employees has a high cost associated with it. Frederick Reichheld's book (1998), "The Loyalty Effect", points out:

"If you are losing employees, you are losing customers. On average, American companies lose half of their employees every four years and half of their customers in five years. This suggests that employee attrition may have a significant impact on customer loyalty."

Going through a Turn-A-Round borders on mastering revolutionary change that requires facing the challenge of creatively destroying and remaking the organization to improve profitability. In order to succeed, the Turn-A-Round must be driven by Lead Wolf type leaders that inspire employee buy in, commitment, and support. They must have fresh ideas and the spirit and guts to make things happen. They must create a way of life by taking a risk and believing in the employees that they have chosen to remain on the team.

---

**Thought Provoker**

**Randy Larrimore (2003) stated in his DREF interview,**

**"I'm convinced that you can change the culture of an organization in under a year, contrary to what a lot of textbooks would say. You can do this by taking an organization through an extensive strategic planning process where you get hundreds of people involved using their knowledge and initiative–creating that environment where their experience and knowledge is considered valuable by ownership and executive management."**

---

Randy Larrimore's comments reference a company that is very successful, not a company facing a Turn-A-Round situation. However, involvement of the employees is critical regardless and changing the culture in a TAR situation becomes mandatory.

Success of the Turn-A-Round or restructuring efforts not only depends on the employees but they are heavily reliant on the executive team and management structure leading the effort.

This effort will demand a variety of different skills from team leaders. They must possess the Lead Wolf mentality. The plan must be articulated clearly enough that it is understood by all and is strategically sound. The executive management team must be aligned in support in their hearts as well as their minds. This team not only demonstrates their competence in practical skills but more importantly they must demonstrate a superior competence in people skills. The attributes, values, personal beliefs and competencies are all important in carrying out the plan. Politics, ownership prejudices, personal feelings and biases must be set aside.

Winning organizations continuously build leaders at every level in their organization. Leaders who actively attempt to mentor and build other leaders gain respect throughout the organization and transfer knowledge, ideas, values and attitude about success; that's the Lead Wolf way. The executive team must:

- Demonstrate a sense of urgency
- Project and articulate the vision
- Create stretch goals
- Develop trust and a spirit of teamwork
- Develop realistic expectations for success
- Promote an environment of success, trust and belief
- Commit honesty—to tell the truth—to do the right thing— with no hidden agendas
- Demonstrate Integrity and respect—responsiveness—recognizing employee value—empowerment

- Be passionate about success

- Motivate and inspire

- Be committed

The executive team must have an edge. They must be courageous enough to take risk and have an unrelenting readiness to act. Popularity is not a requirement but the ability to generate respect from the employees is without a doubt one of the most critical attributes. They must be relentless in their efforts, unconscious about personal sacrifice of their time and the willingness to go beyond normal expectations. Tough decisions are commonplace; uncharted territories will be the norm. Honesty and impeccable character is a must.

*Every single member of the management team has to make a difference. It's the price to play the game. It's part of the rules. Don't pay, don't play, it's as simple as that. Leadership, especially in a Turn-A-Round situation is not in a position to be overly patient with team members that can't "Bump Bellies and Grunt" to get things done in such a way that they command the respect of the employees. <u>Leading the Pack means knowing when to exercise autocratic judgment and when to be a servant transitional type of leader. This is critical. The Lead Wolf model during a TAR restructuring must be resilient and flexible.</u>*

## The New Vehicle For Success

A historic shift has been created with the Turn-A-Round restructuring plan. Employee morale and buy-in should increase every day. A cardinal rule that exists for restructuring is, "There

is no room in the organization for loyal, yet incompetent people." Gardening must become a way of life. Continuous pruning will keep the company on track as the team rises or falls to the occasion.

Confidence in execution means the company is on the winning side of turmoil and confusion. A vehicle has been created that can take the company where it needs to go. More importantly, there is a roadmap to get there.

The company now has the vehicle, the process, the initiative and the team to execute. The company is now prepared to play the game to win, rather than playing the game not to lose. This vehicle has provided the following:

- A definitive plan with clarity of purpose and participation of the employees
- A raised bar with relevant accountability
- A definitive marketing and sales strategy
- Best practices and determination to reside in the upper quartile for performance once recovery is secure
- A measurement of success through activity management

Execution becomes the priority. The sales process is at the heart of success. Labor costs and executive effort invested in this process during recovery often exceed 25% of total gross margin dollars. It is both complex and subjective because it deals with both customer management relationship activities and recovery initiatives.

The new vehicle (The New Restructured Organization) is now made up of four distinct processes that communicate the new culture being created.

- Change Process
- Work Process
- Organizational Behavior Process
- Leadership Process

## Manage the Change Process

The change process begins with the strategic restructuring of the organization, which was required to "Stop the Bleeding." This process starts with the immobilization of the old culture. This is mandatory, as introduction of change into any existing culture is difficult at best. Introducing change into a losing or stagnant culture is almost impossible. This change must deal with organization theory, social psychology and business history. It must be dynamic and include the introduction of fresh new leadership. This is a behavioral process. People can create change but people also resist change. The change process introduced must answer the question, "How do we get from here to there?" The answer to that question is your new vehicle for success. This vehicle includes the restructuring plan, individual one-year departmental plans and every strategic initiative developed by the new management team. Most importantly, this new vehicle is submerged in the empowerment theory releasing individual employee initiative. The plans must

be unified, simple, consistent and universally understood by everyone. Most of the change that has been introduced must be induced change versus autonomous change. Autonomous change has a life of its own. It proceeds due to internal dynamics and follows its own course. It is not easily controlled as it forms its own dynamics. Induced change is calculated and planned. It can be controlled if buy in is generated through sincere communication and employee involvement. Each step along this path will be accompanied by distinct challenges. As questions arise, management must be prepared to answer openly and honestly. While the old culture is suspended, change can thrive under the right circumstances. It is the responsibility of the executive team to insure that these circumstances exist. The primary ingredients that create the right circumstances include open honest communication, empowerment, risk taking, acknowledgment and reward.

## Work Process

The work process is the engine of the new vehicle. This is how the objectives established in the Turn-A-Round plan will be accomplished. It involves measurement and accountability. It employs best practice principles. It begins with a powerful idea. Success will be created through  hard work linked through chains of activities by different groups that synergistically unite into one cohesive effort with common objectives. This activity is cross-functional and does not allow for silos or political agendas. Restructuring is about survival.

The work process involved will create, produce and deliver according to the specific stated objectives. Processes that do not deliver the desired output, those that don't follow best practice principles, will be easily identifiable and must be corrected immediately. Both operational and administrative processes are included and must support each other. Their activities are linked even though they may be interdependent. Together they transform into cohesive outputs. The work process is probably the most familiar process to line managers. It relies heavily on the process of reengineering and quality. It is easily understood and unlike the change process, it is very tangible and measurable. It becomes recognizable that most prior processes may have gone unchecked with little rationale and planning. This creates inefficiencies. The work process is a major factor in the production of tangible results.

Most processes in the work environment of a failing company are not preplanned or designed. They just happen and no one pays attention or questions them. Consequently, redesign of most work processes is an essential part of the new vehicle for success. The redesign of work processes allows management the opportunity to address work fragmentation and encourage cross-functional integration. This also generates bench strength for future growth. This process also identifies new targets for improvement as managers' focus on the underlying process and not on structures or roles.

*Work processes are only part of the new vehicle, the engine; success will not come with process redesign alone. Management, change, organization, recruitment, retention and strategic planning are all a part of the total package.*

## Organizational Behavioral Process (OBP)

This is basic to creating change, and it becomes an important part of the new vehicle for success. OBP may be described as the wheels of the new vehicle. This process will carry the organization on to new heights, new accomplishments. Organizational behavior has its roots in organizational theory and group dynamics. People are the most important ingredient to every organization and the organizations behavior. People and how they are treated will reflect the organizational characteristics; the way it acts and interacts with its own people.

Empowerment, the decision making process and the communication channels are examples of how the organization interacts with its people. Organizational behavior is not easy to change. This is why it is so important, as mentioned earlier, to immobilize the old culture to introduce change. The behavioral process of the organization can withstand personnel changes. In other words, changing out management does not guarantee change in organizational behavior. You must take proactive steps designed to create new organizational behavior. The new vehicle is part of that. It includes, focused specific objectives, open channels of communication, empowerment and a sincere respect for the individual employee and his/her contribution to the organization.

Organizational behaviors become generalizations. They are discovered from observations of everyday work habits and they have no independent existence apart from the work processes in which they appear. They are difficult to identify but they are extremely important. They affect the form, the substance and the character of the work processes themselves. They actually affect the way the work process is carried out. They are different from culture because they represent more than just values and beliefs.

They actually are involved in the sequences producing work. The decision making process is a major characteristic of the behavioral process. The decision making process is a much studied process beginning with the studies of Chester Barnard and Herbert Simon who argued that organizational decision making was a distributed activity, extending over time and involving a number of people. In other words, decision-making is not the personal responsibility of a single manager but a shared, dispersed activity that they only need to orchestrate and lead. This is still a surprising and often unaccepted theory of managers today.

## The Lead Wolf Impact
## Leadership Process

Leadership is often described as the art of getting people to accomplish specific objectives. However, organizations are complex social entities with widely distributed responsibilities and assets. Unilateral action toward specific objectives is seldom sufficient in itself to create the kind of success required in a Turn-A-Round situation. Managers spend the majority of

their day working with and managing the activities of many people. The challenges include how to get the organization moving in the desired direction, the direction that has been clearly stated by the restructuring plan and the new vehicle for success. The Lead Wolf model of leadership is essential to generate the allegiance required, the commitment necessary and the sacrifice desired to meet the new objectives?

Effective leadership, the Lead Wolf model of leadership, is key to harmonizing diverse group interest into a focus specific mode that supports the mechanics of execution. The focus is on the way managers orchestrate activities and events and engage others in tasks so that the desired results are realized. Action is key and is implicitly equated to professional leadership. This skill is subjective and often artistic. It varies with every situation and every individual. Leadership skills can be enhanced and fine-tuned but a basic ingredient of humanistic understanding must exist to create a platform for leadership development. Best practice in itself will not produce a high level of performance unless it is accompanied by above average leadership, the Lead Wolf style of leadership.

Lead Wolf executives are skilled in communication. They use that skill to gain influence. The key to their success, verified by NAW interviews of seven of the most successful leaders in wholesale distribution, is demonstrating integrity by matching what they say with what they do. They are explicit, consistent, concise and sincere. They generally have an abundance of charisma although some leaders gain success with a quieter influence. Leaders take charge and are not afraid of responsibility or risk. Most people want to follow them. A good leader develops openness, honesty, clarity of purpose and a sincere caring for the people they lead. They gain commitment and trust by demonstrating respect for the individual. They have a keen sense of understanding. They believe in their task, they understand the objectives, they communicate clearly and they honestly project the understanding that they need the efforts of everyone to succeed.

# Chapter XIV

---

# $R^2$ = EOC (Recruitment and Retention = Employer of Choice)

The previous chapters on Turn-A-Round restructuring clearly emphasized the important role employees' play in creating success. Employees are a company's most precious asset but our return on that asset is directly proportional to effective leadership. This chapter focuses on recruitment and retention which are key components to becoming "Employer of Choice" (EOC). Becoming EOC begins with effective leadership; the Lead Wolf style of leadership. Problems with staffing and retention may not be due to bad hires or a low unemployment rate. In fact, they may be related to poor management insight by not recognizing your employees as a core competency in your business strategy. Although employees may not fit the strictest definition of a core competency, it is a fact that your employees are the ones responsible for creating many of your core competencies. It is an undisputable fact that failure to recognize the importance of employee contributions will lead to failure regardless of your business strategy.

## Recruitment and Retention

Creating a strategic plan and definitive initiatives is the easy part of the formula for success. The difficult part is finding, recruiting and retaining the appropriate talent combination in today's market to carry out that plan.

Recruitment and retention are major issues in industry today. These issues are especially critical to the wholesale distribution industry for two reasons:

- First, the distribution industry is one of our aged-basic industries that don't project the excitement of the high-tech industries and the dot coms of the new millennium (even though many have crashed and burned).

- Second, the number of employees between the ages of 25 and 44, traditionally the bulk of the workforce, will continue to decline in the United States for at least the next five years. The baby-boomers are aging quickly toward retirement.

Under these circumstances, how in the world does a company not only recruit new talent, but protect the talent they have? Questions about compensation, training, incentives, benefits and work environment always come to the forefront. The answer is committing to becoming an EOC with as much tenacity as you commit to being a supplier of choice, always wanting the first call and last look.

## Pay Attention

Many executives pay far too little attention to this part of their businesses. Often the mindset is that this is the "touchy-feely", human resource stuff that's a non-revenue producing necessary evil. Maybe that thought process didn't hurt the company in the 80's or early 90's when unemployment in some areas reached 10%, but that's not the case today where the labor unemployment rate in some markets is less than 3%. When unemployment reaches that level, most people who are unemployed just don't want to work.

As a result, there is a lot of corporate raiding going on. Even with the recent massive layoff announcements by the automotive industry, the airlines and some high-tech industries, unemployment remains at a level that just is not conducive to recruitment and retention.

## So what's the answer?

Going on midnight raids? Offering BMWs as signing bonuses? Paying way above market wages? NO, the answer is building a human resource strategy into your business plan. Get over the old paradigm that human resource departments are too costly and of little value. In fact, those distributors that adopt that philosophy actually spend more money by having highly compensated managers, particularly sales managers, running ads, receiving resumes and doing preliminary interviews when they should be selling. The costs associated with that process as well as the revenue lost due to extended position vacancies inevitably far exceeds the annual costs of dedicated human resource professionals. Secondly, a huge percentage of new hires will jump ship within 18 months if they sense the company is not committed to its employees. They will jump if the company does not accept them into the fold properly by offering initial orientation, subsequent training and a culture that treats the employee as the company's most precious assets.

---

**Thought Provoker**

**The question is not, "Can you afford to invest in this soft touchy-feely stuff?" The question becomes, "Can you afford to not invest in your most important asset, your employees?"**

---

This old paradigm creates a bias against paying attention to the human element of the workforce. Many executives that do strategic business plans initiate from the top down instead of the bottom up often ignoring the real value of a strategic plan. The real value is the involvement and education of your employees in completing the plan, not in the document itself.

## Are you at the mercy of your workforce?

This bias that exists in many companies is almost as though admitting that employees are the most precious of corporate assets will lead to an anarchy on which owners and managers will fall at the mercy of the workforce. Well, shake your head in disbelief if you want to, but the reality of the situation is that you are at the mercy of your workforce. The rules have to continue to change. If you aren't willing to admit that and get your head in the game then you won't survive in the new millennium.

Some companies recognized their dilemma years ago. Many of the top performers in your industry are at the top because they strive to be employers of choice embracing the Lead Wolf model of leadership. These are forward thinking companies that have found solutions to their recruitment and retention challenges. Following in their footsteps requires an initial "gut check." Honestly ask yourself how your employees would answer questions like:

- Do you receive counseling on a career plan?
- Is there a current wage and salary plan in place?
- Do performance incentives exist?
- Do you receive regular training and instruction?
- Do you receive performance updates and recognition beyond a once a year chat with your B.O.S.S.?
- Does customer feedback play a role in performance evaluations?
- Are suggestions reviewed and awarded?
- Is there both a formal and informal communication channel?

These questions relate to the basic core competencies of human resources: staffing, training, rewarding, recognizing and organizing. The business strategic plan cannot succeed without paying attention to this part of the business. You must facilitate your employees' involvement and feedback into this process. This basic premise in implementation across distribution varies according to size. The same plan for a $20 million privately held service center would not work for a $500 million distributor.

## EOC --- Employer of Choice

To solve your recruitment and retention problems you must strive to become an Employer of Choice. To accomplish that objective you must have a human resources strategy that is integrated into your corporate strategic plan that acknowledges and recognizes the employees as the company's most precious asset.　　　**$R^2 = EOC$**

Don't pay lip service to employee development. Walk the talk; Lead the Pack and invest profits into employee development. Hire a human resource executive that is more than a compliance manager. Human resource should become a major focus in your strategic planning process.

---

**Thought Provoker**

"Always treat people with dignity and respect, particularly those who work for you. Not only is this appropriate behavior – if you follow this principle, you will attract and retain talented people, which you will find is essential to your success."

**Raymond V. Gilmartin
CEO Merck and Co.**

---

# Chapter XV

# LEADERSHIP – THE BOARD OF DIRECTORS AND FAMILY SUCCESSION

Family owned/privately held organizations, both small and large, with succession issues, family preparation and second and third generation leadership issues have been subjected to the evolution of leadership. The evolution from the Lone Wolf leadership model to the Lead Wolf leadership model. These organizations are often founded by an aggressive, highly talented entrepreneur. Many of the principles of leadership employed by the founder that helped build the success that the organization enjoyed in the past is not the type of leadership that will maintain that success through generations of ownership. The formation of a board with several outside directors can help ownership cross the transitional divide that often accompanies generational succession.

A Board of Directors, elected by ownership, can provide the kind of support necessary to take the company to the next level. No man is an island and it can become very lonely at

the top. Growing an organization is hard work. The president of the corporation not only has to surround himself with an excellent team but he

must be able to rely on another power to challenge him and his team. The Board of Directors, in exercising its business judgment, acts as an advisor and counselor to the President and his executive team. The Board can help define and enforce standards of accountability. Accountability that is often found lacking in a privately held family run organization. A Board can challenge and help the management team execute their responsibilities to the fullest extent in the best interest of the shareholders.

## A Sounding Board

A Board can have differing types of responsibilities based on its written charter and by laws. However, the typical responsibilities that a Board for a privately held corporation must live up to are generally aligned with ownership/shareholder objectives. Overseeing the  way the company conducts its business to insure that it is managed effectively is one primary responsibility. Selecting, compensating and evaluating the President is another key responsibility. Someone has to have the power to take the President to the woodshed when it becomes necessary. No one person has all the answers and the board can provide the kind of advice and insight that may circumvent mistakes or validate the direction the President is taking the company in. Boards can be structured under a wide range of responsibilities and personalities. They can be very formal with strict procedural requirements or they can be very informal, made up of predominantly family members without the necessity of following "Roberts Rules of Order" in conducting its business. It's the opinion of this author that every Board including the "Family Advisory" Board needs to have several outside directors elected. These outside board members are not the company accountant, the company attorney or best buddies with the owners. They are proven successful business people that can serve the Board in an uncompromising objective manner. The Board can support management in the development of organizational planning, succession and resource management. The most effective Board will be a group of professionals with a wide variety of skills. Ideally, these board members will have backgrounds that differ from the management team but compliment their skill sets.

## The Board Personality

Just like management, a Board of Directors success and how supportive it is to management is directly related to their personality traits and their character. Selecting directors for board membership is critical and the process should

*"This is not the type of board member you want."*

313

not be taken lightly. These directors must perform the role of governance, although their primary role is one of a supporter, a coach and even mentors. They must also assume the role of questioners and monitors of company performance. As supporters they must provide guidance and advice while living up to their governance responsibility which insures the long term health of the organization. This role includes succession planning and holding the President and the management team accountable for the success of the organization. This is why the director's character is so important. A character that embraces the following:

- Honesty
- Integrity
- Enthusiasm
- Open mindedness
- Competence
- Trustworthiness
- Analytical thinking
- Being a team player
- A sense of humor

*Any board member that does not possess these characteristics does not provide value to the organization. In fact, a board member that does not demonstrate honesty, integrity and trust worthiness could do irreparable harm to the company.*

# Strategic Planning

Every company needs to think about its future. Developing a long term strategic plan is a key best practice within wholesale distribution. A Board of Directors has the responsibility of reviewing, approving and monitoring the success of the company's strategic plan. The President and ownership is responsible for the company vision.

The executive team should create the roadmap, the strategic plan and the Board will review and approve it. Monitoring the company's financial performance, reporting policies and accounting practices are part of this process. Compliance and risk management also become a part of the Board's responsibilities.

# So What Does the Management Team Do?

It sounds like the management team will spend most of it's time trying to keep the Board happy. Not true. The role of the President and the management team is quite clear. They run the company. The company's day-to-day business will always remain the responsibility of its employees under the direction of senior management and the President.

The President is held accountable, as he should be, by the Board of Directors. Once the management team creates the strategic plan and it is approved by the Board, they are fully empowered to execute the plan.

# Role of the Director

Directors are expected to demonstrate the kind of character that is beyond reproach. They must always act in the best interests of the business and fulfill their fiduciary responsibilities. They must always act honestly, ethically and with integrity. They must always maintain a courteous and respectful attitude. They will act in good faith exercising sound judgment, competence and due diligence. They must maintain the confidentiality of the organization and avoid any conflict of interests. Being a director should never be taken lightly. It requires time, attention and dedication. They are expected to attend all the scheduled meetings and serve on necessary committees that are in the best interest of the organization.

# Leadership Development

Differing opinions and even controversy over direct contact and relationships between board members and members of the management team still exists today. However, it is widely recognized that one of the board's responsibilities is not only succession planning for the President but also succession within the ranks of executive management. It would be extremely difficult for any board member to make a contribution in the succession planning process if they had absolutely no contact with the management team at all. This doesn't mean that any director should encourage or support the circumvention of authority but private meetings dealing with specific committee issues are not out of the ordinary.

The board may invite individual management team members to board meetings asking for a specific presentation on important issues. This can also help the board in evaluating individual management team members. Coaching, mentoring and leadership development can be a significant contribution a director can make to the future success of the company.

A Board of Directors should not perform an adversarial role but a supportive role to the President and the management team of the organization. The right board members can be significant part of the success of the organization. The power the board has is dependent upon its charter and it's by laws. Remember, the board is elected by the shareholders. In a privately held corporation, this means that ownership determines the make up and type of board they want to govern the organization. Successful owners and Lead Wolf executives understand the value a board of directors can provide.

## Succession in the Family Business

A family held business with multiple family members working in the business often creates unique leadership and succession issues. This requires unique processes and policies to develop effective leadership and generational succession. These processes and policies may include but not be limited to:

1. Statement of Legacy
2. Board of Directors Charter
3. Family and Non-Family Members' Pre-Employment Qualifications
4. Compensation Policy for XYZ's Family Employees
5. Performance Issues

6. Succession

7. Sample Buy/Sell Agreements

Family members should agree to hold quarterly shareholders' meetings and that these meetings would include an agenda to guide discussion on important family and business issues.

Additionally, a Board of Directors should be formed with three non-family members to help guide the strategic direction of the company. The family is committed to putting principle and process in place of power and politics. Board responsibility will include mentoring and management development.

## Statement of Legacy:

The following is a sample statement of legacy written as the fictitious Fred's Quarry Company and the Flintstone family.

Fred's Quarry Company will be the high value/low cost, easy to do business with supplier of choice. The company is to understand, accept, meet and exceed the service output demands of our customers.

The Flintstone family is dedicated to serving the business; the business is not run to serve the family. The family recognizes that the business is important and, at the same time, the family is a strong element in contributing to the company's success. The Flintstone family is dedicated to retaining the ownership of the business and will not consider selling the business. Fred's Quarry Company will provide employment opportunities for family members who meet established entrance criteria and continue to meet established performance criteria. To help family members enter the business and succeed at the company, we will endeavor to provide advice to family members on the standards necessary to succeed.

## Board of Directors Charter----For Privately Held Distributors

The owner of a privately held distributor will frequently set up and use a formal Board of Directors. The key difference between a typical board of family members along with professional service providers and a formal board is participation by outside directors with distribution industry experience.

This structure essentially creates a situation where the owner reports to a "higher authority." The key advantage is creating a process to balance the needs of the owners and the needs of the business.

The most powerful reason that compels many owners down this path is the ability to get experienced judgment from an outsider that does not have any personal agenda beyond helping the owner be successful.

## CHARTER

- The outside directors have no involvement in running the business. Their key task is to approve plans by the operating management and insure effective execution of these plans.

- The Board has no fiduciary responsibility to any constituency beyond the owners of the capital. This

responsibility is clearly limited to providing their best advice. The company will provide appropriate outside director liability insurance or an indemnification agreement for each Director.

- The Board has the responsibility (with approved power of attorney) to execute the owners succession plan in the event of untimely death or major disability.

- The Board has the responsibility to provide the owner with frank, honest, and considered opinions with respect to owner actions, decisions, and general behavior. This consists of pre-decision counseling and post decision criticism.

- The Board of Directors is concerned with "the direction of the tide" rather that "the size of the waves." The board needs to be focused on supporting steady improvement in strategy, vision, leadership, and operational execution.

- Through a series of scheduled Board Meetings, the outside directors provide several support services to the owner that include:

  1. Providing a "Corporate Challenge" to the operating management team to insure that their plans are realistic and challenging. Part of this process is to insure that the operating management team has developed adequate contingency plans and responses to competitive threats and opportunities.

  2. Providing their advice and counsel directly to the President and his or her direct reports. Senior

Executive employees are encouraged to have direct involvement and personal relationships with the Outside Directors so those Directors have multiple sources of information to provide considered advice. Directors limit their involvement with Senior Executives to providing advice on how said Executive can approach the problem on their own.

3. Providing Audit Committee services to the owner where the outside accounting firm is actually hired by the Audit Committee. This is intended to improve the "arms length" relationship that needs to exist between the owner and the outside CPA firm.

4. Providing Compensation Committee services to the owner where determinations are made on all compensation packages, incentives, and related programs for President and President direct reporting positions. Where appropriate this group includes all relatives and children of the owner. This "arms length" relationship allows the owner to deal with these problems as an "Agent of Limited Authority."

5. The scheduled Board Meetings range from 2 to 4 each year, excluding any need for emergency meetings. Operating managers have a clear deadline to prepare answers and presentations for Board consideration. In a 2 meeting/year structure, the annual plan would be presented in one meeting

and a mid year review would be conducted in the second meeting.

## DIRECTOR ROLE

The Director signs on for a two-year term that may be renewed if both parties desire to extend the relationship. The owner, after several years of replacements and renewals, would ideally replace one director each year with continuity within the other positions.

The Director receives a complete set of financial statements each month from the company which are reviewed at Director Convenience. The Director will normally speak to the owner monthly to review progress and discuss outstanding issues and problems.

The Outside Director is a coach and mentor for the owner and selected management personnel. The advantage of not being personally involved and also not being held hostage to past history, coupled with extensive distribution management experience creates a powerful source of objective judgment.

The Outside Director serves as a trusted advisor to the owner and much of the input provided is over an informal lunch, or a phone call.

## DIRECTOR SELECTION CRITERIA

The ideal Outside Director is in his/her mid to late career in a distribution business that is not a competitor of the owner. If the owner made a list of the key areas of strategic importance

where the company was weak, i.e. Information Technology, each Outside Director would have a personal experience base aligned to the weaknesses.

The owner should avoid any providers of professional services in Board positions. Even though they are trusted, the potential conflict of interests (I can fix that problem and you give me money) needs to be avoided. Specific occupations that should be avoided include the company's accountant, attorney and banker due to the potential conflict of interest. If the owner feels strongly that one of these individuals needs to serve, there should be a moratorium on provision of any professional services for the duration of the appointment.

Normal compensation for Outside Directors in privately held distributors is between 15 to 20 thousand dollars each year. This is normally paid in quarterly installments at the beginning of each quarter. If Outside directors are asked to get involved in the business due to a special situation, additional compensation of $1,500 to $2,500/day is normally provided. In some cases the compensation is as low as $1,000 per meeting. There are senior executives who have become professional outside directors. These individuals, if chosen, typically are provided compensation significantly above the levels quoted. Of course, all fees listed are relative to the size of the company involved, what they can afford and what is reasonable.

## BOARD MEETINGS

Board meetings are run under Roberts Rules of Order, but normally in a very relaxed atmosphere. Decision making, after

appropriate deliberation, is made with motions being presented and voted.

Board meetings are scheduled many months in advance, unless there is a substantive crisis. In a crisis situation, a Board Meeting can be conducted via conference call.

Directors will be provided with a Board Book that contains all information to be discussed along with an enclosed agenda for each meeting.

Directors are provided all background material for discussion at least one week in advance. It is poor form for an Outside Director to become aware of a major decision in a Board Meeting.

A key element of a Board Meeting is a private discussion late in the day between the outside Directors and the owner. In this situation, the owner/president can receive private coaching, counseling, and the occasional "ball peen" adjustment. A sample agenda would be:

Evening Before:     Joint dinner with Board Members and Senior Operating Executives

8:00 – 8:30 AM     Refreshments

8:30 – 9:30 AM     Review financial results

9:30 – 11:00 AM     Review of current action plans provided by Senior Operating Executives

11:00 – 12:00 PM     Review of Strategic Initiatives

12:00 – 1:00 PM     Working Lunch

1:00 – 2:30 PM     Discussion of issues on previously published agenda

2:30 – 3:30 PM     Private feedback to owner from outside directors

3:30 PM     Adjourn

## Family Members' Pre-Employment Qualifications:

The company has established the following set of pre-employment criteria for incoming third and fourth generation family members. The board of directors reserves the right to review each individual on a case-by-case basis. The criteria are for family members seeking long-term, full-time employment.

In general, family members seeking employment must meet the same requirements as non-family member applicants. However, additional requirements include:

1. A job opening must be available. Positions will not be created for the sake of family.

2. Qualifications must reasonably match job requirements.

3. There must be evidence of success outside the family business.

4. Family members must have at least three years of continuous full-time work experience outside of the company in a middle management position.

- Family members must achieve a minimum level of education. We encourage family members to receive a four-year college degree. The amount of education required depends on the specific position, but to be promoted to the level above line supervisor, family members must have four-year college degrees. To aspire to the position of President, an MBA is required.

5. Members must accept the company's policies and Family Legacy Statement and family doctrine. In some cases a "code of conduct" may apply..

6. Members must meet the company's other entrance criteria.

## Non-family Member Pre-Employment Qualifications:

The company's commitment to non-family employees' needs is critical to future success. Commitment to our non-family employees will engender a commitment in return to Fred's Quarry Company, our customers and products. Committed family members working side by side with committed non-family employees work smarter, more efficiently and help create a culture of innovation, initiative, empowerment and success.

Recognition and respect are the principle ingredients in creating this unified culture. Employees of Fred's Quarry Company must believe in the family's commitment toward fairness in treatment of opportunities. Career paths for executive potential employees both family and non-family must be clearly defined.

Non-family member employees, especially in middle and upper management positions want to grow professionally. Fred's Quarry Company is committed to the financial investment necessary to provide training and educational opportunity to all employees who demonstrate leadership qualities in alignment with current and future company needs. Fred's Quarry Company understands that well trained and educated employees provide the company with succession opportunity, strength and flexibility.

Opportunity for growth increases employee retention. This investment is an investment in the company's future that has an expected return. Motivated, trained and educated employees, both family and non-family are essential ingredients for growth and future success.

## Compensation Policy for the Flintstone Family Member Employees

Compensation for actively employed family members includes two components, salary and bonuses. Family members will be compensated in the following manner:

1. It is our intent that salary should be set at fair market value (FMV). However, cases may occur where a family member is compensated above FMV. In a case such as this, total compensation (salary and bonuses) will not exceed the limits set by our Board of Directors' compensation committee.

2. All family member performance reviews and recommended compensation increases and productions will be reviewed by the Board of Directors' compensation committee for approval and recommendations.

## Framework for Dealing with Family Member Performance Issues

The company believes that developing a framework for dealing with under performing family members first requires that we develop a policy on how family members should be evaluated and by whom.

## How should we evaluate family member performance?

For the benefit of the rest of the company's employees in particular, it is important and generally accepted that family members' performance should be evaluated in the same manner as other employees. In essence, family member employees should not receive preferential or different treatment. Evaluations allow the supervisor (company) to provide helpful feedback to the family member. This flow of communication is important because:

1. It opens lines of communication between the company and the family member.

2. It limits surprises in performance evaluation and provides benchmarks to the family member for continued growth.

3. It allows family members to make changes to their work product or ethic that are more in line with the company's goals.

4. It helps the company develop its family members both technically and professionally.

5. Family members must contribute and not be a burden. They need to be in the right seat on the bus.

## Who should evaluate family member performance?

Family member supervision is an especially sensitive topic, particularly when the family member is also a stockholder at Fred's Quarry Company. Recognizing the difficulty this poses to family members wearing two hats while at the company, we encourage family members, especially shareholders, to subordinate their special role to the extent that they are able, and to follow the company's present supervision and review policies. Family members should be reviewed in the following manner:

1. By their immediate supervisor.

2. If the immediate supervisor is NOT at a key level or position, then an additional supervisor at a key level (non-family preferred) may be beneficial to help ensure that the immediate supervisor is doing the job properly.

3. Other family members will not review family members. There may be cases in which a board member is asked to participate in the review process.

This policy allows proper channels for supervision and professional development without playing favoritism or undermining the important role of all supervisors at Fred's Quarry Company. We will, however, provide informal mentoring support to family members at the company to help ensure and supplement their professional development. The appropriate mentors will usually be specifically assigned executives who will provide informal counsel and support to newer family member

employees and/or their supervisor. Dealing with nepotism perceptions will be part of this coaching process.

It is important to manage the perception of other associates and the immediate supervisor if an additional mentor is used. Without proper orientation, the immediate supervisor may feel undermined and other associates may resent what they perceive as preferential treatment toward the family member.

It is important to ensure that supervisors and subordinates are properly coached on methods of review and evaluation. This will help enable participants to effectively give and receive constructive feedback. This process includes coaching, counseling, education, training, corrective action, planning, the probationary process and termination if necessary.

## The Family Doctrine

It is often times advisable to clearly define what the family stands for. A doctrine that outlines the family philosophy can be an effective tool when dealing with family leadership issues within the organization. This doctrine may be referred to in reminding family members that their behavior may not be in accordance with the intent of the family and the founder of the business.

## Exhibit XIX     Sample Family Doctrine
## "The Johnson Family Doctrine"

The Johnson family lead by Ken Johnson (3rd generation) have built a reputation in the industry for fairness and integrity. The company was founded by Ken's Grandfather in 1917. The family believes that they must strive to reach the status of "Employer of Choice" by treating their employees with respect and recognizing their contributions to the company's success not only with praise but also with promotion and monetary rewards.  Human resources must play a leading role in this endeavor. The company profit sharing plan is generous to employees but is only one vehicle for recognition.   Ken wants to carry on the family and business tradition including the culture shift that had begun just prior to his appointment as President in 2005.  A shift more toward a family oriented, employee recognition environment that encourages individual growth, empowerment, development, continuous improvement and an attitude for winning. The family philosophy which is intended to be supported by the management is very simple. Create an environment that makes people want to come to

work, an environment of fun being at work and an environment that encourages people to reach their maximum potential. It is based on the following principles:

- Respect for the individual
- Integrity and fairness in all our dealings
- Ethical behavior and hard work
- Winning—success breeds success
- Safe and healthy workplace
- Open communication without fear of reprisal
- Pride in our work, our company and our individual contributions
- Relationship equity with our vendors
- Prioritizing customer service. Customer service that creates competitive advantage.
- Policy and procedure that clearly define responsibilities providing functional guidelines to all employees
- Knowledge transfer through the sharing of information and communication

Caring about people is the cornerstone of this Johnson Doctrine, a doctrine that continues to create and develop a culture that embraces these core values, a culture that encourages and supports leadership development. We must manage our processes but Lead our People. Every one of our employees should not only be encouraged to develop their own leadership skills but as an organization we have an obligation to demonstrate effective leadership at every management level within the company.

This means we must be willing to invest in the leadership development and skill level of every employee that is in a management position at our company (including family members) and at the same time offer opportunities for advancement to all of our employees.

*Although we expect our employees to demonstrate a passion for success and a commitment to getting the job done, we cannot expect any of our employees to "Live to Work" but recognize that employees "Work to Live." This means that we must not only understand that every employee has family obligations but we must encourage employees to seek a balance in their lives and at a minimum give their own family life the priority necessary to* maintain that balance.

Our ownership is committed to making our company a learning and evolving organization that believes in a family atmosphere and recognizes individual contributions toward success and demonstrates that recognition by providing job security and appropriate financial reward. This doctrine promotes the concept of exceptional performance by exceptional employees by not allowing our compassion and commitments to a family atmosphere gravitate toward acceptance of substandard performance at any level in the organization. Additionally, the Johnson family recognizes the importance of being a diligent corporate citizen that reaches out through various endeavors to support the needs of the communities that we do business in.

This doctrine should be signed by all family members.

# Succession

According to John C. Bruckman, PhD, less than 15% of companies address the need for succession planning. This is especially true at the executive level. When disaster strikes, which may include unexpected death or resignation, there is little time for the Board of Directors to meet and select new top executives.

Fred's Quarry Company does not want to put itself in a vulnerable position with unexpected circumstance. Additionally, the company believes that succession planning throughout the management ranks is a recognized best practice. This stabilizes the company's consistent future success. Good leaders plan for the future. Companies lose top talent because there is no clearly defined career path. They may view the company as having an absence of opportunities.

Fred's Quarry Company will hold its Board of Directors accountable for development of our executive level management succession while the company holds all other management personnel accountable for the development of bench strength and future leadership within the management rank itself.

Succession and bench strength will become a part of the company's strategic planning phases. Clearly, as stated previously, genetic bond is not a pre-requisite to succession. Members of the "lucky sperm club" must meet the minimum criteria for employment and advancement. Future family leadership is not ordained. Fred's Quarry Company will hold the following standards for family member succession:

- Minimum middle management experience at another company of three years or more.

- Four-year degree for executive level management.

- MBA degree for Presidential consideration.

- Competence – performance must be equal to or clearly superior to non-family employees in a similar position.

- Non-family leadership – the company as a matter of policy will ensure that a balance exists between family and non-family members in key management positions.

- Top-level executive leadership succession will be documented to avoid crisis planning in the event of an unexpected death or disaster.

## The Code of Conduct

Succession to second, third or fourth generation leadership may lead to family conflict, jealousy, mismanagement and a disruption in the business that is so dramatic that the business may face imminent failure. If this situation develops, it generally happens when multiple family members work in the business and they don't get along well at all. The named successor as President may not have the support of other family members resulting in a division of leadership that effects employee performance. Sometimes this division of leadership is so apparent that employees begin to take sides. If that occurs, the business suffers dramatically and the situation must be corrected quickly. Failure to resolve these issues will result in the failure of the business or the necessity to sell the business.

A first step in dealing with this type of situation is the family code of conduct.

The following is a sample "Code of Conduct."

## "Family Code of Conduct"

### I Will Always:

1. Deal with family members with integrity, honesty and respect and never criticize another family member's decision in public.

2. To the best of my ability attempt to demonstrate courtesy, respect and friendship in dealing with other family members to show employees that the family is united.

3. Be a professional listener allowing each other to express their views without interruption and challenge.

4. Make decisions based on the principles outlined in our family business doctrine.

5. Invest in a minimum of one consecutive week per year in personal management and leadership development offered outside the organization.

6. Be willing to discuss issues openly and honestly.

7. Support the decisions of the President and other senior managers publicly

8. Address any problem with a family member directly with that person.

9. Follow through on all my commitments to other family members unless I notify them in advance

10. Be open to constructive feedback from family members with positive follow-up dialog without shutting down and fostering feelings of resentment.

11. Function in my role within the realm of my responsibilities and will not usurp authority or circumvent authority.

12. Respect the position of other family members performing their duties as outlined by their personal job responsibilities and support their decisions even if I disagree.

13. Be committed to act in conformance and support of this code of conduct.

## I will never:

1. Openly challenge a family member in front of other employees about a decision they made. I can disagree and discuss issues without being disagreeable and confrontational.

2. Get so angry that I walk away or tune out from a family discussion unless we call a time out to allow emotions to settle.

3. Disregard a decision made by another family member performing in their respective role with the authority defined by their role.

4. Go behind the back of another family member with the intention of soliciting support from employees to challenge the authority of the other family member.

5. Talk about the competence or the attitude of another family member with any employee in our company. Family respect will always be the top priority.

6. Intentionally withhold information that is relevant to the business from another family member.

**Signed by all Family members**

# Chapter XVI

# *Bringing It All Together*

We covered a wide swath of the leadership landscape in the preceding chapters starting with the Lone Wolf leadership model and how leadership has changed going into the twenty first century. The B.O.S.S. syndrome was discussed along with the five principles necessary to avoid this autocratic Machiavellian style. Planning is the key to leadership and scenario planning, strategic planning and even `contingency planning was covered in earlier chapters. Leadership focus and how it applies under a variety of situations is explored throughout the chapters in this book. Economic turbulence and the creation of a Turn-A-Round plan supported by transitional Lead Wolf leadership were explored in depth. Recruitment and retention, becoming Employer of Choice and even corporate recreational mating become challenges the Lead Wolf executive faces in today's business environment. The Lead Wolf executive not only has to see what's possible but they have to describe those possibilities in a clear concise compelling manner in order to engage employees to deal with individual situations that may occur. The Lead Wolf model of leadership has to inspire employees to create a willingness in

them to release their discretionary energy focused on company success. Remember, discretionary energy is the energy an employee gives voluntarily that is above and beyond what is expected for normal acceptable performance. It can not be demanded as it is controlled solely by the employee's willingness to release it.

To bring it all together we need to understand that leadership is the process of influencing employees to do things. This influence must be directed at accomplishing corporate goals. A true Lead Wolf executive understands the directional style of their personal influence. Leadership is not just about your influence on your subordinates. Leadership is an entity in itself and can be demonstrated in a variety of ways even in situations that may or may not involve the corporate hierarchy. Expertise, charisma and relationship power all determine the effectiveness of leadership in any given situation. Have you ever been in a group situation where the highest ranking individual in the group was not the one that demonstrated the leadership for the group? When this occurs, it is an example of charisma, presence and relationship power that is stronger than the position power of the highest ranking individual.

A Lead Wolf will constantly evaluate the performance needs of their subordinates and determine what kind of support and resources are necessary for them to achieve success. It is essential to understand the readiness factors that indicate an employee's willingness and ability to accomplish what it takes to be successful.

---

**Thought Provoker**

"It is not the critic who counts, not the man who points out how the strong man stumbled, or where the doer of deeds could have done better. The credit belongs to the man who is actually in the arena; whose face is marred by dust and sweat and blood; who strives valiantly; who errs and comes short again and again; who knows the great enthusiasms, the great devotions and spends himself in a worthy cause; who, at the worst, if he fails, at least fails while daring greatly, so that his place shall never be with those cold and timid souls who know neither victory nor defeat."

Teddy Roosevelt

---

## Three 21st Century Lead Wolf Approaches

There isn't much doubt that most effective high impact leaders are driven by a model. This is true even when that effective leader doesn't take the time to define his personal unique model but acts instinctively. A model is a tool that leaders use to predict future outcomes of current decisions; a tool that not only enhances personal creativity but encourages creativity in the minds of their employees. An executive's model is built from the sum of their experiences, knowledge, deeds and, in fact, many of their mistakes. Best practice alone will not get the job done. Effective model driven leadership utilizing best practice is a combination that is an absolute must. It is the Lead Wolf model of leadership that is flexible and resilient enough to support a variety of approaches. Different leaders create their models through different approaches, some knowingly

and some instinctively. Each model is unique to the individual but the following three examples explain the different types of platforms that models can be built on.

## The Competitive Desire Approach

Some leaders strongly shape their Lead Wolf model by working in every aspect of the business and also from learning the business from the ground up. They always carry a strong desire to compete and win. The Leaders competitive instincts are generally tempered by personal humility and respect for the individual managers on his team. Listening skills and genuine interest in what is right for the business are key tools in building a consensus. Belief in the employees is a guiding principle in leadership style. This same approach is used with both suppliers and customers to find the innovative win-win solution. Make no mistake; this approach is very different than typical negotiation approaches used in many wholesale-distributors.

It becomes a discipline. This discipline circumvents growth mistakes so common in the industry. The other implication of this model is providing significant autonomy to the executive team. The leader makes sure the executive team has a detailed and shared vision of the business objectives and goals. He believes his role as chief executive is to provide the shared vision and make sure that it is clear and also current.

## The Elegant, Powerful Win-Win Innovation & Creativity Approach

Another variation of the Lead Wolf servant style of leadership is the elegant, powerful, and simple approach. This approach starts with an open and clear balance between the various stakeholders whether they are customer/owners, employees, or suppliers. It is a true win-win approach without the destructive negotiations experienced by many other distributors. Using this foundation and a long established set of core corporate values and best practice the leader consistently reminds each stakeholder group of the key messages while continually focusing the organization on innovation and creativity. Innovation becomes a key strategic initiative for growth. It is exciting to see the accumulated economic power that can be developed by a constantly evolving innovative business model and effective leadership combined with best practice utilization.

## The Strategic Shift Approach

A third example of Lead Wolf leadership modeling is about managing a strategic shift from being a traditional box-moving wholesaler with limited growth prospects to a logistics powerhouse that provides significant value in the supply chain.

Strategy is said to be obvious once you've had it explained. It is also said that customers don't see strategy, they only see execution. This Lead Wolf approach like the other examples platform a strong sense of curiosity about other companies and how to apply lessons learned in their own organizations. The answers needed for major change and organizational renewal lie outside the enterprise and effective Lead Wolf leaders using this approach are able to take prior "lessons learned" and on-going bench marking to generate success.

Over ninety percent of the reasons companies fail can be traced to ineffective leadership. It's not because of the economy and it is not because of the competition. It is a failure to learn. Effective leadership will overcome these obstacles, and they'll be looking down the road at what needs to be done to grow with the current model or change it once the model is no longer 'grow-able. Attention is paid to the lessons learned.

## What is a High Impact Leader?

High impact leaders, regardless of their personal model demonstrate a curiosity that can not be satisfied without personal examination of what exactly were the causes of any failure to meet expectations. Non-performance is just not acceptable. Leadership is a key in every instance to creating an attitude, structuring an environment and developing employees as the very essence of success. Although individual leadership models differ in some specific approaches the common thread that links every model together is respect for the individual employee and the willingness and ability to listen with an understanding that embellishes their own leadership contribution to the organization. That is the essence of the Lead Wolf model. Best practices are a part of every successful leadership model but best practice alone will not create the level of success demonstrated by the high impact upper quartile performers.

The Lead Wolf model creates a culture where employees can express themselves and fight for what is right; employees become responsibly fanatical about aligning their resources to add value to the customer and the company. That's what "Leading the Pack" is all about.

## Effective Leaders Don't Have To Know It All

A mistake many leaders make is the self imposed responsibility to have all the answers. This is just not true. It is okay to admit to not having all the answers. Good leaders are willing to show their imperfections. Surround yourself with a solid executive team and you don't need all the answers. No one expects perfection, just leadership. Being President doesn't grant you supreme knowledge.

## The Ego Factor

Stagnant growth, lost market share and panic response management are more likely to occur if strategic growth objectives are Ego driven vs. Profit driven which often leads to putting personal needs ahead of business needs. This is a common symptom of the lack of leadership in the organization. Leadership is quite different then management.

Steve Kaufman in his DREF interview, NAW's leadership series (2003), stated that he did not invent the phrase "Servant Leadership" but he leans heavily toward that methodology.

The academics tell us a leaders role is to serve those people that report to him. He or She is not a dictator but their ultimate role is to serve, to allow those people to achieve their goals. It's a style that starts by asking; What do you want to accomplish rather than telling them what you want to accomplish." I would say that the servant leadership model is the one that I like to talk about. I like to talk about the most effective leaders being those that have volunteer followers not those–that have draftees. And if your team could vote for a leader rather than be assigned a leader, would they still vote for you. Steve Kaufman, CEO Arrow Electronics

Servant-leadership, being a Lead Wolf, encourages collaboration, trust, foresight, listening, and the ethical use of power and empowerment. Warren Bennis, leadership scholar believes American corporations are over managed and underled. Great leaders get exceptional efforts from their employees simply because they recognize that they don't have to have all the answers. Knowing this they make a concerted effort to leverage the intelligence, the creativity and the innovation of their employees. For this process to be successful, effective leaders must have vision and they must communicate that vision with crystal clarity. A visionary leader has a clear sense for the future with the ability to turn their vision into results. This could not be accomplished if they let their ego get in the way. Communication is critical to the process used to inspire others to act.

A Lead Wolf, servant leader, "Leading the Pack" makes a conscious choice to lead by being a servant first. He or she is sharply different from the person who is leader first, perhaps because of the need to assuage an unusual power drive or to acquire material possessions. The leader-first and the servant-first are the two extreme boundaries. Between these two extremes is where you find the most effective leaders. Your style is determined by you, your environment and the specific situation you face. But, if you stay in the grid between these two extremes but closer to the servant-first boundary, the Lead Wolf model, your effectiveness as a leader will be obvious. Good managers get employees to respect them, Lead Wolf executives get employees to not only respect them but more importantly they get them to respect themselves.

## The Servant Leadership Presence – The Core of the Lead Wolf Model

Although situational leadership is the predominant methods demonstrated when dealing with economic challenges, the transitional style is necessary to manage the change in those circumstances. However, I believe that servant leadership is the predominant style of this century's Lead Wolf executives. Servant leadership is the foundation of transitional leadership and it also plays a role under certain circumstances in a restructuring Turn-A-Round situation. It is clearly evident in all three leadership modeling approaches discussed previously. It is necessary to be an effective listener in this environment to understand when to employ specific leadership techniques. The Lead Wolf executive is an exceptional listener. When employees feel that they are really being heard, that their thoughts and opinions matter, they begin to trust their leader and believe in their ability to lead them to success. Listening is the starting point to introduce cultural change in the organization. Listening must be accompanied by an empathetic attitude so that we can see things from the employee's perspective. The Lead Wolf executive must be continuously aware of his surroundings, the environment, the attitude of his employees and the resistance to change. This is a never ending process. Conceptualization and persuasion become the working tools of an effective leader. The Lead Wolf executive must be able to conceptualize their vision and persuade the employees to execute on that vision. This requires buy in and buy in starts with effective communication.

The Lead Wolf isn't born a Lead Wolf. They are trained throughout their career and adopt a style based on their own personal exposure to leadership mentors, coaches, education and training they receive along the way upon which they build their personal model. Passion and a sense of urgency can be seen early on in their career. They have a special energy that gets people excited. They walk the walk and demonstrate a high ethical standard for others to follow.

The power a Lead Wolf seems to have over people is earned. It is earned by showing trust, respect and confidence in their employees. A key instinct Lead Wolf executives employ is the ability to distinguish poor leadership techniques applied by former B.O.S.S.es and its impact on the employees. They study leadership and work on their skill sets. Most have had at least one specific mentor in their career that has guided them, helping them develop their own leadership style. Formal training and education is second nature and they seek it out. Their focus is not on the past, not on the present but their focus is on the future.

A Few Key Characteristics of the Lead Wolf model include:

- Utilizing interpersonal skills and building relationship equity with their employees
- Employee needs are the highest priority
- Visionaries with the ability to communicate that vision
- Employees are involved in future planning and they are empowered to execute
- Leadership by example with high integrity
- Character
- Compassion for and recognition of employee efforts
- Trust
- Integrity

## Learning from Mistakes

Effective leaders learn from their mistakes and they do make mistakes. It's called experience. Experience creates good judgment. Good judgment is proactive not reactive. Current reality is the baseline utilized for mentoring and coaching employees to serve a nobler cause, a cause that does not recognize defeat or sub par performance. The status quo is not an option as they help redefine what the organization is capable of and what is expected from the organization to achieve the vision of the future. The Lead Wolf leaders demonstrate an unhesitant curiosity to achieve greater success taking people out of their comfort zones. The discovery of new possibilities by everyone becomes the challenge of the day.

---

**Thought Provoker**

**"Hard work, of course is critical. But you have to have balance that with time for your family and friends. One dimensional people are rarely successful over the long haul."**

**G. Richard Thoman**
**President Xerox Corp.**

---

Fundamentally, Lone Wolf executives that employ old style autocratic methodologies are no longer effective in this century, Leadership is much more difficult today. Generational diversity

demands understanding and fundamental change in how organizations are led. This makes it virtually impossible for a Lone Wolf leader to excel in this environment long term. Soft leadership skills, those skills embraced by the Lead Wolf model of leadership are essential to success. These soft skills lead the way with trust, respect, empathy, empowerment and communication. Effective leadership is absolutely central to organizational success. Today, more and more importance is being placed on leadership development. Leadership today, the Lead Wolf model of leadership is defined as a process that

engenders. It releases the power of the people and recognizes that any organizational success is directly related to the abilities, creativity and innovation that is released in the employees by effective leadership. Leadership is about creating competitive advantage.

And never forget, an effective leader is only as good as the team that he surrounds himself with.

*Become a Lead Wolf executive and leverage the power of your people. It will create competitive advantage and competitive advantage is the key to increased profits.*
*Good Luck in "Leading Your Pack."*

*Rick Johnson*

# APPENDIX I

## End Game Examples

This document contains five different examples of end games to help you write your organization's own End Game Vision during your strategy development process.

## Example #1

Successful companies are willing to do what their competitors are not willing or able to do. The key to our success, then, is in the hands and creative minds of our employees.

We are committed to continually developing our employees' personal skills and technical abilities to meet the rising challenges of our competitors and the increasing service expectations of our customers.

Exceeding our competitors' service levels and customers' expectations adds value to the products we sell and develops the trust and loyalty of our customers. Our goal is to do every job right the first time.

We are an independent, small-town, employee-owned distributor.

Our success as a company and as individuals will be possible only as long as we are recognized by our suppliers and customers as "People doing what they say they are going to do!" Our core values and respect for people will be observed at all times.

ACME is market-driven with "same store" mentality. We intend to keep our "profitable" customers reaching for much deeper penetration in our identified strategic partner accounts, converting customers with high potential to strategic partners while encouraging prospecting of potential future customers. Our T.L.S. sales strategy will be our baseline for this program. ACME recognizes that our growth has a significant dependence upon our vendor base as well as our customer base. As a result we have identified our strategic customer criteria and our strategic vendor criteria. Geographical expansion is a critical part of our strategy and will be documented in each independent segment plan. This geographic growth could include Greenfield startups.

## Example #2

The ABC Company will manage our business to maintain a market valuation tracking in the upper quartile of the industry. The interest of our stockholders will continue to be a priority, and at the same time we will drive toward a culture built around positive reinforcement and achievement.

## Growth and Market Leadership

- We have established core initiatives that incorporate revenue growth of 5% per year. We expect to maintain a minimum margin of 17% while establishing a return on sales of 2.5% and greater.

- Continued development and implementation of our business system

- Regionalized distribution

- Business segmentation
- Geographic expansion
- Employee development

## The Company Vision/Mission Statement

Successful companies are willing to do what their competitors are not willing or able to do. The key to our success, then, is in the hands and creative minds of our employees.

We are committed:

- To meeting or exceeding the expectations of our customers with quality products and quality service

- To working in a partnership with our suppliers in aggressively and effectively reaching our target markets

- To providing employees opportunities for personal growth, recognition and reward and empowerment in the continuous improvement process

- To providing our shareholders with a fair return on their investment through consistent growth and increasing market share, constant improvement in resource management and ongoing commitment to the continuous improvement process

- To being responsible and involved citizens both corporately and personally, utilizing our time and resources

Exceeding our competitors' service levels and customers' expectations adds value to the products we sell and develops

the trust and loyalty of our customers. Our goal is to do every job right the first time.

Our success as a company and as individuals will be possible only as long as we are recognized by our suppliers, our customers and our community as "People doing what they say they are going to do!" Our core values, business principles and respect for people will not be compromised.

- Ethical Business Practice. Our principles of right and wrong are derived from traditional business practice, civil law, and the Bible.

- Respect for the individual. Each employee is regarded as a unique, created being, to be treated as such in the conduct of the affairs of the company.

- Open and Honest Communication. Each employee has access to anyone in the Company and is both permitted and expected to communicate and be communicated to in a clear, factual and meaningful manner.

- Progressiveness and Innovation. The Company seeks out and encourages ideas that will result in beneficial change and is willing to take risks in anticipation of improvement.

- Professionalism. Each employee is expected to meet or exceed standards for behavior, effectiveness, efficiency and job knowledge in responding to the needs of internal and external customers.

- Teamwork. The Company nurtures an environment in which people work productively together to achieve desired results.

- Responsiveness. We respond in a timely and complete manner to the opportunities presented to the Company.

- Consistency. The Company strives to apply these principles in a consistent manner.

# Example #3

## QRS Company – Strategic End Game

## Success

QRS Company's success in meeting our long-term objectives is directly dependent upon maintaining and enhancing our reputation among our customers and suppliers, and within our industry. We believe that our strong reputation results from two factors, present since our inception:

1. Our company's core values, including ethical business principles and respect for people
2. The dedication of our employees to our company and to our customers

Therefore, our continued success depends on an uncompromising commitment to our core values and the creativity and effort of each and every one of us.

Recognizing these principles will guide us in establishing human resources management as a core competency at QRS .

Employee development, continuous improvement, performance measurement and accountability will be a central part of our strategic planning process.

## Growth

Growth at QRS Company will come from the efforts of dedicated, hard working employees striving to meet objectives. One key objective is an internal growth rate of eight to ten percent annually. This equates to a revenue stream approximating $29 million by the year-end 2007. Additionally, we expect growth through acquisition to add another $21 million in revenue over the same period. Therefore, our revenue target is $50 million by year-end 2007. We must clearly recognize that, due to our industry's stagnant growth rate, our expansion must come at the expense of our competition.

Since acquisitions are very opportunistic in nature, we will not charge our strategy team with developing an acquisition strategy. We will assign this responsibility to our president. Our strategy team will focus on attaining eight to ten percent internal, organic growth annually.

## Profitability

We challenge our entire team with the responsibility for maintaining or improving our gross margin rate of 24%, while achieving an ROS of at least 4%, with stretch expectations of 6%.

## Customer Service, Quality and Business Segmentation

QRS Company must continue to strive to introduce at least one new product line annually, with a willingness to investigate creative alternatives to our base line business segments. Quality and service must continue to be the platform that we use to increase market penetration. We must develop an evolving process for selectively pruning and adding customers and product lines. Additionally, we must focus on growth by building on our established relationships with existing high potential customers. Finally, we must generate increased recognition of the QRS Company brand throughout the marketplace to develop new customers.

This "End Game" can only be achieved by consistently being aggressive, innovative and dedicated to maintaining QRS Company basic business principles. We must continue to be a sales and marketing driven company that recognizes our employees as our most precious asset and our customers as the key to our success.

## Example #4

## ABC Company's Vision of the future

The shareholders have initiated a board of governance and are committed to ensuring the company is always lead by a competent Board of Directors. The shareholders are going to determine the applicability and potential roles of outside directors as a possible structure in 2005. The shareholders are seeking to complete the board creation process on or before December of [Year]. The primary responsibility of the Board

is to assure the organization is lead by qualified and effective executive leadership today and in the future.

Shareholders will be responsible to ensure that proper accountability is maintained throughout the ABC organization. Shareholders will create a board, the board will hold the executive committee accountable, and the executive committee will hold the management team accountable.

The shareholders are challenging the strategy team to establish a development and succession process necessary to support the Board's objective of having qualified executive leadership and recognize that this will require a monetary investment for personnel development. To ensure qualified executive leadership (i.e. senior managers and above) in the future, it is possible that executive leadership may not be a part of the ownership group.

The strategy team will propose a new organizational structure that supports the "Vision of the Future" and the strategy to achieve it. The shareholders have an expectation that managers will solve most problems between peers rather than brining problems to the next higher level. Operating four different Strategic Business Units (SBUs) within one management structure is part of the company's competitive advantage. This inherently places a high premium on effective interdependence. The shareholders expect that this will be a strength that continues to develop over time. As a part of this strategy group and regional decisions at the SBU level will be made ensuring that they are in full support of the firm's Vision of the Future.

The shareholders' "Vision of the Future" includes several objectives beyond financial performance. The first is to accomplish a shift in the management culture of the firm. The shareholders are challenging the management team to develop a culture of manager accountability that operates at a high level of personal initiative. The clear job responsibilities defined by the new organizational structure and measured by Key Performance Indicators will support accountability and empowerment. While preserving entrepreneurial spirit the company will transition from being "entrepreneurially driven" to being "strategically driven." Managers will have the authority and the responsibility to take action, including probation and termination, in cases of persistent under-performance. In all cases, these actions will be in accordance with published company policy. We will not allow our compassion for individuals to limit our ability to succeed as an organization.

In the future, family members of shareholders who express an interest in senior management positions will participate in formal and structured development programs inclusive of a four-year bachelor's degree and two to three years working for another company. A formal review process within the guidelines of our management-training program will ensure they have the requisite skills and experience appropriate for the needs of the company.

The shareholders have financial objectives with respect to their collective investment. The standards will include sales and gross margin goals by location and strategic business units. Expectations will be included in the proposed standards. Guidelines for corrective actions will be included for poor performance at the location, SBU or department level. Critical core initiatives will include specific performance and progress measurements.

The shareholders have an expectation that the strategy document presented for approval will provide clarity and include specific growth and margin goals.

ABC is committed to provide top quartile managerial compensation for top quartile performance.

There are two minimum financial performance criteria that must be met independent of the discussion described. The shareholders are charging the management team with the responsibility to monitor financial performance carefully and take the decisive actions necessary to produce an operating profit, expressed as net profit divided by sales (ROS), of 3.0% minimum on an annual basis. The strategy team is charged with creating a process that brings all compensation structures, including incentives, into alignment with the strategy once it is approved.

The second minimum performance criterion is the debt exposure that the shareholders are willing to accept. High profit successful companies in our industries operate with debt to equity levels that range from 1.0 to 1.0 up to 1.3 to 1.0. The shareholders are willing to sustain a higher level of capital risk to grow the firm. The shareholders expect the company to operate at a debt to equity ratio between 1.5 and 2.0, calculated prior to any shareholder distributions.

Given these higher risk tolerances, the shareholders expect that the strategy team will develop a process to ensure that these risks are prudent and responsible over the entire economic cycle. There will be times when the company needs to take unusual capital risks to meet strategic objectives. These circumstances may include acquiring another company. The shareholders are willing to incur additional debt to support strategic objectives up to a debt to equity ratio of 3.05. In these circumstances, the shareholders expect the executive management team to seek approval from the Board of Directors, in advance, by presenting a financial plan that includes the timeline and actions necessary to return to the normal debt to equity levels.

High levels of customer service are essential to assure the future of the firm as an independent. It is the responsibility of the management team to create processes to ensure that every ABC employee understands the Mission Statement and that the employee has the ability to provide a high level of service to all customers, suppliers, and peers. We will formally and regularly conduct satisfaction surveys of our stakeholders (customer, suppliers and employees) and act on the results.

ABC represents significant value to our suppliers as an alternative to the national chains. The shareholders expect the management team to develop strong strategic relationships with key suppliers by performing as an excellent partner. The management team must also create the capability in the firm to effectively present the ABC value proposition to suppliers. Relationships should be maintained between all levels of our organizations, from the Presidential level down, to effectively present our value proposition as a corporation.

## Example #5

## The XYZ Company "End Game"

The long-term success of any organization lies with an effectively communicated and shared vision of the future for its employees, products and financial goals. XYZ has formed a Strategic Planning team to analyze, develop, implement and move the organization forward, with a shared sense of urgency, vision and purpose, to establish and achieve the next set of goals for the Organization, as agreed to here and in the Strategic Plan.

The Widget family of products is the single-most important factor for XYZ's long and short-term success. Our #1 goal is to drive Widget to become the customer-specified brand in our chosen and/or preferred geographical markets over the next 3 years. Global market dominance will be supported by Sales, Manufacturing and/or Patent Licensees in areas outside those identified as "chosen" or "preferred." All new licensees and production facilities will be based on maintaining agreed upon financial and operational goals agreed to in this document and the overall Strategic Plan. In the next 5 years, the Widget family of products should grow to represent over 70% of all revenue sources. Non-Widget products are to be used in a "support role" to help reduce delivery cost and entry barriers when introducing Widget to new customers or markets. To emphasize the importance of Widget to our future success, XYZ will change its name to Widget Express (DBA Widget), if desirable, after consulting experts in such matters

The second key factor to XYZ's long-term success is a well-defined Plan for an orderly transition to the next generation of leadership. This Plan will identify all key leadership positions and the void(s) left behind from any potential promotions. This Plan includes, but is not limited to, techniques utilizing internal and external support mechanisms, professional training, and coaching, mentoring and "on-the-job" practical experience. The goal is to over the next 2 -3 years, provide the necessary training and support to XYZ employees that allow them the opportunity to become the best-qualified option in the marketplace for the above identified leadership positions. The plan to implement both leadership and ownership succession will be driven by a clearly defined business strategy currently being developed in the Strategic Plan. This strategy will include clearly defined models to grow the company (EBITDA) with Widgets as the primary focus. The management team will also be charged to include strategic performance metrics that track success.

The measurement criteria for success over the next three-years will be an average annual MINIMUM EBITDA growth rate of at least 10%, with a targeted average annual EBITDA growth rate of at least 15%, while maintaining a long term debt to equity ratio of no more than 1.5 to 1.

An effectively managed strategic planning process is necessary to preserve the economic strength and continued growth of the business. The Board of Directors (the Board) and current Owners are the final authority in approving the details of the Strategic Plan. In doing so, the Board and current Owners realize that, in approving the Strategic Plan, they are empowering the Strategy Team to guide and control the execution of the initiatives within the framework of the approved plan. This is not an abdication of responsibility, but rather a clear charge to the Management Team with the responsibility to execute the agreed upon plan. Managers will have well thought out solutions to problems. Managers will be expected to take initiative and clearly explain rationale for decisions/actions to the Board and current Owners.

XYZ recognizes its employees are critical to future growth and prosperity and that they will be the driving force behind achieving objectives set forth in the Strategic Plan. XYZ will continue to promote and maintain an honest concern for the well-being and respect for all individuals. The Management Team (Strategy Team) is charged with the responsibility of developing processes to make the above stated goals and objectives a reality and to ensure success by achieving the minimum measurement criteria. Tools used can include, but are not limited to:

- Future leadership development
- Applicable seminars and training for all employees
- Regular performance reviews for all employees utilizing a coaching and mentoring approach
- New or modified existing company-wide incentive programs

In summary, the vision for the next five years is to have a dynamically growing organization with a highly trained workforce, predominantly selling patented products to a national and international customer base, operating from a highly efficient and intrinsically valuable facility in Anywhere,

USA, with the next generation of leadership in place, returning an above average profit (EBITDA) to its investors.

# Appendix II

## Discovery Analysis – Recruitment and Retention

This questionnaire is designed to stimulate a thought provoking process which should direct you to focus-specific areas within your management organization that need attention. The Owner/President, and the executive team should complete this discovery analysis. A second analysis can be completed by line management for comparative purposes.

A discovery team meeting should be conducted to review the objectives of this process. Each team member should prepare an independent S.W.O.T. (Strengths, Weaknesses, Opportunities and Threats) analysis based on his responses after completing this questionnaire. Only the three most critical areas in each category should be recorded:

*Strengths:*      The three biggest strengths that create an ability to utilize company resources to recruit and retain talent.

*Weaknesses:*      The three most critical areas that create confusion, dissatisfaction and lack of understanding as to overall recruitment and retention issues.

*Opportunities:*      The three biggest opportunities that may increase understanding, satisfaction and loyalty of current employees. The three biggest opportunities to recruit for upgrading.

*Threats:*    <u>The three biggest threats</u> to effective recruitment and employee retention.

## Recruitment and Retention Discovery Analysis:

- Do you have an employee assistance program?
- Do you use a recruiter to find talent or do it yourself?
- Do you pre-test potential employees using one of the personality profile methods?
- Do you have a Human Resources department?
- Do you have a new employee orientation program?
- Do you provide career counseling?
- Do you have a formal wage and salary program?
- Do you provide regular training outside the office?
- Do you conduct monthly performance reviews?
- Do you communicate and share staff meeting minutes, financial overviews?
- Do you have formal job descriptions and job functions in place?
- Do you have an employee skill data bank in place?

## Discovery Analysis – Human Resources

This questionnaire is designed to stimulate a thought provoking process which should direct you to focus-specific areas within your management organization that need attention. The Owner/President, and the executive team should complete this discovery analysis. A second analysis can be completed by line management for comparative purposes.

A discovery team meeting should be conducted to review the objectives of this process. Each team member should prepare an independent S.W.O.T. (Strengths, Weaknesses, Opportunities and Threats) analysis based on his responses after completing this questionnaire. Only the three most critical areas in each category should be recorded:

*Strengths:*      <u>The three biggest strengths</u> that create an environment that treats employees as your number one asset.

*Weaknesses:*      <u>The three most critical</u> areas that create confusion, dissatisfaction and lack of understanding as to overall individual performance and understanding of company goals.

*Opportunities:*      <u>The three biggest opportunities</u> that may increase understanding, satisfaction and job performance.

*Threats:*      <u>The three biggest threats</u> to effective leadership based on low human resource planning and adapt ion.

- Do you have an employee assistance program?
- Do you use a recruiter to find talent or do it yourself?
- Do you pre-test potential employees using one of the personality profile methods?
- Do you have a Human Resources department?
- Do you have a new employee orientation program?
- Do you provide career counseling?

- Do you have a formal wage and salary program?
- Do you provide regular training outside the office?
- Do you conduct monthly performance reviews?
- Do you communicate and share staff meeting minutes, financial overviews?
- Do you have formal job descriptions and job functions in place?
- Do you have an employee skill data bank in place?
- Do you offer any training to managers in dealing with diversity in the workplace?
- Do you have a documented Human Resource strategy that is part of your strategic plan?
- Do you have a strategic plan?
- Do you have a Human Resource vision?
- Do you have employment and non-compete agreements?
- Do you thoroughly explain benefits during orientation?
- Is your benefits package competitive within your industry and market?
- Do you make it fun to come to work?
- Do you recognize accomplishment of individual employees formally?

## Discovery Analysis– Compensation

This questionnaire is designed to stimulate a thought provoking process which should direct you to focus-specific areas within your management organization that need attention. The Owner/President, and the executive team should complete this discovery analysis. A second analysis can be completed by line management for comparative purposes.

A discovery team meeting should be conducted to review the objectives of this process. Each team member should prepare an independent S.W.O.T. (Strengths, Weaknesses, Opportunities and Threats) analysis based on his responses after completing this questionnaire. Only the three most critical areas in each category should be recorded:

*Strengths:*  The three biggest positives related to the structure of and amounts realized by your pay practices.

*Weaknesses:*  The three areas where what pay or how we pay is producing unsatisfactory results.

*Opportunities:*  The three areas where adjusting pay levels or changing compensation programs would increase the probability of attaining corporate objectives.

*Threats:*  The three biggest threats to the company if pay levels are in appropriate or pay structures are misaligned.

## Compensation Discovery Analysis:

- Do you pay too much or too little to your employees?

- Do employees have any incentive to 'go above and beyond?'

- Does an entrepreneurial spirit exist with your organization?

- Are you receiving acceptable returns on your investment in human resources?

- Is the process by which pay levels are adjusted clearly communicated?

- Do employees feel they are adequately compensated?

- Does your company employ salary grades?

- Are any of your employees at or near their maximum pay level?

## Discovery Analysis ---- Inventory Management

This questionnaire is designed to stimulate a thought provoking process which should direct you to very focus-specific areas within your purchasing, logistics and inventory management organization that need attention. The Owner/President, Director of Purchasing, Logistics, Operations and Marketing should complete this discovery analysis.

A discovery team meeting should be conducted to review the objectives of this process. Each team member should prepare an independent S.W.O.T. (Strengths, Weaknesses, Opportunities and Threats) analysis based on his responses after completing this questionnaire. Only the three most critical areas in each category should be recorded:

*Strengths:*        The three biggest strengths that create competitive advantage and customer

satisfaction

*Weaknesses:* The three most critical areas that create customer dissatisfaction, reduced fill rates and create a competitive disadvantage.

*Opportunities:* The three biggest opportunities that may increase customer satisfaction, improve market share or create competitive advantage.

*Threats:* The three biggest threats to effective inventory management including external influences such as vendor support, dual distribution, multiple new channels or supplier apathy.

- How much time is spent expediting orders?
- Do you do a lost order report?
- Do you track fill rates? How?
- What is the biggest excuse given for stock outs?
- Do you use EDI or E-business?
- Do you cycle count?
- How do you justify doing a physical inventory if you still do one?
- Do you track turnover by product line?
- Do you classify inventory - A, B, C?
- Do you track turnover by classification?
- Do you formally measure vendor performance?

- Do you know which vendors enhance margin and which detract from it?

- Do you have a formalized dead or aged inventory process?

- What measures are taken to reduce dead and aged inventory?

- Do you pay incentive or SPIF to move dead inventory

- Does your operations department truly understand the impact of inventory management?

- Does your sales department really understand the importance of accurate forecasting?

- Are they held accountable?

- What process does your company use in gaining customer feedback in demand change?

- Does accounting or finance pressure inventory management to maximize turns? At the expense of customer service?

- Does accounting or finance understand transaction costs associated with too high of a turn rate?

- Do you use EDI or E-business?

- Do you cycle count?

- How do you justify doing a physical inventory if you still do one?

- Do you track turnover by product line?

- Do you classify inventory - A, B, C?

- Do you track turnover by classification?

- Do you have a formalized dead or aged inventory process?

- Does your operations department truly understand the impact of inventory management?

- Does your sales department really understand the importance of accurate forecasting?

- Are they held accountable?

- What process does your company use in gaining customer feedback in demand change?

- Does accounting or finance pressure inventory management to maximize turns? At the expense of customer service?

- Does accounting or finance understand transaction costs associated with too high of a turn rate?

- Does your executive management team understand the benefits of consignment?

- Does your executive management team understand the benefits of DMI?

- Does your executive management team understand the benefits of VMI?

- Have you ever approached a vendor requesting inventory management support?

- Has a customer ever approached you asking for J.I.T., Consignment or DMI?

## Discovery Analysis - Customer Service Improvement

This questionnaire is designed to stimulate a thought-provoking process, which should direct you to very focus-specific areas within your sales organization that need attention. The Owner/President, Vice President of Sales, Sales Managers and both inside and outside sales representatives should complete this discovery analysis.

A discovery team meeting should be held to review the objectives of this process. Each team member should prepare an independent S.W.O.T. (Strengths, Weaknesses, Opportunities and Threats) analysis based on his responses after completing this questionnaire. Only the three most critical areas in each category should be recorded:

| | |
|---|---|
| *Strengths:* | The three biggest strengths the company has that create competitive advantage. |
| *Weaknesses:* | The three most critical weaknesses that must be addressed to maintain or create new competitive advantages or at a minimum put you on a level playing field with the competition. |
| *Opportunities:* | The three biggest opportunities for your company to create competitive advantage, improve market share, increase revenues or create cost reduction through process improvement. |
| *Threats:* | The three biggest threats created by either the internal or external environment. |

This may include government regulations, internal politics, competition activity, poor process control or other external influences.

All responses should be collated from each group. Common areas of concern should be highlighted. A minimum of a one-day retreat attended by all management and key personnel is encouraged to ensure that proper attention and discussion is given to every area of concern that is identified through this discovery analysis.

From this session, major initiatives should be identified in conjunction with completion of the diagnostic tool:

- What are the most commonly heard customer complaints?

- Have the common types of complaints changed over the past few years?

- How are your customers' expectations of your performance set?

- How much time does your management team spend "putting out fires" related to customer service issues rather than working on root causes?

- How much pricing power would you gain if your customer service were to become uniformly excellent?

- Do you know how often scheduled delivery dates are changed? How often they're changed at the customer's request? How often they're changed to match your ability to deliver?

- Does all your information about your customer service come through your sales team?

- Do you currently have any cross functional teams working on customer service improvement? If so, how are they doing?

- Do you have people within your organization who are experienced in managing improvement projects?

- Do you have up-to-date and detailed documentation of how you're key processes, like order entry, credit processing, and warehouse activity, really work?

- Has anyone in your organization been publicly recognized for making significant process improvements within the last year?

- Do you tend to spend management meetings debating symptoms of problems or looking for solutions?

- Do you have simple measurements of your performance upon which everyone agrees? Are measurements lacking? Is the reliability of your measurements contested by your management team?

- Is there a lot of disagreement among your management team as to your most serious customer service issues?

## Discovery Analysis – Warehousing Operations

This questionnaire is designed to stimulate a thought-provoking process, which should direct you to very focus-specific areas within your sales organization that need attention. The Owner/President, Vice President of Sales, Sales Managers and both

inside and outside sales representatives should complete this discovery analysis.

A discovery team meeting should be held to review the objectives of this process. Each team member should prepare an independent S.W.O.T. (Strengths, Weaknesses, Opportunities and Threats) analysis based on his responses after completing this questionnaire. Only the three most critical areas in each category should be recorded:

*Strengths:*       The three biggest strengths the company has that create competitive advantage.

*Weaknesses:*    The three most critical weaknesses that must be addressed to maintain or create new competitive advantages or at a minimum put you on a level playing field with the competition.

*Opportunities:*  The three biggest opportunities for your company to create competitive advantage, improve market share, increase revenues or create cost reduction through process improvement.

*Threats:*        The three biggest threats created by either the internal or external environment. This may include government regulations, internal politics, competition activity or other external influences.

All responses should be collated from each group. Common areas of concern should be highlighted. A minimum of a one-

day retreat attended by all management and key personnel is encouraged to ensure that proper attention and discussion is given to every area of concern that is identified through this discovery analysis.

From this session, major initiatives should be identified in conjunction with completion of the diagnostic tool:

- Do you consistently have a "clean floor" in your warehouse at the end of the day, meaning that all items received during the day have been completely put away and all orders picked during the day have been completely shipped?

- Do you consistently ship all orders received the same day?

- Do you consistently complete the put away and data entry for all receipts on the same day they arrived?

- How long does it typically take to research and resolve picking or shipping errors?

- If you randomly counted the inventory in 100 locations, how many would have the exact product and quantity shown in your computer system?

- Do your warehouse managers spend most of their time helping to get product out the door or working with other company managers?

- Do you have customers visit or tour your warehouse or do you try to hide it from them?

- Do you have dedicated inventory management staff to count inventory and research problems?

- Do you have to inspect all your shipments to ensure they are correct?

- Do you consider order picking optimization when selecting a put away location or do you just move the receipt to the easiest spot in the warehouse?

- Are there processes or workstations in your warehouse that everyone always complains about?

- How high is the turnover in your warehouse, especially at the supervisory level?

- Do you have a formal process for training warehouse staff and determining their compensation?

## Discovery Analysis– Technology

This questionnaire is designed to stimulate a thought-provoking process, which should direct you to very focus-specific areas within your sales organization that need attention. The Owner/ President, Vice President of Sales, Sales Managers and both inside and outside sales representatives should complete this discovery analysis.

A discovery team meeting should be held to review the objectives of this process. Each team member should prepare an independent S.W.O.T. (Strengths, Weaknesses, Opportunities and Threats) analysis based on his responses after completing this questionnaire. Only the three most critical areas in each category should be recorded:

*Strengths:*  The three biggest strengths the company has that create competitive advantage.

*Weaknesses:* <u>The three most critical weaknesses</u> that must be addressed to maintain or create new competitive advantages or at a minimum put you on a level playing field with the competition.

*Opportunities:* <u>The three biggest opportunities</u> for your company to create competitive advantage, improve market share, increase revenues or create cost reduction through technology improvement.

*Threats:* <u>The three biggest threats</u> created by either the internal or external environment. This may include government regulations, internal politics, competition activity or other influences.

All responses should be collated from each group. Common areas of concern should be highlighted. A minimum of a one-day retreat attended by all management and key personnel is encouraged to ensure that proper attention and discussion is given to every area of concern that is identified through this discovery analysis.

From this session, major initiatives should be identified in conjunction with completion of the diagnostic tool:

- Do you have in-house experts who understand most of the functionality in your business system?

- How much outside expert advice do you receive on your existing technology tools from training courses, user groups or consultants?

- How often do you discuss your technology issues with your peers in other companies? Do you belong to any organizations for this purpose?

- Where in your business processes do you seem to need a lot of cumbersome "work arounds?" Have you asked other companies or your software vendor for advice on how to handle these processes?

- How long does it typically take for a transaction like a receipt, shipment or stock check to be recorded into your business system after it occurs?

- How often do your managers have to request new or special reports from your IT guru? How easy is it for everyone to get information for themselves when they need it?

- When is the last time someone in your company checked your responsiveness to phone calls, faxes and emails? Have you ever hired a "secret shopper" to audit your staff?

- Do you really offer a consistent face to your customers, whether they contact your through phone, fax, email or website?

- Is your responsiveness to customers largely determined by the individual involved or do you have consistency throughout your company?

- Have you ever actually tested your company's disaster recovery procedures? Do you know they work?

- What would happen to your company if there were a major natural disaster like a flood, fire, hurricane or earthquake?

- What would happen to your company if an angry employee attempted to steal customer information or delete critical files from your systems?

- What would happen to your company if a 14-year-old hacker broke into your systems and viewed or deleted critical files?

- When you look at new technology do you have a process to relate it back to business objectives or do you buy the "coolest" stuff?

- Have you ever implementing a technology solution that never really solved the problem as intended? Do you examine proposed technology solutions to be sure that there are no underlying organizational or process problems that won't be fixed by technology?

## Discovery Analysis – Strategic Planning

This questionnaire is designed to stimulate a thought provoking process which should direct you to focus-specific areas within your management organization that need attention. The Owner/President, and the executive team should complete this discovery analysis. A second analysis can be completed by line management for comparative purposes.

A discovery team meeting should be conducted to review the objectives of this process. Each team member should prepare an independent S.W.O.T. (Strengths, Weaknesses, Opportunities and Threats) analysis based on his responses after completing this questionnaire. Only the three most critical areas in each category should be recorded:

*Strengths:* The three biggest strengths that create an ability to define and develop a long term strategic plan.

*Weaknesses:* The three most critical areas that create confusion, dissatisfaction and lack of understanding as to overall company objectives.

*Opportunities:* The three biggest opportunities that may increase growth opportunities over the next five years.

*Threats:* The three biggest threats including external influences such as vendor support, bank financing and internal controls that may create road blocks to achieving our objectives.

- Describe a clear vision statement
- Describe a mission statement
- Do you understand the difference between a mission statement and a vision statement?
- What is a SWOT analysis?
- What is strategic planning?

- What are the key concepts and definitions in strategic planning?

- What are the basic steps in a strategic planning process?

- What do I need to know before I start the planning process?

- What are the individual roles in a planning process?

- What is a situation assessment?

- How can we do a competitive analysis report?

- What is a strategy and how do we develop one?

- What should a strategic plan include?

- How do you develop an annual operating plan?

- How do we increase our chances of implementing our strategic plan?

- Should I use an external consultant?

- How do I use retreats in the planning process?

## Discovery Analysis – Cash Is King

This questionnaire is designed to stimulate a thought provoking process which should direct you to focus-specific areas within your management organization that need attention. The Owner/President, and the executive team should complete this discovery analysis. A second analysis can be completed by line management for comparative purposes.

A discovery team meeting should be conducted to review the objectives of this process. Each team member should prepare an independent S.W.O.T. (Strengths, Weaknesses,

Opportunities and Threats) analysis based on his responses after completing this questionnaire. Only the three most critical areas in each category should be recorded:

*Strengths:* The three biggest strengths that create positive cash flow within your organization.

*Weaknesses:* The three most critical areas that create customer dissatisfaction, reduced revenues and reduce positive cash flow.

*Opportunities:* The three biggest opportunities that may increase customer satisfaction, improve market share and provide opportunity to increase positive cash flow.

*Threats:* The three biggest threats to cash flow including external influences such as economic decline, lack of vendor support and lack of internal control and understanding of cash flow.

## Cash Management Discovery Analysis:

- Do you have a system to review and evaluate your RGAs (Return Goods Authorization)?

  - *Do you charge for restocking?*

  - *Are you getting the optimum discounts from your supplier and are you keeping the discounts as profit?*

  - *Have you done a supplier profitability analysis?*

- *Are your customers profitable?*

- *Do you have significant supplier error?*

- *Do you have a vendor returns program and do you manage it well?*

- *Do you track your own and your suppliers on time delivery?*

- *Are you selling the right products to the right customers?*

- *Do you have an outcall program?*

- *Does your inside sales force understand the concept of up selling?*

- *Do you have a freight recovery program or do you fold under pressure and give it all away?*

- *Do you rank and evaluate your customers by gross margin dollars and gross margin percentages?*

- Do you have an incentive program that is tied to gross margin growth both in dollars and percentages?

- Do you track your cash to cash cycle?

- Do you create a monthly or quarterly cash flow analysis?

- Do you have specific programs to improve inventory turns?

- Do you not only track ageing of receivables but also have a proactive program to reduce aging?

- What is your bad debt as a percentage of sales?

- Do you aggressively attack waste to plug profit leaks?

- How do you make inventory management a significant source of competitive advantage?

- Does your company have a clear and collective agenda for building inventory management into a competitive advantage?

- Do you have a specific collection policy?

- Are your accounts receivable personnel trained in collection procedures?

## Discovery Analysis – Margin Management

This questionnaire is designed to stimulate a thought provoking process which should direct you to focus-specific areas within your management organization that need attention. The Owner/President, and the executive team should complete this discovery analysis. A second analysis can be completed by line management for comparative purposes.

A discovery team meeting should be conducted to review the objectives of this process. Each team member should prepare an independent S.W.O.T. (Strengths, Weaknesses, Opportunities and Threats) analysis based on his responses after completing this questionnaire. Only the three most critical areas in each category should be recorded:

*Strengths:*     The three biggest strengths that create competitive advantage and customer satisfaction.

*Weaknesses:*     The three most critical areas that create

customer dissatisfaction, reduced margins and create a competitive disadvantage.

*Opportunities:* <u>The three biggest opportunities</u> that may increase customer satisfaction, improve market share, increase margins or create competitive advantage.

*Threats:* <u>The three biggest threats</u> to effective margin management including external influences such as vendor support, dual distribution, multiple new channels or supplier apathy.

## Margin Management Discovery Analysis:

- *Identification -What is a profitable customer for your company?*

- *What methods and processes do you use to identify customers?*

- *What methods and processes can you use to identify customers?*

- *What methods and processes should you use to identify customers?*

- *What criteria should you use to identify customers?*

- *Is this process a formalized process? What information is needed? Why?*

- *What information is gathered, where is it stored, and how is it used?*

- *How is the information gathered?*

- *Who gathers the information?*

- *Who reviews information?*

- *What is the review cycle?*

- *How is information utilized and shared to create knowledge?*

- *Can all the information needed be obtained through current processes?*

- *Do you know what information should be gathered?*

- *What are the expectations of current processes?*

- *Does the current process effectively meet your expectations? Alternatives?*

- *Have you identified what types of customers you want to do business with?*

- *What types of customers are you currently succeeding with?*

- *Who decides what customers you target? Have you identified target markets?*

- *Is it currently measured? How?*

- *Who reviews customer profitability?*

- *How is it used?*

- *How do you measure customer retention rates?*

- *How do you track retention of desired customers?*

- *How do you track lost customers and the reasons why you lost them?*

- *How do you determine which customers to "let go"?*

- *How should you measure customer retention rates?*

- *How is information used?*
- *How do you prospect?*
- *What percentage of prospects do you turn into customers?*
- *Are you focused on quantitative growth of sales or qualitative growth of profitable customers?*
- *How can you better target the X% or group of customers who will generate the majority of your new growth in the next few years?*
- *Do you require a certain number of accounts to be identified and pursued?*
- *What criteria should you use to select such accounts?*
- *How do your customers rank the value of each of your value elements? How do you rank them?*
- *How does your company disseminate and utilize information from customers?*
- *What criteria are used?*
  - Accuracy -Error rates for item and item count, delivery, price, shipment
  - Methods, invoicing
  - Value-added kitting and customized services
  - Responsiveness
  - Technical Support
  - Dependability
- *Are analysis methods and credit policies consistent with customer retention?*

- And development objectives ?
- *Are credit policies formally documented?*
- *How often are they reviewed?*
- *Which suppliers can meet the performance requirements of your company and your customers?*
- *Should you pursue minimum pricing-levels by supplier or products?*
- *What are the supplier's capabilities? Limitations?*
- *Do they meet your criteria?*
- *Do they fit your corporate objectives?*
- *What are the supplier's commitment to distribution and past loyalties?*
- *What is their reputation in the marketplace ?*
- *Do you formally evaluate your suppliers?*
- *How do you define supplier on-time shipments?*
- *Shipment quality*
- *Paperwork accuracy*
- *Response time*
- *Vendor profitability*
- *GMROI*
- *Inventory turns*
- *Key Factors in Lead Time Variability*
- *What is the effect of your processes on supplier performance?*
- *What information do they use?*

- *How do they use it?*

- *What information do you send?*

- *What information do they need?*

- *Why do suppliers place you at a lower level than their direct customers?*

- *Supplier's Profitability via Distributor vs. Direct Shipment to Customer*

- *Do you have APR issues?*

- *Lead-time Variability*

- *Consistency*

- *Lot-sizing*

- *Minimum Orders*

- *Computer capabilities*

- *Terms*

- *What is your pricing strategy?*

- *Do you understand sensitivity pricing?*

- *Do you have a break-even analysis?*

- *How do you fire unprofitable customers?*

## Discovery Analysis – Sales Planning

This questionnaire is designed to stimulate a thought-provoking process, which should direct you to very focus-specific areas within your sales organization that need attention. The Owner/ President, Vice President of Sales, Sales Managers and both inside and outside sales representatives should complete this discovery analysis.

A discovery team meeting should be held to review the objectives of this process. Each team member should prepare an independent S.W.O.T. (Strengths, Weaknesses, Opportunities and Threats) analysis based on his responses after completing this questionnaire. Only the three most critical areas in each category should be recorded:

*Strengths:* The three biggest strengths the company has that create competitive advantage.

*Weaknesses:* The three most critical weaknesses that must be addressed to maintain or create new competitive advantages or at a minimum put you on a level playing field with the competition.

*Opportunities:* The three biggest opportunities for your company to create competitive advantage, improve market share, increase revenues or create cost reduction through process improvement.

*Threats:* The three biggest threats created by either the internal or external environment. This may include government regulations, internal politics, competition activity or other external influences.

All responses should be collated from each group. Common areas of concern should be highlighted. A minimum of a one-day retreat attended by all management and key personnel is encouraged to ensure that proper attention and discussion is

given to every area of concern that is identified through this discovery analysis.

From this session, major initiatives should be identified in conjunction with completion of the diagnostic tool.

- Do you record and monitor customer complaints?
- Do you maintain a customer complaint database to track patterns and identify recurring problems?
- Do you use this information to improve performance and increase customer satisfaction?
- Do you use external customer surveys?
- Do you solicit customer feedback?
- Do you provide customers with a single point of contact?
- Do you track customer satisfaction with internal operating statistic fill rates?
- Can you identify waste in operating costs, such as the high cost of errors?
- Do you receive phone system statistics to analyze calling behavior?
- How do you measure customer satisfaction? Do you have a formal system; such as a report card?
- Does your sales force involve suppliers in the selling process?
- Do you use integrated supply arrangements to "lock in" the customer?
- Do you understand integrated supply?

- Can they get shipping or tracking information 24X7 off your web site?

- How much price negotiation do the sale representatives do?

- Do they have discretion in pricing?

- Is it based on a percentage or dollar amount?

- How do negotiated prices fit into their commission or incentive program?

- Is the pricing simple, easy to understand and easy to calculate?

- Is there a system in place for maintaining customer pricing for use by inside and outside sales and insuring consistency for all customer locations?

- What opportunities do you provide to allow you to get to know your clients better at all levels of their organization?

- Have you held a conference, forum or social event involving several non-competing customers?

- Do you know your customers' top 10 customers?

- Do you have joint planning of growth objectives with customers?

- How are you helping customers to be more profitable?

- Do you document customers cost savings that you generate?

- Can you prove how you were able to make improvements in speed, cost or quality?

- Can customers reach their sales representative easily?

- Which communication tools are currently utilized: cellular phone, beeper, email, paging off of web site?

- What is your company's current position in the marketplace?

- What changes have had a significant impact on your business? Please describe recent trends.

- Manufacturers are selling direct?

- Electronic commerce?

- Reducing duplicate inventories and sales force.

- What trends are affecting your industry?

- How can you reposition yourself to take advantages of the changes?

- What strategic decisions are needed?

- What's new in the external environment on which you can capitalize?

- What are your competitors offering that your do not?

- Why do your largest customers buy from you?

- What new products and services can you offer to provide new growth opportunities? To existing customers? To new customers?

- Do you evaluate re-order frequency to determine if a customer is current and active or departing?

- How have the sales to your top customers changed?

- What volume do the top 10% represent?

- How many of your customers represent 80% of your revenue?

- How has this changed over time?

- Have you looked at average gross profit per customer?

- What trends are affecting specific territories or specific sales representatives?

- How do you refocus their energy and give them feedback?

- How do you promote generating increased business from existing accounts?

- Are you growing current customers?

- Are you losing or gaining compared to competitors?

- Is management involved with the sales to top/target customers?

- Is management involved in partnering relationships?

- How does your company compare to your association statistics (par reports)? If you don't measure it you can't manage it.

- What plan is in place to offer premier accounts extremely high levels of service?

- Are these accounts designated in the computer and on every printed document so that everyone will discriminate in favor of these target accounts in service and related support?

- Do you drive smaller accounts with a higher mark-up and charge for value added services?

- How do you determine which customers get which services?

- What special services do you offer your best customers?

- How do you generate prospective sales leads?

- What are your methods for gathering competitive intelligence?

- What competitive advantages do your competitors have?

- Do you use a combination of outside sales, inside sales and focus specific outcall customer service to facilitate growth?

- What part of the field sales representative's job could be delegated to allow more time to generate new business?

- Have you made any investments in sales force automation?

- How would you define your company's competitive advantages?

- Do customers value your core competencies?

- Are you the most efficient and effective source of supply for existing product service offerings? If not, why?

- What meaningful statistics are you using to measure your sales team? Your customers?

- How do you rate your sales representatives?

- What type of performance statistics are you maintaining?

- Which of these are part of your planning and feedback?

- Monthly territory review

- Monthly training activity - minimum of twelve non-product subjects

- Quarterly planning – meet with salespeople to agree on priorities?

- Annual sales conference – to make announcements; give recognition, training, play?

- Annual performance reviews? Written?

- Do you publish a calendar?

- Does each sales representative have a key account plan for their top 15 customers?

- Do you use weekly call plans? Daily call reports? Monthly performance reports?

- Do you use a quarterly call budget to see if you do what you planned? Quarterly call budget ties in with the business strategy and the annual business plan, look at total available sales calls for each 3 month/13 week period, use to evaluate monthly performance, actual to plan, call frequency to opportunity.

- Do all your sales employees know and understand your business strategy?

- How does the role of your field sales representatives fit into that business strategy?

- How does the role of your inside sales representatives fit into that business strategy?

## Discovery Analysis - Sales Personnel

This questionnaire is designed to stimulate a thought-provoking process, which should direct you to very focus-specific areas within your sales organization that need attention. The Owner/ President, Vice President of Sales, Sales Managers and both inside and outside sales representatives should complete this discovery analysis.

A discovery team meeting should be held to review the objectives of this process. Each team member should prepare an independent S.W.O.T. (Strengths, Weaknesses, Opportunities and Threats) analysis based on his responses after completing this questionnaire. Only the three most critical areas in each category should be recorded:

*Strengths:* The three biggest strengths the company has that create competitive advantage.

*Weaknesses:* The three most critical weaknesses that must be addressed to maintain or create new competitive advantages or at a minimum put you on a level playing field with the competition.

*Opportunities:* The three biggest opportunities for your company to create competitive advantage, improve market share, increase revenues or create cost reduction through process improvement.

*Threats:* The three biggest threats created by either the internal or external environment.

This may include government regulations, internal politics, competition activity or other external influences.

All responses should be collated from each group. Common areas of concern should be highlighted. A minimum of a one-day retreat attended by all management and key personnel is encouraged to ensure that proper attention and discussion is given to every area of concern that is identified through this discovery analysis.

From this session, major initiatives should be identified, with completion of the diagnostic tool.

- Do you record and monitor customer complaints?
- Do you maintain a customer complaint database to track patterns and identify recurring problems?
- Do you use this information to improve performance and increase customer satisfaction?
- Do you use external customer surveys?
- Do you solicit customer feedback?
- Do you provide customers with a single point of contact?
- Do you track customer satisfaction with internal operating statistic fill rates?
- Can you identify waste in operating costs, such as the high cost of errors?
- Do you receive phone system statistics to analyze calling behavior?

- How do you measure customer satisfaction? Do you have a formal system? Such as a report card?

- Does your sales force involve suppliers in the selling process?

- Do you use integrated supply arrangements to "lock in" the customer?

- Do you understand integrated supply?

- Do customers purchase off your web site?

- How much price negotiation do the sale representatives do?

- Do they have discretion in pricing?

- Is it based on a percentage or dollar amount?

- How do negotiated prices fit into their commission or incentive program?

- Is the pricing simple, easy to understand and easy to calculate?

- Is there a system in place for maintaining customer pricing for use by inside and outside sales and insuring consistency for all customer locations?

- Do you know your customers' top 10 customers?

- Do you have joint planning of growth objectives with customers?

- How are you helping customers to be more profitable?

- Do you document customers cost savings that you generate?

- Can you prove how you were able to make improvements in speed, cost or quality?

- Can customers reach their sales representative easily?

- Which communication tools are currently utilized: cellular phone, beeper, email, paging off of web site?

- Why do your largest customers buy from you?

- Do you do regular territory reviews?

- Do you remove or revitalize unprofitable accounts?

- Do you use a quarterly call budget and break it down into weekly call plan with weekly reports?

- How do you promote generating increased business from existing accounts?

- Are you growing current customers?

- Are you losing or gaining compared to competitors?

- Is management involved with the sales to top/target customers?

- Is management involved in partnering relationships?

- How does your company compare to your association statistics (par reports)? If you don't measure it you can't manage it.

- What plan is in place to offer premier accounts extremely high levels of service?

- Are these accounts designated in the computer and on every printed document so that everyone will discriminate in favor of these target accounts in service and related support?

- Do you drive smaller accounts with a higher mark-up and charge for value added services?

- How do you determine which customers get which services?

- What special services do you offer your best customers?

- How do you generate prospective sales leads?

- What are your methods for gathering competitive intelligence?

- What competitive advantages do your competitors have?

- Do you use a combination of outside sales, inside sales and focus specific outcall customer service to facilitate growth?

- What part of the field sales representative's job could be delegated to allow more time to generate new business?

- Have you made any investments in sales force automation?

- How would you define your company's competitive advantages?

- Do customers value your core competencies?

- Are you the most efficient and effective source of supply for existing product service offerings? If not, why?

- What meaningful statistics are you using to measure your sales team? Your customers?

- How do you rate your sales representatives?

- What type of performance statistics are you maintaining?

- Which of these are part of your planning and feedback:

  - Monthly territory review

  - Monthly training activity - minimum of twelve non-product subjects

  - Quarterly planning – meet with salespeople to agree on priorities?

  - Annual sales conference – to make announcements; give recognition, training, play?

  - Annual performance reviews? Written?

- Do you publish a calendar?

- Does each sales representative have a key account plan for their top 15 customers?

- Do you use weekly call plans? Daily call reports? Monthly performance reports?

- Do you use a quarterly call budget to see if you do what you planned? Quarterly call budget ties in with the business strategy and the annual business plan, look at total available sales calls for each 3 month/13 week period, use to evaluate monthly performance, actual to plan, call frequency to opportunity.

- Do all your sales employees know and understand your business strategy?

- How does the role of your field sales representatives fit into that business strategy?

How does the role of your inside sales representatives fit into that business strategy?

**Lead Wolf Leadership Creed:** BY: Rick Johnson

- *A leader doesn't follow others footprints—he is always first in line creating a new road map to follow*

- *A leader doesn't panic in a crisis he becomes a pillar of strength for others*

- *A leader doesn't look for the light at the end of the tunnel—he carries the light*

- *A leader doesn't flaunt his title—he finds the time to be more than his title*

- *A leader doesn't get up early to make himself better—he gets up early to  help make others better*

- *A leader has a vision—he doesn't dream—he is the dream and he communicates his vision*

- *A leader isn't arrogant but he commands a presence. He is confident.*

- *The leader is not the one taking credit for success first but he's the first one to credit those who helped create success*

- *The leader may not be the most valuable player but he is the player most valued*

- *The leader does not like being called the reason for success— He realizes success depends on the*

*people you surround yourself with--after all he is
the leader*

# Bibliography

## Literature

Ahlrichs, N. (2000). <u>Competing for Talent</u>. California: Davies-Black Publishing.

Anderson, A. (1995). <u>Facing the Forces of Change</u>. Washington, DC: DREF/NAW Publication.

Becker, B.E. Husfield, M.A. and Ulrich, D. (2001). <u>The HR Scorecard</u>. Harvard Business School Press.

Benfield, S. and Baynard, J. (2001). <u>Pricing Management</u>. Illinois: Loran Nordgren and Co.

Collins, J. (2001). <u>Good to Great</u>. New York: Harper Collins Publisher, Inc.

Daft, R. (2001). <u>Organization Theory and Design</u>. Ohio: South Western Publishing.

Daniels, T. and Spiker, B. (1994). <u>Perspectives on Organizational Communication</u>. Iowa: Brown and Benchmark.

Ford, J. E. and Samuelson, J. (2003). <u>Wholesale Distribution Equity Research</u>. New York: Harper Collins Publishers.

Greenleaf, R. (1970). <u>Servant As Leader</u>. San Francisco: Berrett-Koehler Publishers.

Douglas Berry , "Wisdom of a Young CEO (2004) Running Press Book Publishers

Llewellyn, J. (2000). Coming in First. Georgia: Long Street Press, Inc.

McGuinness, B. (2000). Cash Rules. D.C: Kiplinger Washington Editors.

McLagan, P. and Nel, C. (1995). The Age of Participation. California: Berrett-Koehler Publishers.

Pearce, J. A. II and Robinson, R. B. Jr. (2000). Formulation, Implementation and Control of Competitive Strategy, New York: McGraw – Hill Companies, Inc.

Quinn, R. E. (1996). Deep Change. California: Jossey-Bass, Inc Publishers.

Schermerhorn, J. (2002). Management. Massachusetts: John Wiley and Sons Inc.

Shelton, K. (1998). Integrity At Work. Utah: Executive Excellence Publishing

Tracy, J. A. (1994). How to Read A Financial Report. Canada: John Wiley and Sons, Inc.

Womack, J. P. and Jones, D. T. (1999). Banish Waste and Create Wealth in Your Corporation. New York: Simon and Shuster.

# Dr. Eric (Rick) Johnson Biography

Rick Johnson has over 35 years of experience in distribution sales and operations. Rick's career can be broken down by decades. The **first ten years** of his distribution career were spent with the largest steel-processing distributor in the world (Joseph T. Ryerson). Rick started in Inside Sales, grew into the Merchandise Manager's position, spent five years as an Outside Salesperson, two years as Sales Manager, and the final year at Ryerson, Rick was General Manager at their Dayton, Ohio facility.

The **second ten years** began with Rick starting his own processing distribution center from scratch. In the first year, sales reached $1 million dollars and had grown to $25 million in its tenth year when Rick sold the business to one of the major national chains.

The **third ten years** of Rick's career began almost by accident after a year of retirement when a former customer asked Rick to close an acquisition that was losing money. Rick agreed to spend six months working in the business and evaluating the possibility of a Turn-A Round (TAR) or closure. After six months, the plant began operating at break even and actually ended that year with a small profit. In the third year after Rick's TAR efforts, the plant was very profitable and the decision was made to sell the operation. This began Rick's career in dealing with financially troubled Turn-A-Round companies. During this decade of Rick's career, he completed four TAR's.

The smallest company had annual revenues totaling $50 million and the largest TAR Rick competed had a revenue stream of $400 million. Rick's position as a change agent in these companies included Chief Executive Officer (CEO), President, Chief Operating Officer (COO) and Vice President of Sales and Operations.

After completing ten years of TAR work, Rick decided a decade of acting like Darth Vader was enough. He had met Mike Marks, founder of Indian River Consulting Group (IRCG), after selling his own company. Rick joined Indian River in 2000. At IRCG, Rick specialized in Sales Management, Sales Effectiveness, Strategic Planning, Turn-A-Round restructuring and Organizational Design. Rick started CEO Strategist LLC in July of 2005 a company that focuses on providing value through Board of Directors representation, executive coaching, team coaching and education and training.

Rick received an MBA from Keller Graduate School in Chicago, Illinois and a Bachelor's degree in Operations Management from Capital University, Columbus Ohio. He also served in the United States Air Force. Rick recently completed his dissertation on    Strategic Leadership and received his Ph.D. on April 15th, 2005. Rick is frequently published in *NAW Smart Brief, Material Handling Wholesaler, Modern Distribution Management,* and many other distribution industry publications, with over seventy different articles published to date. He's also a published book author with the following titles to his credit:.

- Naw – "The Toolkit for Improved Business Performance"

- NWFA and NAFCD "Roadmap" - A Guide to Success in the Flooring Distribution Industry
- "Shattered Innocence" - A fiction novel about teenagers.
- "Conquering the Counter Conundrum" - A workbook for training counter professionals in wholesale distribution.
- "Lone Wolf---Lead Wolf" - The Evolution of Sales
- Leadership Guide to Coaching and Mentoring